Race and Redistricting

LANDMARK LAW CASES

&

AMERICAN SOCIETY

Peter Charles Hoffer
N. E. H. Hull
Series Editors

TINSLEY E. YARBROUGH

Race and Redistricting

The *Shaw-Cromartie* Cases

UNIVERSITY PRESS OF KANSAS

Published by the University Press of Kansas (Lawrence, Kansas 66049), which was organized by the Kansas Board of Regents and is operated and funded by Emporia State University, Fort Hays State University, Kansas State University, Pittsburg State University, the University of Kansas, and Wichita State University

Library of Congress Cataloging-in-Publication Data

Yarbrough, Tinsley E., 1941–

Race and redistricting : the Shaw-Cromartie cases / Tinsley E. Yarbrough.

p. cm. — (Landmark law cases & American society)

Includes bibliographical references and index.

ISBN 0-7006-1218-1 (cloth : alk. paper) — ISBN 0-7006-1219-x (pbk. : alk. paper)

1. Apportionment (Election law)—United States.   2. United States. Congress. House—Election districts.   3. Election districts—North Carolina.   4. Gerrymandering—North Carolina.   5. African American legislators—North Carolina.   I. Title.   II. Series.

KF905 .Y37 2002

342.756'053—dc21   2002007024

British Library Cataloguing in Publication Data is available.

Printed in the United States of America

10 9 8 7 6 5 4 3 2 1

The paper used in this publication meets the minimum requirements of the American National Standard for Permanence of Paper for Printed Library Materials z39.48-1984.

To Ben

CONTENTS

The series of cases that opponents of North Carolina's Twelfth Congressional District brought over the course of the 1990s makes a wonderfully complex and immensely intriguing tale. In one sense, the story begins with the Voting Rights Act of 1965. In another, it goes back to Reconstruction and the progressive, debilitating denial of political rights to African American citizens of North Carolina. Lambasted as the "I-85" district by its critics (for its tortuous boundaries along the interstate highway), defended as the only way that African American voters could select one of their own to represent them in Congress, the Twelfth District and its story bring together a remarkable cast of characters. By the time the suits reached the U.S. Supreme Court for the third time, local politicians, civil rights advocates, historians, political scientists, the Democratic and Republican National Committees, a phalanx of federal judges, and eleven members of the Supreme Court's bench had spoken. Even a spectator in court got the chance to register an opinion by a nod of the head. One might say that history played its part, for the changing demographic composition of the state, the success of the civil rights movement in its precincts, and the rise of the African American bar also spoke in the *Shaw-Cromartie* cases.

There were good folks on both sides — people who hated prejudice and worked for equal protection of the law for all races. But was the creation of one or two majority-minority districts the appropriate way to ensure that people with a long-standing lack of political power could finally exercise such power? Was taking race explicitly into consideration an illegitimate step for the legislature? Or were the legislators simply engaging in the time-honored (and legally acceptable) practice of partisan gerrymandering of districts, ensuring that the balance between Democrats and Republicans in the state's congressional delegation would not be disturbed by the additional seat the 1990 census had given the state? These were critical constitutional questions, but when they were heard in court they took on a partisan tinge.

The federal district courts, whose three-judge panels heard the various suits three times, seemed to divide on partisan grounds. That is, the Democratic appointees to the bench favored the two majority-minority districts, while the Republicans opposed them. So, too, when the case went to the High Court, race and partisanship crisscrossed each other. The Court divided five to four twice, then flipped its ruling in a final five-to-four division. Nevertheless, throughout the oral presentations, the key question remained whether the legislature could arrange electoral boundaries to ensure that a preponderance of voters of one race resided within the district. At the same time, the snakelike shape of the Twelfth District played a role in its fate, as considerations of compactness and contiguity, though not mentioned in the Voting Rights Act and the Constitution, influenced the voting of more than one judge.

Fortunately, the complexities of the cases have met their match in the author of this book. Tinsley Yarbrough is one of the country's foremost students of the courts and brings to this study not only a mastery of the details but also a personal familiarity with many of the participants. His great respect for all of them shines through this balanced and authoritative essay. He makes the most difficult legal arguments and factual disputes compelling and clear.

But the story, as the author reminds us, is not really over, for in the 2000 census, North Carolina gained another congressional seat. And in other states the federal requirement that redistricting not deny to any racial group its right to participate fully in the political process will surely lead to more oddly shaped districts and more cases challenging them, as it did in Georgia and Louisiana. All these factors make this book must reading for students of our politics, past and future.

ACKNOWLEDGMENTS

The assistance of a number of individuals and institutions was critical to the completion of this project. I am tremendously appreciative to Judge Robinson O. Everett for making pertinent files available to me, and to his associate Seth Neyhart and secretary Francesca Burns for graciously assisting me in collecting and copying briefs, oral arguments, trial transcripts, and related documents. Frances Carraway of the North Carolina attorney general's office was similarly helpful in providing materials relevant to my research. For giving so freely of their time and experiences in recorded interviews, I am grateful not only to Judge Everett and Seth Neyhart but also to Dan T. Blue, Thomas Farr, W. Edwin McMahan, Ruth O. Shaw, Melvin Shimm, Tiare Smiley, Eddie Speas, and Adam Stein. Sincere thanks are also extended to the staffs of the Southern Historical Collection at the University of North Carolina at Chapel Hill and East Carolina University's Joyner Library, to Cynthia Manning Smith for flawless clerical assistance, and to Michael Briggs and his superb staff at the University Press of Kansas. Finally, as always, I cherish the love and encouragement of my family, especially our latest addition, grandson Benjamin Cole Ratner, to whom "Gramps" affectionately dedicates this book.

Race and Redistricting

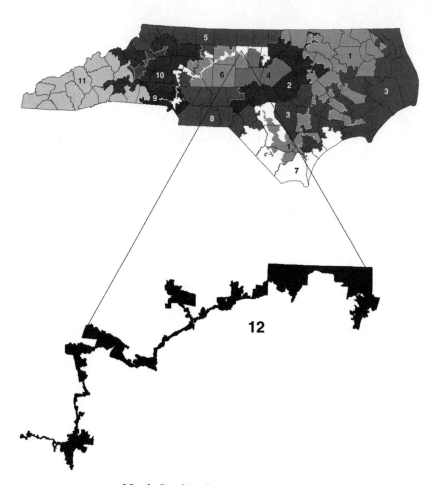

1992 North Carolina Congressional District Plan

In 1992, the North Carolina General Assembly, under pressure from the U.S. Department of Justice, created two majority-black congressional districts, greatly improving chances for the election of African Americans to the state's delegation in the U.S. House of Representatives for the first time since the beginning of the century. At first glance, Robinson Oscar Everett seemed an unlikely prospect to challenge North Carolina's "majority-minority" districts. The Duke law professor, Durham attorney, and former chief judge of the Court of Military Appeals was, after all, a specialist in military law, not voting rights disputes. He had never argued any case before the U.S. Supreme Court, much less a civil rights suit of potentially far-reaching significance. In fact, he had devoted much of his attention over the years to his family's extensive real estate holdings and broadcasting interests. Like his parents, both of whom had also been prominent members of the North Carolina bar, Everett had long been active in the civic, political, and cultural life of Durham and his native state. Like them, too, he was at least a moderately liberal Democrat who for years had enjoyed close relations with the leaders of Durham's African American community.

The chances for victory in a suit challenging majority-minority districting as an unconstitutional racial gerrymander also appeared doubtful. Despite the obvious distaste of certain Supreme Court justices for race-conscious policies of virtually any sort, the Court's response to affirmative action programs and related practices had been mixed, with a number surviving challenge. Moreover, when the Court held in *Mobile v. Bolden* (1980) that the federal Voting Rights Act of 1965 prohibited only election procedures with a racially discriminatory *intent*, even though their *effect* was to exclude all African Americans from elective office, Congress moved to amend the law in 1982. The Voting Rights Act's revised Section 2 made it clear that nothing in the law entitled racial minorities to proportional representation. Under the new provision, however, a voting rights violation was established "if, based on the totality of the circumstances, it is shown that the political processes leading to nomination or election [were] not equally open to participation by members of a [protected] class of citizens in that its members have less opportunity than other members of the electorate to participate in the political process and to elect representatives of their choice." The extent to which a racial minority had been elected to office was one factor in determining whether Section 2 had been violated.

Even before Section 2's modification, the Supreme Court had upheld a New York state legislative districting plan based on racial criteria as a constitutional means of securing Justice Department approval for redistricting covered by the Voting Rights Act. Speaking for a plurality in *United Jewish Organizations [UJO] v. Carey* (1977), Justice Byron R. White emphasized that the plan did not underrepresent white voters relative to their share of the population, but instead was an appropriate means of "seeking to alleviate the consequences of racial voting at the polls and to achieve a fair allocation of political power between white and nonwhite voters."

The Supreme Court's membership had changed considerably, however, since *UJO* was decided, and at least three justices — Chief Justice William H. Rehnquist and Associate Justices Antonin Scalia and Clarence Thomas — seemed opposed to nearly all race-conscious laws. Speaking for the *UJO* plurality, moreover, Justice White himself had stipulated that legislatures drawing majority-minority districts must employ "sound districting principles such as compactness and population equality." North Carolina's new majority-minority Twelfth District, which snaked along the state's Interstate 85 corridor for 165 miles from Durham to Gastonia, was hardly a model of geographic compactness. Indeed, it was one of the least compact legislative districts ever drafted.

Most important perhaps, Robinson Everett's courtly southern demeanor masked an exceptionally tenacious personality. An old-style liberal who believed that discrimination against African Americans was abhorrent, he found race-conscious policies that were beneficial to blacks, including candidates for elective office, equally objectionable. Acting as chief counsel as well as plaintiff, and enlisting a longtime Duke law school colleague, one of his sons, an old friend, and a secretary in his firm to act as co-plaintiffs, Everett not only filed his suit but also went on to win two impressive Supreme Court victories in *Shaw v. Reno* (1993) and *Shaw v. Hunt* (1996). When further redistricting prompted by *Shaw I* and *II* removed him and the other original plaintiffs from North Carolina's disputed districts but failed to satisfy his notion of a "color-blind" Constitution, Everett was hardly dissuaded. Instead, he rounded up new plaintiffs; filed another suit, *Cromartie v. Hunt;* and continued the battle, albeit with less successful results. Drawing primarily on interviews, court transcripts, other documents, and newspaper files, this book chronicles the politics of majority-minority districting in North Carolina, *Shaw-Cromartie*'s protracted journey through the courts, the cases' significant impact on election law, and the fascinating interplay of law, politics, and human conflict the dispute has generated.

CHAPTER I

Preclearance Politics

The Fifteenth Amendment, adopted in 1870 in the aftermath of the Civil War, proclaims, "The right of citizens of the United States to vote shall not be denied or abridged by the United States or by any State on account of race, color, or previous condition of servitude." The amendment also confers on Congress the power to enforce its provisions through "appropriate legislation." Nearly a century later, however, various states and counties, especially in the South, were still resorting to stratagems designed to defeat the amendment's purpose. Indeed, in a number of counties of the Old Confederacy, not a single voting-age African American was registered to vote, while more than 100 percent of their white counterparts—living and dead—remained on the voter rolls.

Over the years, the Supreme Court had abolished some of the more egregious discriminatory election devices. After indulging for a time the fiction that party primaries held to nominate candidates for elective office were private affairs beyond the Constitution's reach, a majority in *Smith v. Allwright* (1944) struck down the Texas Democratic Party's all-white primary. In *Allwright* and later cases, the justices declared that primaries were elections in the constitutional sense if they were regulated by the state—as was the case with Democratic primaries throughout the post–Civil War South—or effectively controlled the election choice.

In *Gomillion v. Lightfoot* (1960), the Court intervened further in state election practices, invalidating a state law that had redrawn the boundary lines of predominantly black Tuskegee, Alabama, thereby excluding all but ten of its African American voters from the town and further participation in its elections. Prior to the law's adoption, Tuskegee had been essentially square in shape; afterward, it had twenty-eight sides, roughly resembling a stylized seahorse. The justices unanimously branded the scheme a transparently unconstitutional racial gerrymander.

Judicial decisions had little impact, however, on devices used to restrict black voter registration. Discriminatory application of literacy and education tests, disqualification of applicants for spelling and other technical errors on registration forms, strict application of voucher requirements for would-be African American registrants, and severe limitations on the number of days registration offices were open each month were but a few of the stratagems to which voting officials resorted. In certain areas, blacks with the temerity to visit a registration office faced intimidation and violence.

Finally, Congress moved slowly and cautiously to action. The 1957 Civil Rights Act authorized Justice Department attorneys to seek injunctions against voter registrars. When many registrars resigned in a ploy to frustrate such suits, Congress in 1960 amended the statute so that states could be made defendants in voter discrimination cases. Although directed primarily at discrimination in public accommodations, employment, and federally funded programs, the omnibus Civil Rights Act of 1964 also contained a number of voting provisions, including a ban on the disqualification of voter applicants for irrelevant errors on registration forms. The next year, however, Congress passed the most formidable voting rights safeguards ever enacted.

The Voting Rights Act of 1965 suspended literacy and related tests in all states and counties in which less than 50 percent of the voting-age population was registered in November 1964 or actually voted in that year's presidential election. The law also authorized the attorney general to dispatch federal examiners to covered areas with the authority to register voters where necessary to protect against continued discrimination or intimidation by local officials. Under the "preclearance" requirements of Section 5, the Voting Rights Act's most controversial provision, state and local jurisdictions subject to the voter test ban were required to secure the approval of the attorney general or the U.S. District Court in the District of Columbia before enforcing any new election or voting law. The law's "bailout" provision exempted state and local governments from coverage only if they could convince the district court that their officials had not engaged in discriminatory voting practices for the past five years.

Based on its triggering formula, the Voting Rights Act initially applied to Alabama, Georgia, Louisiana, Mississippi, South Carolina, Virginia, portions of North Carolina, and Alaska. Alaska was eventually permitted to take advantage of the bailout provision. Given their long histories of voter discrimination, the southern states covered by the law were hardly in a similar position. Instead, South Carolina invoked the Supreme Court's original jurisdiction in a suit contending that the Voting Rights Act exceeded Congress's constitutional authority. Speaking for the Court in *South Carolina v. Katzenbach* (1966), however, Chief Justice Earl Warren rejected each of the state's claims, upholding every provision of the statute and emphasizing the broad scope of congressional power to enforce the Fifteenth Amendment's prohibition on racial discrimination at the polls.

While concurring in the Court's judgment with respect to other parts of the law, Justice Hugo L. Black vigorously objected to the preclearance provisions, charging that they violated state reserved powers under the Tenth Amendment. But the Alabama native dissented alone. So long as a federal statute's provisions were rationally related to the elimination of racial discrimination in the suffrage, the Court held, they fell within Congress's power to enforce the Fifteenth Amendment, and outside the states' reserved powers.

In subsequent years, Congress extended the Voting Rights Act's life and made its ban on voter tests nationwide. Supreme Court decisions also made it clear that Section 5's preclearance provisions covered electoral boundary lines as well as voting requirements. Section 5 stipulated that new election laws must "not have the purpose . . . [or] the effect of denying or abridging the right to vote on account of race or color." And in *Rome v. United States* (1980), the Court upheld the Justice Department's refusal to grant preclearance to electoral changes and annexations in a Georgia community, even though the attorney general had found no discriminatory purpose but only that Rome had failed to prove that the annexations would not have the effect of diluting the African American vote. Under Section 5's "plain language," Justice Thurgood Marshall concluded for the Court, new election laws must have neither a discriminatory purpose nor a discriminatory effect to withstand a preclearance challenge.

The *Rome* case involved an application of Section 5. *Mobile v. Bolden*, decided the same day, raised issues under Section 2 of the Voting Rights Act, which forbade any "voting qualification or prerequisite to voting, or standard, practice, or procedure . . . imposed or applied by any state or political subdivision to deny or abridge the right of any citizen of the United States to vote on account of race or color." The *Bolden* majority upheld at-large elections for members of Mobile, Alabama's county commission, even though no African American had been elected to the commission since its creation in 1911. Finding no racially discriminatory intent behind the scheme, the Court concluded that neither Section 2 nor the Constitution prohibited election procedures with a merely racially disparate impact.

The *Bolden* decision became a major focus of debate when Congress considered further extension of the Voting Rights Act in 1982. Over the opposition of the Reagan administration, the law was extended for twenty-five years. In addition, a covered state or political subdivision was required to show that it had not been guilty of voting discrimination for the past ten years and had made efforts to improve the rate of minority voting. Most significantly, Congress replaced the *Bolden* Court's interpretation of Section 2 with a results standard. Section 2(a) prohibited voting regulations that "result[ed]" in denying or abridging the right to vote on account of race, and Section 2(b) provided that a Section 2(a) violation was established when the "totality of the circumstances" revealed that election processes were not equally open to all races, and minorities had less opportunity than other voters to participate and elect representatives "of their choice."

A Senate Judiciary Committee report on the 1982 amendments to the Voting Rights Act listed "typical factors" that might warrant a finding of a Section 2 violation. Among them were an area's history of racial discrimination in voting; the degree of racially polarized voting there; the extent to which unusually large districts or other arrangements enhanced the opportunities for discrimination against minorities; the degree to which minorities were denied access to candidate slating processes; the effects of discrimination in education, employment, and other fields on minority participation in the political process; the presence of racist appeals in political campaigns; and the degree to which minority candidates had been elected to public office in the area in question.

In *Thornburg v. Gingles* (1986), a North Carolina case that gave the Supreme Court its first opportunity to construe the revised Section 2, the Court drew on such considerations in announcing conditions necessary to establish a Section 2 vote dilution claim. The same year that Section 2 was revised, North Carolina's General Assembly had adopted a redistricting plan for state house and senate seats. In *Gingles*, African American voters contended that one single-member district and six multimember districts in the plan impaired their ability to elect representatives of their choice, in violation of Section 2. Applying Section 2's "totality of the circumstances" test, a three-judge federal district court held that the plan resulted in the dilution of minority votes in each of the disputed districts.

Speaking through Justice William J. Brennan, the Supreme Court concurred in the lower court's judgment with respect to all but one of the districts at issue. The *Gingles* Court also established three conditions that must be met for a Section 2 vote dilution violation to prevail in a challenge to multimember districts. "First," declared Brennan, "the minority group must be able to demonstrate that it is sufficiently large and geographically compact to constitute a majority in a single-member district. . . . Second, the minority group must be able to show that it is politically cohesive. . . . Third, the minority must be able to demonstrate that the white majority votes sufficiently as a bloc to enable it — in the absence of special circumstances, such as the minority candidate running unopposed . . . — usually to defeat the minority's preferred candidate."

Against this background, North Carolina and other states began the redistricting process necessary to comply with the results of the 1990 census. Under the Constitution, the national government must conduct a census of the population every decade. Based on those census results, the 435 seats in the U.S. House of Representatives are reapportioned among the states, with certain state delegations gaining seats, some losing representation, and others retaining their previous allocation of House seats. Next, states are obliged to redraw the districts from which House members, state legislators, and most other officials elected by district are chosen. In the process, they must comply with the Supreme Court's "one-person, one-vote" rulings requiring districts of substantially equal population, as well as with other Court decisions and the Voting Rights Act.

States derive their responsibility for congressional districting primarily from Article I, Section 4, of the Constitution, which provides that "the times, places, and manner of holding elections for Senators

{ *Race and Redistricting* }

and Representatives, shall be prescribed in each state by the legislature thereof." But that provision also stipulates that "the Congress may at any time by law make or alter such regulations." In 1842, Congress required each state with more than one House member to elect its representatives by single-member districts "composed of contiguous territory," rather than at large. In an effort to limit gerrymandering — the drawing of districts to favor the electoral chances of one political party or group over others — Congress in 1901 and 1911 also required that congressional districts be "compact." A major apportionment act adopted in 1929, however, omitted any requirement for contiguous, compact, or equally populated districts. From that point until the Supreme Court's reapportionment rulings of the 1960s and passage of voting rights legislation, the state congressional redistricting process was subject to virtually no federal oversight.

In North Carolina, as in most other states, the legislature assumes responsibility for redistricting rather than placing that task in the hands of a commission or some other agency. Always a complicated, politically sensitive process, congressional redistricting in North Carolina following the 1990 census was especially problematic. First, the state's population growth entitled it to an additional U.S. House member; its eleven districts had to be redrawn not only to reflect population shifts since the last census but also to accommodate a new Twelfth District. Second, interests both internal and external to the state pressed for the creation of one or more districts in which African Americans would constitute a voting majority. Finally, since a portion of North Carolina was subject to Section 5 of the Voting Rights Act, the state's congressional redistricting plan was subject to Justice Department preclearance.

External pressure for the creation of majority-minority districts came primarily from the Justice Department's Civil Rights Division. Some suggested that staff attorneys with no partisan political interests simply believed that the 1982 amendments to Section 2 of the Voting Rights Act, as well as the *Gingles* ruling, required such districting to guard against minority vote dilution. Democratic officeholders in North Carolina and elsewhere in the South, however, charged that the campaign for majority-minority districts was part of a Bush administration "Max-Black" campaign, largely orchestrated by Republican National Committee counsel Ben Ginsberg. The plan was to pack African American voters — by far the most reliable members of the

Democratic Party's electoral bloc—into a few districts, leaving other districts predominantly white and more likely to elect white Republican candidates to office. Whatever theory is correct, members of the North Carolina General Assembly and state attorney general's staff began the redistricting season with the knowledge that adoption of at least one majority-minority congressional district, not to mention a number of state legislative districts, would be critical to North Carolina's survival of the Justice Department's preclearance process.

Interest in majority-minority congressional districts was not confined entirely to the Bush administration or the Republican Party. North Carolina had not had an African American in Congress since George White of Edgecombe County, in the state's rural eastern Black Belt, left his House seat in 1901. State legislative redistricting in the 1980s had increased the number of blacks in the General Assembly, and members of the legislative black caucus considered their race long overdue for seats in the U.S. House. Leaders of the state National Association for the Advancement of Colored People (NAACP) shared that sentiment, as did Dan T. Blue, a Raleigh attorney who in 1991 became the first African American elected speaker of the North Carolina house of representatives.

Dan Blue had grown up in rural Robeson County, in the southern part of the state. His father was a farmer and factory worker, and his mother was a housewife who worked in the fields alongside her husband and their five children. A high achiever with a zeal to succeed, Blue was valedictorian of his high school class, where he also played in the school band, was an officer in the state chapter of the Future Farmers of America, and participated in school plays and oratorical competitions. The Soviet launching of *Sputnik* when Blue was in elementary school led to a sustained interest in the U.S. space program and dreams of becoming a physicist or engineer. When he left Robeson County in 1966 to attend North Carolina Central University, a predominantly black school in Durham, he chose, not surprisingly, to major in mathematics.

By his senior year at Central, however, Blue's admiration for lawyers involved in the civil rights struggles of that period convinced him to seek a law degree at Duke. One of his professors was Walter Dellinger, a former clerk to Supreme Court Justice Hugo L. Black and future acting solicitor general in the Clinton administration, who would later represent the state before the Supreme Court in the districting suit. Another was Robinson Everett. Everett, Blue later recalled, "was the kind of professor you could talk with. . . . He shared a lot of my views on civil rights, the effort to be inclusive. There were not a lot of black students at Duke then. There were seven at the law school. Robinson was held in high esteem by the black students. He was helpful when he could be."

After graduating from law school in 1973, Blue joined the Raleigh firm of Terry Sanford, the former North Carolina governor then serving as Duke's president. In 1976, however, Blue and two associates left to open their own Raleigh firm. Blue eventually became the firm's managing partner, but he also had an abiding interest in politics. In 1980, he was elected to the state house of representatives and has been reelected ever since, serving as speaker from 1991 to 1994.

Other key players in the redistricting and preclearance process included the three co-chairs of the house redistricting committee, one of whom was Milton F. ("Toby") Fitch, Jr., an African American whose father had figured prominently in North Carolina's civil rights protests of the 1960s and had been a field coordinator for Martin Luther King's Southern Christian Leadership Conference.

As committee counsel, Blue chose Asheville native Leslie Winner. Winner had clerked for James B. McMillan, the pioneering U.S. district court judge who ordered massive desegregation of Charlotte schools. Later, Winner became a partner in Ferguson, Stein, the firm that represented the black parents in the Charlotte suit, Ferguson, Stein had been founded by Julius Chambers, North Carolina's leading African American civil rights attorney. Winner's firm had successfully sued the state in the *Gingles* case, and she was considered one of North Carolina's premier experts in election law. In the state senate, president pro tem Henson Barnes chose Winner's brother Dennis to chair the redistricting committee. Among legislative staffers, Gerry Cohen would play a central and ultimately controversial role in the redistricting process and the subsequent litigation.

Staff members from the North Carolina attorney general's office also played a major support role in preclearance negotiations with the Justice Department. Eddie Speas was head of the attorney general's special litigation unit at the time. Speas had been raised in Boonville, a Yadkin County village in the North Carolina foothills. After obtaining an undergraduate degree in history and a law degree from Wake Forest, he joined the attorney general's staff, where he would remain throughout his career. For the first fifteen years of his tenure, Speas worked in the education section, defending, as he later put it, "many of our fine institutions of higher education" in a variety of suits. In 1990, he became head of the special litigation section, a unit created by Attorney General Lacy H. Thornburg in 1986 and staffed by lawyers with at least ten years of trial experience to handle major cases not covered by other divisions in the state's justice department. Later, he was named North Carolina's chief deputy attorney general.

Speas would play a significant part in the majority-minority districting litigation. But Tiare Smiley, an assistant in his office, was the special litigation section's point person in both the lawsuits and the protracted preclearance negotiations with the U.S. Justice Department, including compilation of the voluminous documentation required for preclearance proceedings. Smiley's parents were New Englanders. She had been born in Florida and spent part of her childhood in North Carolina, but much of her life prior to college was lived elsewhere. Her family returned to the state when her father, a newspaper man, acquired two papers in western North Carolina. Largely to satisfy her father, Smiley majored in journalism at the University of North Carolina at Chapel Hill but quickly realized that she had no interest in pursuing his profession and took a job as a retail clothing buyer while her husband completed law school. She then finished law school at Chapel Hill in 1977. After a brief stint in private practice, Smiley joined the state attorney general's staff in 1978.

Before going into the special litigation section, Smiley worked in the antitrust, labor, education, and corrections divisions. She obtained her first experience with redistricting litigation when the *Gingles* suit was filed in 1982, prior to the creation of the special litigation unit. Private counsel largely argued the state's case in *Gingles*, but Smiley and two other staff attorneys did the legwork and prepped Attorney General Thornburg to argue the case before the Supreme Court. Given her involvement in *Gingles*, Smiley seemed a logical choice to work with the General Assembly in securing preclearance for North Carolina's redistricting plans adopted after the 1990 census.

Through all of North Carolina's modern history to that point, Democrats had controlled both houses of the General Assembly.

Speaker Blue, president pro tem Barnes, and other influential Democrats in the legislature were convinced that districts should be created that would improve minority chances for election to state legislative and U.S. House seats. But they did not necessarily want to maximize the number of such districts that could be drawn. "Since North Carolina had not had an African American congressman since George White in 1901," Blue later said, "we figured that there had to be some effort made to create an opportunity for minority citizens to slate and elect a minority candidate if they so chose. And so we went into it, with the understanding of the senate leadership as well as the people who were putting together the congressional redistricting plan in the senate, that we would go through all means to create at least one majority-minority district."

Major improvements in computer technology since the 1980s made sophisticated manipulation of district lines almost as simple as the click of a keyboard digit. Gerry Cohen, the General Assembly's chief redistricting architect, composed plans with the help of a $200,000 software program that enabled him to sort quickly though census data and election and voter registration statistics, as well as something called the Topologically Integrated Geographic Encoding and Referencing System, an elaborate geographic database. TIGER, as the database was known, was essentially an atlas of North Carolina that allowed Cohen to call up computer screen images of districts containing the names of streets, roads, railroads, rivers, and even the homes of incumbent state legislators and members of Congress.

At 2:35 A.M. on June 20, 1991, Cohen completed work on 1991 Congressional Base #4. Consistent with the Supreme Court's one-person, one-vote precedents, the plan divided North Carolina's 6,628,637 residents as evenly as mathematically possible, with seven districts containing exactly 552,386 residents; the other five districts had an additional resident each. It also included one majority-minority district. For many years, North Carolina law had forbidden the splitting of counties in legislative and congressional districting, but reapportionment decisions and the Voting Rights Act had prompted an end to that tradition. The congressional districting plan then in effect split only four of the state's hundred counties; the plan Cohen created split thirty-four. District One, the proposed majority-minority district, took in eleven entire counties and portions of fourteen additional counties.

Although largely concentrated in the northeastern corner of the state, one portion of the district ran south, and another ran west along North Carolina's northern boundary, encompassing part of the Raleigh-Durham metropolitan area. The First District's proposed new boundaries made it less likely that Walter B. Jones, Sr., the district's veteran Democratic congressman, could win reelection against an African American challenger. But Jones, who had served in the House since 1966, was seventy-seven years old and was expected to retire. The redistricting kept all of the state's seven Democratic and four Republican incumbents in separate districts, but it also made two GOP incumbents — the Eleventh District's Charles Taylor and the Sixth's Howard Coble — more vulnerable to Democratic challenge by removing Republican-leaning counties from their districts and, in Coble's case, adding several Democratic-leaning counties. The proposal gave Democratic congressmen William Hefner and Stephen Neal of the Eighth and Fifth Districts safer seats by removing several Republican-leaning counties from their districts, but the plan placed two other Democratic incumbents — Tim Valentine and Martin Lancaster — in new districts that contained only about half their current constituents.

African American legislators praised the plan. Howard Hunter, Jr., a black house member residing in the proposed majority-minority district, told a reporter that "it will give us a chance to elect somebody who understands the needs of minorities in this state, someone who will try to address those needs and concerns." But Walter B. Jones, Jr., a white member of the state house and son of the First District's incumbent congressman, objected to the way the plan split many counties and towns to achieve the desired white–black population ratio in his father's district. Jones, Jr., who would later switch to the Republican Party and win a U.S. House seat from the Third District after losing a First District runoff primary to his black opponent, complained that the configuration of the proposed First District was "like trying to put a jigsaw puzzle together." House leaders rebuffed the junior Jones's proposal for an alternative plan that would have left more eastern counties intact. But Jones did not vote against the plan the General Assembly adopted; he was simply absent when the measure came up for a vote. He later explained that he had been called to the senate to discuss an ethics bill he was sponsoring. Others suspected that he feared black voter backlash should he seek election to his father's congressional seat in a majority-minority district he had voted to defeat.

Republican legislators and party officials were critical of both the state legislative and the congressional districting plans, primarily because of the electoral advantage they gave incumbents, most of whom were Democrats at that point. Raleigh GOP house member J. Arthur Pope complained, "When you look across the state, many of those strangely drawn districts are due to partisan gerrymandering and protecting the incumbents. The districts shouldn't be drawn for the incumbents. They should be drawn for the people of North Carolina, respecting traditional counties, cities, and towns and other smaller communities." House minority leader Johnathan Rhyne told a reporter that his party intended to file a lawsuit if necessary but predicted that the congressional plan would not survive preclearance, since it included only a single majority-minority district.

Tiare Smiley would eventually become adept at compiling the voluminous documentation the Justice Department required for preclearance, but preparation of the more than twenty large notebooks that accompanied the 1991 state legislative and congressional plans proved to be, she later remembered, a "bear of a project." In October, Blue, Smiley, Leslie Winner, and other staffers and legislators took a state plane to Washington for a meeting with officials in the Justice Department's voting rights section. "We told them," Blue later said, "what our reasoning was, what the process was, and that we had for the first time minorities [in the General Assembly] drawing the districts, or at least some minorities in charge. . . . In our group, we had two African Americans, two Jewish legislators, a Jewish staffer, and two white eastern North Carolina legislators. And all of us went to Washington to [support a single majority-minority district. But] . . . it was rather clear after we had talked that the . . . Bush administration was going to . . . push us toward creating a second majority-minority district. It was clear in our minds. [And] we had not intended to do that. . . . The thing that occurred to us was that we were going to have to have huge geographical expanses to put together 550,000 people, at least 250,000 to 300,000 of them having to be minority," in creating a second majority-minority district.

Neither Smiley's submissions nor the state officials' Washington trip would have the desired effect. In late October, two weeks after

Blue and the others returned to Raleigh, the Justice Department sent the state a seven-page request for information. Under the Voting Rights Act, such requests gave the attorney general an additional sixty days to review the state's proposed plan. The documents sought included correspondence with members of the General Assembly's redistricting committees and maps of alternative plans the legislature chose not to adopt. Henson Barnes tried to be optimistic, telling a reporter, "I think they just needed more time. . . . The nature of the information they asked for was pretty broad. There were not a lot of specific requests that would indicate a specific problem they were looking at." But Laughlin McDonald of the Atlanta office of the American Civil Liberties Union (ACLU) said that requests for further information were often a prelude to the Justice Department's rejection of proposed changes in a state's election laws.

The ACLU, along with the North Carolina Republican Party, had supported creation of a second majority-minority district stretching from Charlotte in the state's piedmont to Wilmington on the coast. Asked why Democrats and the legislative black caucus had opposed that arrangement, Democratic house member Toby Fitch, the African American co-chairing the redistricting committee, asserted that the Republicans simply wanted to pack minorities into a handful of districts, diluting their influence in the rest. "It's not that they're for the Voting Rights Act. It's because they believe their numbers will be better."

In early November, Smiley responded to the Justice Department's request for additional information. Later that month and in December, she submitted responses to ten further requests, but to no avail. In a letter to Smiley dated December 18, 1991, John R. Dunne, the assistant attorney general in charge of the department's voting rights division, concluded that the state legislative and congressional plans would require further modification before qualifying for preclearance. Alternatively, North Carolina could exercise its option under Section 5 to attempt to convince the federal district court in Washington that the plans had "neither the purpose nor will have the effect of denying or abridging the right to vote on account of race or color." Or the state could ask the attorney general to reconsider his objections.

Early paragraphs in Dunne's six-page letter summarized the requirements for preclearance. The state had the burden "of showing that each of the legislative choices under a proposed plan [was] free of racially discriminatory purpose or retrogressive effect" and would not result in minority vote dilution, which was forbidden by Section 2 of the Voting Rights Act. Drawing on judicial precedents and the Justice Department's administrative guidelines, Dunne also noted that "we cannot preclear those portions of a plan where the legislature has deferred to the interests of incumbents while refusing to accommodate the community of interest shared by insular minorities, . . . or where the proposed plan, given the demographics and racial concentrations in the jurisdiction, does not fairly reflect minority voting strength." Such concerns, he added, were "frequently related to the unnecessary fragmentation of minority communities or the needless packing of minority constituents into a minimal number of districts in which they can expect to elect candidates of their choice." As stipulated by the Voting Rights Act's language, however, the assistant attorney general also conceded that the law did "not require that any jurisdiction guarantee minority voters racial or ethnic proportional results."

After indicating that the North Carolina proposals "in large part" met Section 5 preclearance requirements, Dunne turned to the weaknesses he saw in each. Referring to the congressional redistricting plan, he suggested that the First District's "unusually convoluted shape" had not been necessary for the creation of a majority black district, that, in fact, "at least one alternative configuration was available that would have been more compact." He concluded, however, that the First District's "irregular" shape had neither "the purpose [n]or effect of minimizing voting strength in that region."

The state's failure to create a second majority-minority district was a different matter. Dunne noted the "significant interest on the part of the minority community" in the creation of a second minority district. Several plans had been developed, he wrote, proposing one for the south-central to southeast area of North Carolina, including at least one proposal introduced in the General Assembly. Both the NAACP and the ACLU had endorsed such a plan. Yet the legislature had rejected a second minority district, Dunne observed, "for what appears to be pretextual reasons." Some of those who submitted comments on the plan the legislature adopted, he added, "have alleged that the state's decision to place the concentrations of minority voters in the southern part of the state into white majority districts attempts to ensure the election of white incumbents while minimizing minority electoral strength." Finding that North Carolina had submitted "no convincing evidence to the contrary," Dunne rejected the congressional plan. Based on similar reasoning, he objected to the state house and senate plans as well.

———

Opponents of North Carolina's redistricting plans greeted the Justice Department's decision with enthusiasm. Kelly M. Alexander, Jr., president of the state NAACP, praised the decision, adding that "it's been a long time since I concurred with the [GOP-controlled] Justice Department." Alexander and other prominent African Americans also faulted the willingness of Dan Blue, Toby Fitch, and other members of the legislative black caucus to support plans with fewer minority districts than could have been created. "The difference between where I am and where some of them are," the NAACP head declared, "may be that I don't have to defend political compromise."

Howard Clement III, a black Republican member of the Durham city council, echoed Alexander's sentiments. "I think those folks are more concerned about their standing in the Democratic Party than they are concerned about the needs and aspirations of the minority community. If we get the numbers, at least we will have people there who can articulate more clearly the needs and aspirations of the minority community. At this stage in our history, that is very important." Nor was Clement concerned about the division that debate over the plans had created within the African American community. "White folks don't agree," said Clement, "so black folks don't have to agree. We are not a monolithic community."

The Reverend Thomas L. Walker, a black Democrat and eastern North Carolina county commissioner, asserted that members of his race could not afford to worry about the motives of the leadership in either political party. "It's a sad commentary on white Republicans and white Democrats," said Walker, "but we are not going to get any blacks elected unless we have majority black districts. We have to look out for our interests first and the party second."

Black and white Democratic leaders in the General Assembly saw the Justice Department's decision as further evidence of a Republican plot to pack minority (and overwhelmingly Democratic) voters into a few districts, enhancing the electoral prospects of white Republicans elsewhere in the state. Fitch had first won election to the state house of representatives in 1985 from a minority district created after the 1980 census. But taken too far, Fitch warned, the movement for majority-minority districts could end up confining blacks to "political reservations," reducing their influence in state politics as a whole. "Obviously they would elect their representatives, but all the other representatives around them would be of a different ideology or political persuasion. Thus [minorities] would not be able to build [their] coalitions."

Speaker Blue chided the Republicans for championing additional majority-minority districts after years of refusing to support blacks on other legislative issues, including recognition of a paid holiday for state workers in honor of Martin Luther King, Jr. "I am supportive of the Voting Rights Act, supportive of its goal," Blue declared. "But I think that what the Republicans are trying to do is corrupt the Voting Rights Act to the extent they can go beyond . . . its goal and mission . . . and use it for political advantage."

Whites in the Democratic leadership directed most of their ire at the Justice Department. Sam Hunt of Alamance County in the North Carolina piedmont, one of the co-chairs of the house redistricting committee, said that the legislature would continue to do "what's best for North Carolina instead of having some bureaucrats in Washington telling us what to do. I am not too impressed with anything I have seen come out of Washington." Henson Barnes was more acerbic. "It always bothers the state," he told a reporter, "for some faceless bureaucrat in Washington to have the power to reject months of hard work on the stroke of a pen. A bureaucrat can dictate a six-page letter and change 12 congressional districts and all the Senate and House districts . . . and that is not right."

Whatever their frustrations over Justice Department policy, the Democratic leadership in the General Assembly bowed to the inevitable, moving to adopt a second majority-minority district. Postponing the candidate filing period for a month, the legislature adopted new plans in late January 1992. But the Democratic majority in the assembly was not about to create a second majority-minority district in the southeastern section of the state, as the Justice Department had suggested. Although that district would have combined Lumbee Indians and blacks to create a district dominated by minorities, those two groups hardly had common interests. More significantly, creation of such a district would have removed reliably Democratic voters from the district of veteran Democratic congressman Charlie Rose, substantially weakening his electoral base.

Instead, Democratic leaders, reportedly with considerable assistance from a Rose aide, drew the new Twelfth District across North Carolina's northern piedmont crescent, along the Interstate 85 corridor from Durham to Charlotte. One of several districting plans proposed by Charlotte Republican representative David G. Balmer had followed that route. While legislative Democrats were examining Balmer's handiwork, "a light went on," as Smiley later put it. They realized that they could pattern the new district after Balmer's plan yet avoid jeopardizing the reelection chances of white Democratic incumbents in neighboring districts. And that is exactly what they did.

Democrats also attacked the Bush administration for forcing states to adopt such districts. Senate redistricting committee chairman Dennis Winner complained, for example, "It looks like what the Justice Department has required is that we go back to 'separate, but equal,'" adding, "That goes against every grain in my body of what society should be." Republicans, in contrast, charged the Democrats with once again seeking, this time under the guise of compliance with the Voting Rights Act, to gerrymander Republican congressmen out of office. "If you don't trust the Justice Department," Republican lieutenant governor James C. Gardner advised assembly Democrats, "take them to court."

In early February, the Justice Department approved the new legislative and congressional districting plans. Under the congressional plan, 43 percent of North Carolina's 1.4 million blacks now resided in Districts One and Twelve, the two majority-minority districts. Black candidates won both seats in the 1992 elections. Eva M. Clayton, a management consultant and former county commissioner, defeated Walter Jones, Jr., in a runoff Democratic primary, then won election to the First District seat over her Republican opponent. Charlotte lawyer Melvin L. Watt, a close friend and campaign manager of former Charlotte mayor Harvey Gantt, won election in the Twelfth District. Well before that point, however, the dispute over North Carolina's majority-minority districts had moved from the political arena into the courts.

CHAPTER 2

"Political Pornography"

To serve their goal of maximizing the electoral strength of certain groups while reducing the political fortunes of others, gerrymanders regularly produce bizarrely shaped districts. North Carolina's majority-minority districts were no exception. Although finding them consistent with the requirements of the Voting Rights Act, Assistant Attorney General John Dunne termed the state's First and Twelfth Congressional Districts "ugly as hell." Others were equally unrestrained. One federal judge would compare the First District to a "Rorschach ink-blot test." A state legislator remarked of District Twelve that "if you drove down [Interstate 85] with both car doors open, you'd kill most of the people in the district."

The *Wall Street Journal* was perhaps most graphic, if not entirely accurate in its reaction. Ridiculing North Carolina's congressional map as "political pornography," a *Journal* editorial described District Twelve as "a long snake that winds its way through central North Carolina for 190 miles, from Durham to Charlotte, scooping up isolated precincts with nothing in common save a large number of minority voters. . . . For much of its length, the district is no wider than the Interstate 85 corridor that links the two cities. In one county, northbound drivers on I-85 would be in the 12th district, but southbound drivers would be in another. The next county over, the districts would 'change lanes,' and southbound drivers would be in the 12th district. How will candidates campaign in such a monstrosity? 'We'll just have rallies at every exit along I-85,' jokes [one African American legislator]."

Comparing its shape to a "bug splattered on a windshield," the *Journal* found the First District "equally senseless. It wanders from the Virginia border almost to South Carolina. Two of its parts appear to be connected only by a river, with the banks on each side in other districts."

Under the circumstances, a lawsuit seemed inevitable. North Carolina Republicans launched the first attack. For those unfamiliar with the outcome of the districting battle in the General Assembly, a Republican challenge to the majority-minority districts appeared ironic. The Bush Justice Department, after all, had forced the legislature's action in the first place. But the districting had not only created two safe seats for African American Democrats; the plan had also done relatively little damage to the future prospects of incumbent congressional Democrats. In late February, the North Carolina GOP, state party chairman Jack Hawke, and Republican house member J. Arthur Pope, joined by forty-one other "aggrieved voters," filed a suit in the federal district court in Charlotte, charging that the district plan was an unconstitutional partisan gerrymander.

In announcing the suit, Hawke complained that the Democratic-controlled General Assembly had packed Republican voters largely into two districts (GOP congressman Howard Coble's Sixth District and T. Cass Ballenger's Tenth District), strengthening the chances of Democratic incumbents in other districts. The new districts, Hawke further charged, were so convoluted and confusing to voters that they would lose touch with their representatives, and the representatives with them. "We have government that is supposed to be based upon the principle of government of the people, by the people, for the people," he exclaimed. "But what the General Assembly of North Carolina has done is created government of the Democratic incumbents, by the Democratic incumbents, for the Democratic incumbents. . . . Drawing lines in this manner to protect incumbents turns the whole system upside down. Instead of voters choosing their representatives, the representatives are choosing their voters. This is undermining, in my opinion, the whole fabric of the representative form of government."

Civil rights leaders, Democratic legislators, and state officials quickly reacted to news of the suit. State NAACP head Kelly Alexander confidently predicted that the plaintiffs "don't have a snowball's chance in Hades" to succeed. Senator Dennis Winner expressed some hope that the courts might relieve states of any obligation to create majority-minority districts that were not geographically compact. He reminded a reporter, however, that a Republican (David Balmer) had first suggested the Twelfth District's Interstate 85 design. "It just seems to me rank hypocrisy to assert that [the plan is unconstitutional] when they were the ones who insisted we put those two minority districts in." House Democrat Sam Hunt of Burlington contended that Republicans had proposed districts that were even more contorted than the ones the General Assembly adopted. "My basic comment," declared Hunt, "would be, 'What the hell are they talking about?' The Republican members of the legislature, and the Republican National Committee that they answer to, and the Republican Justice Department are the ones that caused it to be as bad as it is."

Eddie Speas of the state attorney general's office would have overall responsibility for defending the districts in any lawsuit. "The most notable thing about this complaint," Speas observed, "is: There's not, as far as we are aware, any legal authority for the kind of claim they are making."

Especially in light of the Supreme Court's ruling in *Davis v. Bandemer* (1986), a successful equal protection challenge to partisan gerrymandering did appear extremely dubious. Indiana Democrats complained in *Bandemer* that the state's Republican-controlled legislature had drawn legislative district lines for partisan advantage. Speaking for a plurality, Justice Byron White required plaintiffs in a party gerrymandering case to produce evidence that a particular districting scheme caused "continued frustration of the will of the majority of the voters or effective denial to a minority of the voters of a fair chance to influence the political process" over a significant number of elections. The mere absence of party representation in a legislature proportionate to party voting strength in the electorate was inadequate to establish a constitutional violation. Instead, plaintiffs were obliged to prove that their group had "essentially been shut out of the political process." White spoke only for a plurality, but three other justices concluded that partisan gerrymandering raised the kinds of political questions the Court had traditionally considered inappropriate for judicial resolution.

Relying heavily on *Bandemer*, a three-judge district court, with one judge dissenting, dismissed the Republicans' challenge to the North Carolina districts. Speaking for the majority in *Pope v. Blue* (1992), Judge Sam J. Ervin III of the Fourth Circuit U.S. Court of Appeals reiterated *Bandemer*'s holding that a challenge to partisan gerrymandering must establish a discriminatory intent and effect and that the results of a single election were insufficient to establish discriminatory impact in such a case. "Here," he added, "we do not even have a single election to corroborate the plaintiffs' allegations of disproportionate representation." Moreover, while the plaintiffs could in theory prove that the challenged plan would result in a pattern of disproportionate election results, they could hardly claim that the plan would "shut [them] out of the political process." After all, it had created a number of safe Republican seats. Also, voters could influence members of Congress in ways other than through the election of candidates of their choice, and the General Assembly had made no effort to interfere with Republican voter registration, organizing, voting, fund-raising, or campaigning.

The majority gave even shorter shrift to the plaintiffs' other constitutional claims. Article I, Section 2, merely required congressional districts of equal population, observed Judge Ervin; it did not command that the "inherently political [districting] process" also produce compact and contiguous districts. Although conceding that the challenged plan might discourage some Republicans from campaigning, Ervin also rejected the contention that it imposed a chilling effect on their exercise of First Amendment freedoms. The Constitution simply did not entitle any group to political success. Finally, to the plaintiffs' claim that the "right to live in a regularly shaped congressional district" was among the privileges and immunities of national citizenship protected by the Fourteenth Amendment, Ervin responded that the "largely forgotten" privileges or immunities guarantee had been used, to that point, only once to invalidate a state law, in a precedent overruled a mere five years later. The judge saw "no legal basis for breathing new life into the clause."

The Supreme Court summarily affirmed the district court's ruling in *Pope v. Blue*, with only Justice Harry Blackmun favoring a full hearing of the Republican Party's appeal in the case. But court challenges to North Carolina's majority-minority districts were just beginning. In 1966, Robinson Everett, the Duke law professor and Durham attorney who would become the principal figure in the *Shaw-Cromartie* litigation, represented several North Carolina residents in *Drum v. Seawell*, a reapportionment suit. A three-judge district court in that case had upheld the state's redrawing of districts for both houses of the General Assembly but refused to find North Carolina's congressional districts consistent with the one-person, one-vote formula the Supreme Court had imposed in *Wesberry v. Sanders, Reynolds v. Sims,* and other apportionment cases. In an attempt, among other things, to protect incumbent congressmen, the legislature had drawn districts with "tortuous [boundary] lines" lacking "compactness and contiguity." The district court judges agreed that "rigid mathematical standards [were] not the sine qua non of constitutional validity." Emphasizing the Supreme Court's demand for districts as nearly equal in population "as practicable," however, they concluded that the Constitution did require "practical equality," including regard for compactness and contiguity. The legislature's "overemphasis on factors other than population [such as incumbency protection]" in its redistricting, the court held, had created unconstitutionally "excessive deviation[s]" from the requirement of practical equality.

Ruth Shaw, widow of a Duke sociology professor and longtime friend of Robinson Everett's family, had been one of Everett's clients in *Drum v. Seawell.* When Everett's mother Kathrine died in late January 1992, Mrs. Shaw visited the funeral home to offer her condolences. The General Assembly had recently created the two majority-minority congressional districts, neither of which had boundary lines that were geographically compact or contiguous. When Mrs. Shaw came through the receiving line at the funeral home, Everett, recalling the irregular districts struck down in the *Drum* case, said, "Ruth, they did the same thing all over again. We ought to do something about it." Shaw readily agreed.

On March 12, Everett filed a suit in federal district court. His plaintiffs, in addition to Shaw, included his Duke law school colleague Melvin Shimm, Everett's son Greg, and his secretary Dorothy Bullock. Partly to permit greater latitude for making public statements during the course of the litigation than an attorney would ordinarily be allowed, Everett listed himself as a plaintiff as well as counsel in the case.

Given their backgrounds, none of the plaintiffs seemed particularly likely prospects to challenge a districting plan seeking to increase the number of minority representatives in the halls of government. Robinson Everett's mother Kathrine was the daughter of Henry Robinson, a Fayetteville lawyer. A woman of exceptional ability and drive, Kathrine graduated first in her class at the University of North Carolina (UNC) law school, the only woman in the class of 1920. She went on to make the top score that year on the state bar examination, becoming only the fourth woman licensed to practice law in North Carolina. In October, just a few months after graduating from law school, she became the first woman to win an appeal in the state's supreme court — all that in the same year women first won the right to vote.

In 1926, Kathrine married Reuben Oscar Everett, a Duke (then Trinity College) law graduate fifteen years her senior who was a native of Martin County in eastern North Carolina's Black Belt. After their marriage, she moved to Durham, where Reuben had a law office. Robinson, their only child, was born there in 1928.

The Everetts' firm thrived. Over the years, they also acquired extensive real estate holdings and established UHF television stations in Durham, Greensboro, Wilmington, and Fayetteville. Kathrine and her son continued to enjoy financial success after his father's death in 1971. When she died in 1992, at age ninety-eight, the Kathrine Everett estate pledged $7 million each to the Duke and Chapel Hill law schools, the largest bequest to legal education in the state's history.

Kathrine and Reuben Everett were also heavily involved in the cultural and political life of their community and state. Reuben served five terms in the General Assembly and as chairman of the Durham County board of elections. In 1951, Kathrine became one of the first two women elected to the Durham city council, a position she held for twenty years.

Particularly in the early years, many of their real estate holdings were in marginal, predominantly black neighborhoods. For tardy tenants, they could be harsh landlords. In a general letter written to her tenants in 1954, Kathrine complained of the "considerable losses" she had suffered "through trying to accommodate tenants who, for various reasons, would get behind in rent and ask for additional time to pay . . . , [then,] after getting far behind, would move out of the house without paying." Henceforth, her policy was to be "prompt payment of rent each week. . . . This is to advise you," she added, "if you are behind in your rent, you will have to catch up the back rent AT ONCE, or I will have to ask you to vacate the house you now occupy."

The Everetts apparently enjoyed a warm relationship, however, not only with professional, business, and political leaders in Durham's African American community but also with the black electorate generally. When Kathrine ran for the city council in 1951, she received the endorsement of the local committee on black affairs as well as an overwhelming black vote. Both Kathrine and Reuben also enjoyed reputations as sympathetic whites among Durham blacks. As chairman of the county election board, Reuben had appointed the first African American registrars. Years earlier, in the 1920s, the press reported that he planned to sponsor an antimasking bill aimed at the Ku Klux Klan (KKK). When Klan members came to his office, threatening to end his legislative career if he supported the bill, he had a quick response. "I never knew anything about [the antimasking bill], didn't care about it. But you guys are a bunch of thugs, and I will not only support it, I'll introduce it," which he did. "That was pretty typical of him," his son later said. "He did not like to be pushed, particularly by people who were not good."

An apt student, Robinson Everett graduated from Durham high school at age fifteen, salutatorian of his class and winner of state contests in Latin, mathematics, and history. After a year at Phillips-Exeter and a few months at Chapel Hill, he reluctantly yielded to his parents' urging and enrolled at Harvard, from which he graduated with a major in government. Following law school at Harvard, where he was on law review and graduated magna cum laude, he returned to Durham to practice law and teach at Duke. But he had also applied for a staff position with the judge advocate general (JAG) of the Air Force and soon received his orders to report for duty in Texas. He served two years as a JAG lawyer, then spent another two years as a commissioner with the newly created Court of Military Appeals in Washington. In that post, he developed an enduring interest in military law that would result in a voluminous body of published research, including a 1956 book on military justice in the armed forces. Following his two years in Washington, he went back to North Carolina, where he practiced law and obtained a permanent position on the Duke faculty. In 1980, President Jimmy Carter appointed him chief judge of the Court of Military Appeals, a position he held until 1990.

Politically, the Everetts were staunch Democrats, allied with the North Carolina party's moderately liberal wing. In 1950, Robinson's parents backed Frank Porter Graham, the controversial and racially liberal UNC president who had been appointed the previous year to an unexpired term in the U.S. Senate. They watched in dismay as supporters of Graham's opponent resorted to crude racial smears in bringing about their friend's defeat in the Democratic primary. Graham "had been demonized," Robinson later recalled, in the Black Belt, where some of the family's relatives lived. "I was very sad. As I remember, the primary was the same day North Korea invaded South Korea — a pretty disastrous weekend."

Ten years later, Robinson played an active role in the successful gubernatorial bid of racial progressive Terry Sanford against I. Beverly Lake, one of the state's most outspoken segregationists. As in the past (if not in the not too distant future), victory in the Democratic primary was tantamount to election in North Carolina. Initially Everett had worked for the most liberal candidate in the race, a man who had been involved in a Klan prosecution and won the endorsement of Durham's black political organization. When Sanford and Lake were thrown into a runoff, however, Everett shifted his support to Sanford. In fact, when a former law partner and friend who had managed the Sanford campaign in Durham County had to leave the race, Everett became head of the county campaign. After the election, Everett was associated with Sanford, who later became president of Duke and a U.S. senator, in a variety of causes. He also supported Richardson Preyer, a liberal who later became a federal judge, in his unsuccessful 1964 gubernatorial primary bid against the more conservative Dan K. Moore. At one point, Everett served as counsel to the Senate Subcommittee on Constitutional Rights in Washington, headed by Sam J. Ervin, another influential North Carolina Democrat. In 1972, in his last political foray, he went down to the Democratic National Convention in Miami to support Terry Sanford's unsuccessful effort to win the presidential nomination over South Dakota senator George McGovern.

Like his parents, Robinson remained a "yellow-dog Democrat" for many years, regularly supporting the party's candidates and working in their campaigns. In fact, he met his wife, Lynn, while working in a friend's 1966 congressional campaign, courting her in her Volkswagen on nightly trips to Raleigh to work at the campaign office. "Big guy like me, a little girl like her, it was almost inevitable." After three sons and thirty-six years of marriage, they remain deeply devoted.

In the summer of 2000, Everett conceded that he had voted for a couple of Republicans for local office in the last election and had also voted for a Republican candidate for state supreme court justice over a Democrat who had been twice censured for judicial misconduct. To that point, however, he had never voted for a Republican presidential candidate — although, he confessed, he had been relieved when Lynn supported Richard Nixon in 1972, canceling his vote for McGovern.

Robinson Everett's racial views, like his politics, were also moderately liberal. When the Supreme Court outlawed segregated schools in its 1954 *Brown* decision, he later recalled, he and his parents "did not talk about it that much. Just viewed it as something that had transpired. . . . Our family was probably more allied with black interests than would be true of some. My mother got almost unanimous black votes every time she ran. I don't know whether they thought *Brown* was premature or not, but we just sort of accepted it as the law of the land. . . . We knew from our relatives down in eastern North Carolina that this was pretty traumatic for some of them. So we understood their viewpoint and respected it. . . . [But] I remember prosecuting a case as an Air Force prosecutor that involved racist remarks by the defendants, that we tried to get a heavy sentence for, because it was disruptive. And I think my experience in the Air Force influenced my attitude toward it — that people could live together of different races. My Dad had been opposed to . . . some of the things that groups like the KKK were doing. My mother may have had the most concern of any of us."

The backgrounds of the other major plaintiffs in Everett's suit seemed equally difficult to reconcile with their opposition to districts enhancing the electoral chances of minority candidates. A Minnesota native, Ruth Shaw had moved to Durham in the late 1950s, when her husband, a sociologist, took a position on the Duke faculty. Shortly thereafter, their automobile collided with a lumber truck in Virginia while they were returning to Durham from a professional meeting. Professor Shaw was killed instantly, and his wife was seriously injured. Robinson Everett successfully represented Ruth Shaw in her accident-related lawsuits, and the two became good friends and Sanford Democrats.

Raised in a small Scandinavian community, Ruth Shaw does not remember seeing an African American until she attended the University of Minnesota. She and her husband were racial liberals. When he finished his Ph.D., he took a teaching post for a year at the University of Alabama but also taught at the local black college, refusing to take a salary for his services. Their brief stay in the cradle of the Confederacy gave both of them a vivid and distasteful awareness of southern racial mores. When Ruth picked up the packages of a black woman she had bumped into in a department store, the sales clerks refused to wait on her. "Another time," she remembers, "a little black child offered my daughter a piece of candy in a store. She took the piece, and we thanked her. We had a lot of looks, and again I wasn't waited on."

In Durham, Ruth's two daughters attended all-white elementary schools but graduated from a predominantly black high school. Integration of Durham's public schools had provoked massive white flight to private schools or predominantly white school districts. "My youngest daughter was advised by her pediatrician and some of the faculty to go to a private school." An outstanding student who later joined the mathematics faculty at Syracuse University, her daughter "absolutely refused" to transfer. When Everett first approached Ruth about a court challenge to North Carolina's districting plan, she appeared enthusiastic. Initially, though, she was uncertain whether she wanted to become involved. "I knew it was a controversial thing; I knew it was open to criticism by people who would generalize, who would immediately think it was a racial issue [with us]. I didn't want to hurt my daughters. They had [black] friends from [high] school. But they both said that they understood my position, that they too had complete faith in the Shimms and Everetts, and that if I felt it was the right thing to do, then I should become involved."

Everett's colleague Melvin Shimm came from an even more liberal tradition than his co-plaintiffs did. A native of New York City and a Yale law graduate, Shimm practiced law in New York from 1950 to 1951, then worked for a year as an attorney with the Wage Stabilization Board in Washington. Following a year as a Bigelow Fellow at the University of Chicago law school, he joined the Duke faculty. Although his wife, a psychoanalyst, initially resisted a move to the South, both soon grew to relish their lives in Durham.

As a Columbia University undergraduate, Shimm was a member of the NAACP. In the early 1960s, he signed a petition urging the U.S. House of Representatives to cut off further funding of the House Committee on Un-American Activities. "I remember getting scathing letters, mainly from Duke alumni, who sent copies to the president of the university, calling me a pinko and commie." Shimm regarded himself as "a New Deal, Fair Deal sort of Democrat—sympathizing down the line with people like Harry Truman, a politician who in many ways epitomized the way I viewed domestic and foreign affairs." For a long time, Shimm and Duke constitutional law professor William Van Alstyne were considered "the left wing of the [law] faculty." He was also a Democratic precinct officer.

But in 1972, his national party, in his judgment, moved sharply to the left, while his politics remained the same. That year, McGovern forces packed the Durham delegation to the state convention with their people, giving no representation to supporters of other Democratic presidential hopefuls. Shimm walked out and never attended another precinct meeting. He also passed on the presidential election that year. "I couldn't bring myself to vote for Nixon, and I was very unsympathetic with McGovern for a variety of reasons." In time, "Bill Van Alstyne and I—I won't say we're on the right wing—... but virtually all the older Duke [law] faculty are the more conservative Democrats now.... I still am not, and would not register as, a Republican.... But I never necessarily vote the straight [Democratic] Party ticket."

Among the elements of the "new liberalism" of the national Democratic Party, Shimm was most disturbed by its enthusiasm for racial and related preferences as a means of correcting the effects of past discrimination against various groups in society. "I certainly am very sympathetic to any kinds of approaches that genuinely seek to repair damages done in the past. If someone was denied a promotion because he was black, I certainly think that there's no question that it's incumbent upon the government, incumbent on his employer, to make him whole again. What does go down less easily for me are blanket racial preferences, where the mere fact someone is of a certain race gives him an automatic preference. I think certainly one should make every effort to open up doors and to encourage blacks to apply for jobs, apply for schools. But it seems to me the meritocractic approach is the sound one. I look back on my own background growing up in a family where my parents weren't even high school graduates. I got where I was academically by working hard, and I didn't expect anybody to give me a leg up; I just wanted a fair shot.... I don't think anyone should be given a leg up unless he has been directly prejudiced by virtue of race or something of that sort. I look, for example, here in the law school and the university at large. Not only are, to use the word loosely, American blacks given this particular kind of racial preference. But if you come from Jamaica, if you come from Africa, the mere fact that you are very loosely defined as black, this will give you a leg up. This seems to me to be absolutely unsupportable."

A strong supporter in the past of Dan Blue, Durham state legislator Henry M. ("Mickey") Michaux, Jr., former Chapel Hill mayor Howard Lee, and other prominent African American politicians, Shimm was equally unconvinced that majority-minority districts were necessary for a state in which racially polarized voting made it otherwise practically impossible for black candidates to win election. "I don't think you have to be black to represent black interests," he recently remarked, "and I don't think you have to be white to represent white interests."

Somewhat ironically, given the court challenge to state legislative power he was helping to launch, Shimm had also grown more restive over the years with "the increasing intrusion of the federal government into areas that constitutionally have been reserved to the states, and the contortions and distortions of constitutional provisions that are used to justify it. . . . Hate crimes legislation, for example. Criminal law is preeminently something that's in the province of the states; symbolically, having it federalized is understandable but it seems to me that there is nothing that could be criminalized under federal hate crimes legislation that isn't already criminalized. . . . Not only is the federalization of the criminal law deleterious [to] . . . the federal structure of our government, but it overloads the federal courts." Justice Department pressure on states to create majority-minority districts was another obvious target of such concerns.

Everett had no difficulty recruiting Shimm to the cause. Shimm regularly scheduled early morning classes, and after class he visited the faculty lounge for a cup of coffee, often encountering his colleague there. One morning, they were discussing the bizarre shape of the state's newly crafted Twelfth District. "You know," Everett said at one point, "I think there's a good constitutional case that can be made against it." Everett had taught a good deal of criminal law at Duke. In *Batson v. Kentucky* (1986), the Supreme Court largely reaffirmed the traditional prerogative of counsel to exclude prospective jurors peremptorily, giving the judge no reason for the decision. The seven-to-two *Batson* majority refused, however, to uphold peremptory challenges based on a prospective juror's race. Later, the *Batson* precedent was extended to gender-based challenges. Everett could see no difference between the exclusion of jurors based on their race or sex and the exclusion of voters from a particular district—or their inclusion in a district—on racial grounds. "You know," Shimm responded, "I think you've got something there, Robbie." Everett then asked his colleague if he would agree to become a co-plaintiff in such a case. "'Yes, I would,'" Shimm later remembered answering. "It was as simple as that."

———

In filing his suit, Everett cast a broad net, including among the defendants not only a number of state officials but also U.S. Attorney General William Barr and John Dunne, head of the Justice Department's civil rights division. Although they had not participated directly in the adoption of North Carolina's majority-minority districts, they had used their preclearance authority to pressure the state into creating the two districts and thus, in Everett's eyes, shared responsibility for the state's illegal conduct.

For the first round in the litigation, Everett handled the plaintiffs' case alone. Eddie Speas and Tiare Smiley of the North Carolina attorney general's office had overall responsibility for the state's defense, but presentation of the state's position would fall primarily to one of Everett's Duke colleagues. Jefferson Powell, unlike Robinson Everett, was a constitutional law scholar. When the Republican Party filed *Pope v. Blue*, challenging the majority-minority districts on partisan gerrymandering grounds, Powell was on sabbatical from Duke, assisting the attorney general's office with another legal matter. At Speas's request, Powell took on the *Pope* defense, winning a dismissal of the suit in district court and the Supreme Court's decision summarily affirming the lower court's ruling. When Everett filed his suit, Powell agreed to represent the state in that case as well.

Usually a suit in federal district court is assigned to a single judge. But certain types of cases, including those dealing with federal election law, require the convening of a special three-judge panel, generally composed of one court of appeals judge and two district court judges. *Shaw v. Barr*, as the racial gerrymandering suit was originally titled, was to be heard by a three-judge panel.

The court selected consisted of two Democrats and one Republican. The presiding judge was J. Dickson Phillips, Jr., an eastern North Carolina native, prominent state Democrat, and former dean of the UNC law school. A Carter appointee, Phillips had taken a seat on the U.S. Court of Appeals for the Fourth Circuit, the federal appeals court with jurisdiction over North Carolina cases, in 1978. William Earl Britt, the other Democrat on the panel, had practiced law in the southeastern part of the state until his appointment by President Carter in 1980 as a federal district court judge in North Carolina's eastern district. The lone Republican on the court was Richard L. Voorhees, a Syracuse, New York, native who had settled in North Carolina following military service. Voorhees had practiced law in Gastonia until 1988, when President Ronald Reagan chose him for a seat on the U.S. district court for the state's western district.

In the complaint filed on March 12, three days after another district court panel had dismissed the *Pope* partisan gerrymandering suit, Everett charged the federal and state defendants with violations of Article I, Sections 2 and 4, of the Constitution, as well as provisions of the Fifth, Fourteenth, and Fifteenth Amendments. Article I, Section 2, provides that members of the U.S. House of Representatives are to be elected every two years "by the people of the several states." Article I, Section 4, authorizes state legislatures to determine the "times, places, and manner of holding" congressional elections, but it also empowers Congress to "make or alter such regulations" by statute "at any time." The Fifth Amendment's due process clause, forbidding the national government to deprive persons of "life, liberty, or property without due process of law," had long been interpreted by the Supreme Court to include an equal protection component, prohibiting U.S. officials from engaging in various forms of discrimination. The Fourteenth Amendment imposes due process and equal protection requirements on the states and also proscribes state laws abridging the privileges or immunities of U.S. citizens, and the Fifteenth Amendment forbids national and state officials to engage in racially discriminatory voting practices.

The allegations in Everett's complaint made up in novelty what they may have lacked in supporting court precedent. By pressuring the state into "isolating a large number of black persons into two Congressional Districts separate and apart from the 'people' in the other

34   { *Race and Redistricting* }

ten Congressional Districts," the federal defendants had violated Article I, Section 2, which, Everett claimed, "does not authorize or contemplate the creation of a system of proportional representation by race in the United States House of Representatives." Article I, Section 4, he added, reserves redistricting authority to the states, free from federal coercion, and although the same provision authorizes Congress to modify such regulations, it "by implication" denies Congress and federal administrators the authority to impose "such a system upon the 'people' of any state." In fact, the Voting Rights Act itself specifically provides that nothing in that law "establishes a right to have members of a protected class elected in numbers equal to their proportion in the population." Despite that provision, he declared, Justice Department officials had "coerced the State of North Carolina into creating two amorphous districts which embody a scheme for segregation of voters by race in order to meet a racial quota for [House] representation" — districts "totally unrelated [in their shape] to considerations of compactness, contiguousness, and geographic or jurisdictional communities of interest."

As a consequence, declared Everett, the federal defendants had "abridg[ed] the rights of the plaintiffs and all other citizens and registered voters of North Carolina — whether black, white, native American, or others — to participate in a process for electing members of the House of Representatives which is color-blind and wherein the right to vote is not abridged on account of the race or color of the voters." If the attorney general and his assistants acted on the basis of a misinterpretation of the Voting Rights Act, they were in violation of federal law; if their reading of the statute was correct, Congress had exceeded its constitutional powers in enacting its provisions. The state defendants, by submitting to the Justice Department's "unconstitutional requirements," had become "unwilling, but necessary," participants in the scheme and, Everett declared, were equally culpable.

As relief, Everett not only wanted the judges to declare the 1992 congressional districting plan unconstitutional and forbid the Justice Department to oblige the state to adopt districts in which "persons of a particular race or color . . . would be concentrated in a Congressional district that is in no way related to considerations of compactness, contiguousness and geographic or jurisdictional communities of interest." He also wanted the panel to require the state to adopt a new, color-blind plan and to forbid further congressional primaries or elections until the General Assembly had acted in accordance with the court's decree.

The defendants promptly filed motions to dismiss. Counsel for the Department of Justice argued that the district court in Raleigh had no jurisdiction over the attorney general's preclearance decisions. To guard against possible bias on the part of local federal judges in election cases, Congress had stipulated in the Voting Rights Act that suits challenging the attorney general's enforcement of the statute must be heard in the U.S. District Court for the District of Columbia. In *Morris v. Gressette* (1977), moreover, the Supreme Court had held that the attorney general's exercise of administrative discretion under the act, including preclearance decisions, was not subject to judicial review in any court. When the Justice Department objected to North Carolina's first districting plan creating a single majority-minority district, the state could have requested the attorney general to reconsider his decision, sought preclearance in the federal district court in Washington, or chosen to enact a new plan. Private litigants had a right to challenge the plan the state ultimately adopted, but only through a suit against state officials, not one directed against the attorney general or his subordinates.

In his memorandum supporting the state defendants' motion to dismiss the suit, Jefferson Powell first sought to turn language in Everett's complaint to the state's advantage. Everett had charged the attorney general with coercing the state to adopt majority-minority districts. Under numerous judicial precedents, however, establishing a violation of the Fourteenth Amendment's equal protection guarantee or the Fifteenth Amendment's safeguard against racial bias at the polls required a showing of "an invidious, racially discriminatory intent." The plaintiffs' allegations that the federal defendants used their preclearance powers "to dragoon officials of the state into acting against those officials' wishes," asserted Powell, hardly satisfied the invidious intent standard. "The most those allegations state is a tale of federal overreaching, and perhaps of actionable behavior by the federal defendants, without even a hint of *any* invidious purpose on the part of *any* state official."

Nor, of course, had the state acted out of "discriminatory animus against white voters." The plaintiffs, Powell observed, had naturally not made that "facially incredible" assertion; nor had they claimed that North Carolina's redistricting plan was designed to dilute the political influence of "white or black North Carolinians, or indeed of any other racial or ethnic group." Everett had thus failed to allege "what 'the Supreme Court has repeatedly indicated' is an essential aspect of 'the gravamen of a racial gerrymandering claim,' the presence of an 'exclusionary purpose' aimed at a particular group."

Powell was equally unimpressed with Everett's contention, as he put it, "that the Constitution requires 'color-blind' redistricting and that a state legislature may never take race into account for any purpose (invidious or not) in devising a redistricting plan." Such an "assumption of law," Powell declared, was "flatly incorrect, contrary both to well-established case law and to constitutional principle."

Particularly on point, in his judgment, was the Supreme Court's decision in *United Jewish Organizations [UJO] v. Carey* (1977), upholding a New York state legislative districting plan. Kings County, New York, was subject to the Voting Rights Act's preclearance requirements. When the Justice Department objected to the state legislature's initial 1972 redistricting plan, New York submitted a revised plan that increased the size of the nonwhite majority in several legislative districts, splitting, in the process, a majority white Hasidic Jewish community among various districts with strong nonwhite majorities. Hasidic Jewish voters sued state officials, claiming that the plan constituted racial vote dilution in violation of the Fourteenth Amendment. A seven-to-two Supreme Court majority upheld the plan, concluding that the Constitution does not prohibit a state from taking race into account as a means of complying with the Voting Rights Act.

UJO produced no opinion reflecting the views of a majority of the justices. Speaking for a four-justice plurality, however, Justice White agreed that compliance with the Voting Rights Act would "often necessitate the use of racial considerations in drawing district lines" to "banish the blight of racial discrimination in voting." Neither New York's use of "special numerical quotas" to create majority-minority districts nor the plan's impact on white voters, White concluded, made the state action at issue unconstitutional. Though concurring only in the Court's decision rather than with the plurality's reasoning, Justice Potter Stewart, joined by Justice Lewis Powell, emphasized the lack of evidence that the redistricting plan constituted purposeful discrimination. Stewart also rejected the contention that "racial awareness in legislative reapportionment is unconstitutional per se."

To Jefferson Powell, *UJO* established two important propositions —
first, that racial considerations in congressional redistricting were not
inherently unconstitutional, and second, that a legislature's effort to
comply with the attorney general's interpretation of the Voting Rights
Act was "a legitimate, non-invidious legislative purpose." Citing various rulings upholding affirmative action programs, Powell contended
that the *UJO* principles remained in force and that the court was
bound by them to reject the plaintiffs' assertions that North Carolina's
districting plan was invalid. "The plaintiffs' allegations in the present
case concerning the purposes of the North Carolina General Assembly and of the state defendants," observed Powell, "are precisely the
same as the allegations that the United States Supreme Court found
inadequate to state a constitutional claim in [*UJO*]."

Powell found Everett's other claims even more baseless. Regarding the plaintiffs' contention that the challenged districts violated the
right to vote, one of the privileges or immunities of U.S. citizens that
the Fourteenth Amendment protects from state interference, he
reminded the court that the privileges or immunities guarantee —
often called the Constitution's "idle clause" — had been used only
once at that point to strike down a state law, in a precedent overruled
five years later. The privileges or immunities claim, he added, was
simply the plaintiffs' equal protection claim "under a different label."
Article I, Section 2, which grants the people the right to elect U.S.
House members, had previously been used only to require congressional districts of substantially equal population; the courts had
"rejected attempts to read additional requirements into the clause."
Finally, Powell could not understand how Article I, Section 4, which
grants state legislatures the power to regulate congressional elections,
could be used to create "individual rights *against* State officials." That
clause gives Congress explicit power, he added, to make or alter such
state regulations. Thus, "to the extent that the Voting Rights Act
alters [a] state [redistricting] regulation, that alteration is expressly
authorized by the clause itself. This claim is without merit."

––––––

On April 21, Everett filed his response to the defendants' motions to
dismiss, elaborating on the arguments outlined in the plaintiffs' complaint. Everett also quoted extensively from a 1991 opinion by Chief

Judge G. Thomas Eisele of Arkansas's eastern district on the alleged evils of race-based redistricting. "This case," asserted Eisele, a longtime Republican, "carries the effort to concentrate black voters into fewer and fewer districts a step beyond that already taken in [an earlier case]. If successful, it would leave our nation but one short step removed from a system of representative government based on race, ethnic origin and language (is religion next?), in which system district lines would be irrelevant. We would then end up with a system of pure proportionate representation predicated upon factors that should be completely irrelevant in the political life of a democratic society." Although conceding a "certain logic" in race-based districting, Eisele thought that the net long-term effect of isolating black and Hispanic voters in majority-minority districts would be to reduce their overall political influence, "leaving many white officeholders with little incentive to court them." In drafting the Voting Rights Act, Eisele contended, Congress surely had no intention of promoting the creation of "a Jim Crow system of election districts of whites and districts for blacks" or permitting the Justice Department to rewrite the law "to conform to black separatist notions that can only work to harden the racial and ethnic lines that already divide us. Race may still have much to do with the way people vote. Often too much. But, we build the expectation of racial separation into our basic political structure at our peril."

Everett devoted much of his response, however, to the arguments raised by the defendants in their motions to dismiss. In answering their contention that his opposition to all race-conscious districting flew in the face of overwhelming judicial precedent, he expressed doubt whether certain of those rulings would be accepted on the current Supreme Court. He stressed that the principal opinion in the *UJO* case represented the views of only a plurality of justices, not a majority, and in any event, the "plaintiffs doubt that even the Court's judgment [in that 1977 case] would be the same as it was fifteen years ago."

In their motion to dismiss, the state defendants had asserted that, in his zeal to place responsibility for North Carolina's majority-minority districts on the shoulders of Justice Department officials, Everett had failed to allege any invidious discriminatory intent on the state defendants' part. Everett had then amended the complaint to "eliminate [any notion] . . . that plaintiffs have been unduly kind in describing the purpose and acts of the State defendants." In his response to the motion to dismiss, however, he also dismissed as "incomprehensible" the defendants' contention that his original complaint had not included such a claim. Suggesting that the state defendants "seem obsessed with the word 'invidious,'" he drew on dictionary definitions of the term in arguing that the defendants' failure to challenge the Justice Department's directive in court, as well as their creation of the challenged districts, amply established their illegal intent. "Just as no one escapes liability for joining a conspiracy because it was already in existence or . . . suggested by someone else, the State defendants cannot evade their responsibility by claiming that the Federal 'devil made me do it.'" The court, he declared, should reject such a "Nuremberg defense."

Everett also took issue with the rationale underlying the federal defendants' motion to dismiss. Justice Department officials had contended that suits challenging their preclearance decisions must be heard in the D.C. district court, rather than before local federal judges. In a footnote to their brief, moreover, they had expressed doubt that private plaintiffs had standing to challenge preclearance decisions, since Section 5 of the Voting Rights Act expressly provided only that a state or local government could file suit in the D.C. court, seeking a declaratory judgment invalidating the attorney general's refusal to grant preclearance to a proposed election law. Everett conceded that the Voting Rights Act did not authorize private litigants to challenge preclearance decisions in the D.C. court. Citing another provision of the law, however, he contended that the Voting Rights Act was not intended to exclude private suits brought against the Justice Department in other federal courts to challenge voting practices that had won preclearance. Otherwise, he argued, private plaintiffs "would be left high and dry without access to a forum in which they could challenge the Attorney General's action."

Whether the district court had jurisdiction over Everett's complaint against the federal defendants would depend on a fair construction of the Voting Rights Act. The differences between the plaintiffs and the state were much more fundamental. In a reply brief to Everett's contentions, Powell agreed that "reasonable people no doubt [could] differ over the wisdom of employing race-conscious means in the national effort to eliminate racial discrimination from the political process." But courts, he reminded the three-judge panel, were not "to pass on the wisdom" of governmental actions, only their constitu-

　　　　{ *Race and Redistricting* }

tionality. The *Shaw* plaintiffs had presented "a variety of arguments that race-conscious redistricting is a mistaken or self-defeating policy." They had not established, however, and could not, Powell argued, that their opposition to all race-conscious districting was consistent with Supreme Court interpretations of the Constitution.

Powell took issue as well with Everett's decision to "casually dismiss *U.J.O.* in two sentences." He conceded that no majority opinion had been filed in *UJO*, but seven justices in that case had "expressly rejected the argument that the Constitution absolutely forbids race-conscious redistricting." That proposition remained good law, declared Powell, despite the Supreme Court's recent decision in *Richmond v. J. A. Croson Co.* (1989), striking down a local affirmative action program in the awarding of government contracts. In 1995, the Supreme Court would hold in *Adarand Constructors v. Pena* that federal and state affirmative action regulations would thereafter be subjected to the same degree of strict scrutiny by the courts. But at that point, as Powell pointed out in his brief, the Court was according considerably greater deference to race-conscious action "Congress authorizes or commands a state to take . . . , such as under the Voting Rights Act," than to action a state or locality takes "on its own." Indeed, in *Metro Broadcasting v. FCC* (1990), decided the year after the *Croson* ruling, the Court had cited *UJO* approvingly in upholding a federal affirmative action program and declaring that states could "deliberately creat[e] or preserv[e] black majorities in particular districts in order to ensure that its reapportionment plan complies with" Section 5 of the Voting Rights Act. *UJO*'s facts, declared Powell, were remarkably similar to those in *Shaw*, and under *UJO*, the plaintiffs had no case.

Faulting Everett also for his "curious treatment" of the invidious intent standard in equal protection cases, Powell termed "standard hornbook law" the requirement that an equal protection complaint allege "an invidious purpose." No such claim could be validly raised against the defendants' creation of the First and Twelfth Districts. "As plaintiffs themselves allege," Powell observed, "the legislative purpose was to devise a redistricting plan that would satisfy the Voting Rights Act as interpreted by the Attorney General. The state defendants' argument is not, as plaintiffs mistakenly assert, a claim that impermissibly motivated state action can be justified by relying on 'orders' from Washington: state defendants maintain, rather, that the purpose or intent of the state action here, as described by plaintiffs themselves, was legitimate. This assertion is amply supported by the numerous decisions" upholding the use of racial and ethnic considerations in districting to "advance the goals" of the Voting Rights Act.

—————

North Carolina's party primaries were scheduled for May 5. On April 27, the three-judge panel held a hearing on the federal and state defendants' motions to dismiss Everett's suit. At the outset, Judge Phillips indicated that the court would hear the motions separately, with counsel for the United States going first. Each side would be allowed ten minutes for argument and five minutes for rebuttal.

Rebecca Wertz, an attorney for the voting rights section of the Justice Department's civil rights division, represented the federal defendants. Tracking the arguments in their motion to dismiss, Wertz contended that the court had no jurisdiction over the attorney general's preclearance of North Carolina's disputed districts. Under the Voting Rights Act, a state faced with the attorney general's objections to a proposed change in its election laws could seek a declaratory judgment from the district court in Washington, D.C., granting preclearance to the law. But under the Supreme Court's ruling in *Morris v. Gressette* (1977), Wertz asserted, the attorney general's preclearance decisions were invulnerable to judicial review in any court. Private litigants, she added, had no standing to challenge a precleared election law in any jurisdiction.

At that point, Judge Phillips interrupted Wertz with a question. "If a State . . . were to decide . . . that it was going for its own reasons to construct a district which [had] a working majority, where that took drawing a district a mile wide and a thousand miles long . . . and this plan were precleared by the attorney general . . . , is it your position that no private action lies to challenge that legislative districting?" A person subject to such a plan could file a suit, Wertz replied, "but the proper defendants are the persons who devised that plan" — state officials — not the attorney general and his subordinates. "It is the State whose practice, procedure, whatever it be, . . . it is the State's action which is the target of either an interpretive challenge to the statute's application or to the Constitution; . . . no matter how you view the plaintiffs' challenges to what happened in this instance, with

{ *Race and Redistricting* }

respect to their allegations that the Attorney General somehow applied an unconstitutional standard or acted beyond the scope of his authority in objecting to the initial plan, no matter how you look at it, it is a challenge to the Attorney General's understanding and application of the facts [and] the law to its Section Five determination. And it's just that type of action that *Morris v. Gressette* made clear is not subject to judicial review." In fact, she added, the Court had emphasized in *Gressette* that one of the reasons for concluding that Congress did not intend judicial review of the attorney general's preclearance decisions "was that it does not end the rights of anyone to challenge the [disputed] enactment itself in a federal district court. What they cannot do is challenge in an action against the Attorney General." Given the availability of such suits, moreover, Congress had regularly declined to overrule *Gressette*'s interpretation of the Voting Rights Act through additional legislation.

Everett opened his rebuttal of Wertz with a quote from Robert Frost but quickly turned to blunter language, accusing the state and federal defendants of conducting a "shell game." "The State defendants say," declared Everett, "'Well, we did it because we had to because of the Federal government. Therefore, we do not have any invidious [discriminatory intent].' [The television comedian] Flip Wilson used to talk about 'The Devil made me do it.' We refer to it as the 'Nuremberg defense.'" The federal defendants, in contrast, "say, ' . . . the only people that can sue are the State and the political subdivision.' . . . So the upshot of it is, they say, 'you can't get there from here.' There is no way to contest the abridgment of an important constitutional right."

Everett readily conceded that under *Gressette*, courts should not interfere with the attorney general's discretion in the preclearance process. He contended, however, that the federal defendants were integrally involved in North Carolina's adoption of majority-minority districts — "a proximate cause, indeed, an inducing cause, a principal cause of what has happened. They're the ones, really, who have compelled the result that we maintain is beyond the statute, a sort of proportional representation which is specifically prohibited by Section Two [of the Voting Rights Act], by the Dole Amendment [forbidding racial districting merely to ensure proportional representation], and which we would maintain is also prohibited by the interpretation of the Fifteenth Amendment and tying that together with Article One, Section Two."

Judge Britt pointed out that continuation of the suit against the federal defendants was unnecessary, that the plaintiffs could secure relief through a case against the state defendants alone. In responding, Everett cited the need for judicial economy in urging the panel to keep the attorney general in the case. Were the plaintiffs to win their suit against the state defendants, with the Justice Department subjected to no court order, North Carolina would then be obliged to adopt a new redistricting plan, which would be subject to the preclearance process and the Justice Department's possible insistence that the state again establish majority-minority districts, followed by additional litigation. When constitutional rights were at stake, he added, the presumption was in favor of judicial review.

Judge Phillips was not convinced. The suit before the court, he interjected, involved a state redistricting statute. "It has not to do with anything that the Department of Justice has done with respect to anything else. . . . I think I understand the impulse, the intuitive impulse, to trace out the culprit here as you see the culprit as being ultimately the Attorney General of the United States who gave license, at least to the State, to do what it did. But I'm frankly having difficulty with the idea that somehow, as you now seem to be saying, . . . the Attorney General of the United States is an indispensable party to your claim against the State. I don't see how you can fail to win everything that you claim you're entitled to win on deprived of everybody but the state defendants." Everett had a folksy rejoinder. "There are all these statutes nowadays about truth in lending, truth in this, truth in that. We believe in having truth in the judicial process by having the Attorney General as a defendant."

As he had in his briefs, Powell began his argument in behalf of the state by challenging the plaintiffs' contention that all race-based redistricting was unconstitutional. But Judge Phillips soon interrupted with an observation and a question. "The closest . . . the plaintiffs come [to] stating a claim under current Supreme Court precedent," he suggested, was that the "compactness requirement," which limited the redistricting relief minority voters could seek under the *Gingles* decision, "also sets a limit . . . on what the State permissibly can do in order to secure voting rights. . . . Is it possible," he then asked, "for someone to challenge just an outrageous violation by the State of the constraints that limit the right of minority voters to demand, as a matter granted by the Voting Rights Act, districting which . . . accommodate[s] their right not to be fractured, packed, or submerged?"

Powell agreed that there was a limit to the state's power, but only where it acted with "an improper, illegitimate, invidious — . . . the term is not important — racially discriminatory purpose."

"Just a willy-nilly, going beyond what the Voting Rights Act would require the State to do," Phillips inquired, "is not itself a violation of any . . . constitutionally protected right[?]"

"Well, of course," Powell responded, "we don't see that that's this case. But I suppose purely arbitrary action, or action by the State that had no rational connection to the State's purported goals, is always subject to challenge."

If that were the plaintiffs' contention, interjected Judge Voorhees, the lone Republican on the panel, a trial would be necessary to determine whether the state's action was "arbitrary, unreasonable, improper, invidious," and a motion to dismiss would be inappropriate. But the plaintiffs had not made such a claim, Powell promptly countered; instead, they had contended that a state invariably "acts unconstitutionally when it acts with race consciousness" and that the attorney general also did so when he required or suggested that the state engage in race-based districting. Such a claim, Powell asserted, as he had in his briefs, was "squarely contrary to established law."

In his rebuttal of the state's counsel, Everett readily agreed that the plaintiffs were indeed maintaining that the Constitution, as Justice John Marshall Harlan had argued in his *Plessy* dissent, "is color-blind and that except for a remedial purpose, the use of racial classifications does not fit within" the Constitution. Adopting a more conciliatory stance, however, he also acknowledged that it was "not necessary for the court to go that far" and that the panel "perhaps . . . would rather approach [the issue] on a more limited basis." Declaring that recent precedent supported the plaintiffs, he cited *Powers v. Ohio* (1991), which extended the *Batson* ruling's ban on race-based peremptory challenges of prospective jurors to cases in which the defendant and excluded jurors were of a different race. He also invoked *City of Richmond v. J. A. Croson Co.* (1989) and *Freeman v. Pitts* (1992), a Georgia school desegregation case in which the Supreme Court had held that federal judges could relinquish their control over school systems in incremental stages and had no authority to retain jurisdiction indefinitely over a school system merely to ensure continuing racial balance in its student body.

"But *Croson*," Judge Phillips interrupted, "does not suggest that race-conscious measures are always per se [invalid]."

"What we would suggest," Everett answered, "is that *Croson* does say that there has to be a very searching judicial scrutiny and there's language of that sort which we think would apply." Under that standard, he added, North Carolina's districting plan "just doesn't pass muster."

Judge Britt joined the exchange at that point, questioning whether the plaintiffs had invoked such a standard in their complaint. "You don't make any allegation . . . that the action by the State defendants was on the basis of any invidious or racially discriminatory intent, do you?" The very act of adopting majority-minority districts, Everett replied, was "invidious." "But that gets back to your . . . argument," countered Britt, "that the overall purpose of [the districting plan] was to create a racially minority district, which the Supreme Court has specifically said . . . there is nothing wrong with."

Responding to Britt, Everett pointed out that the Supreme Court had not yet dealt with the issue in the particular context of congressional redistricting. *UJO* had dealt with state legislative redistricting, and the Supreme Court in its one-person, one-vote reapportionment cases had given states greater discretion to deviate from population equality in state legislative districting than in congressional apportionment. Nor was the state remedying past discrimination. "The very fact that they had to create such strange districts this time," Everett asserted, "is a good indication that if [the principle of geographical] compactness in districts had been followed in the past it would have made no difference, there would still have been no minority congresspersons serving from North Carolina."

In closing, Everett could not resist another slap at *UJO*. "The *U.J.O.* case, 15 years old — as Judge Phillips said, I can't speculate — I can at least note that there might be a question as to whether it's still good law." Whatever the force of precedent, moreover, Everett was convinced of the rightness of his cause. North Carolina's districting plan, he declared, "demeans the electoral process. It is wrong, we submit. It is unconstitutional, and that's why we're here."

In his concluding remarks, Powell approached, if he did not match, his Duke colleague's certitude. *UJO*, he maintained, remained controlling precedent with respect to race-conscious districting, and the other precedents the plaintiffs had cited had "nothing to do with this case at all." The plaintiffs had a concern "that the race-conscious measures Congress has mandated and authorized, and the State in this case has undertaken, are bad policy, that somehow they corrupt the electoral process, that they are somehow bad ideas. That very well may be so, but that is not the issue before this court."

———

Judges often delay the announcement of their decision for days, weeks, or months. But North Carolina's spring primaries were only a week away. At the conclusion of the hearing, Judge Phillips asked counsel to "stand by" while "[we] go out and talk a little bit among ourselves. . . . We'll be back in due course and speak to you at that time."

It was 11:15 A.M. Thirty-five minutes later, the panel returned to the courtroom, where Judge Phillips announced the dismissal of the complaint against both the federal and the state defendants. "We will try as speedily as we can, given some other work that all of us are involved in, to get something in writing. We will try to write in a way that deals responsibly with a serious matter. But I do not think it's possible to promise to get that done on any date certain. We will act as quickly as we can on it."

On August 7, Judge Phillips, joined by Judge Britt, issued an opinion in the case. Judge Voorhees filed a dissent. Phillips's opinion essentially tracked the briefs and arguments of the state and federal defendants. He turned first to the plaintiffs' contention that the federal defendants had improperly "coerced" North Carolina into creating its disputed districts by either misinterpreting Section 2 of the Voting Rights Act or, if their reading of Section 2 were correct, enforcing an unconstitutional provision of federal law. The Justice Department had claimed that Section 2 permitted lawsuits only in the D.C. district court, not in local federal courts, and that the *Gressette* decision immunized the attorney general's preclearance decisions from judicial review. Judge Phillips agreed, albeit also emphasizing, as he had during the hearing, that the plaintiffs could still seek relief through a suit against the state.

Going next to the complaint against the state defendants, Phillips addressed in a footnote the plaintiffs' initial contention that the Justice Department's action was "the primary unconstitutional conduct being challenged" in the suit and that the state defendants were mere "'unwilling participants' in a racially discriminatory, hence unconstitutional, redistricting process." When the "state defendants predictably picked up on this 'unwilling participant' theory as an implicit concession by plaintiffs of the lack of any 'invidious intent' on [the state's] part," observed Phillips, "the plaintiffs responded by disclaiming any such effect for the 'unwilling participant' theory, dismissing it . . . as the state defendants' 'devil-made-me-do-it' theory." Phillips found this "questionable logic, given that it was [the plaintiffs'] own" theory. But the court, he reported, had declined to give that anomaly "any ultimate significance" in assessing questions about the state defendants' intent.

Attempting to harness the plaintiffs' broad-ranging constitutional claims, Phillips reduced Everett's case to essentially two propositions. "In its most sweeping, but simplest, form, it baldly asserts that any state legislative redistricting driven by considerations of race — whatever the race, whatever the specific purpose, whatever the specific effect — is unconstitutional. . . . To the extent the Voting Rights Act authorizes *any* race-conscious legislative redistricting, the Act is facially unconstitutional." The plaintiffs' alternative theory "seems to assert," wrote Phillips, that even were race-conscious districting not inherently invalid, "race-based redistricting which is specifically intended to assure proportional representation of minority (or any?) races and fails properly to observe (undefined) considerations of contiguity, compactness, and communities of interest in drawing congressional districts to achieve that purpose — i.e., racial gerrymandering — is unconstitutional."

Everett had based his claims on Article I, Sections 2 and 4, of the Constitution, as well as on the Fourteenth and Fifteenth Amendments. The court found the equal protection claim raised by the plaintiffs under the Fourteenth and Fifteenth Amendments "the only relevant, or most inclusive, one under developed constitutional doctrine respecting voting rights." Terming the plaintiffs' Article I, Section 4, challenge a "novel claim in voting rights jurisprudence," Judge Phillips rejected that claim as lacking any support in precedent. Article I, Section 4, he asserted, simply conferred power on states to regulate congressional districting, subject to congressional veto or modification. It thus "operate[d] to validate, rather than restrict, the state's redistricting action here." The Supreme Court had construed Article I, Section 2's provision for popular election of House members to require equally populated congressional districts. But no court had ever extended the clause beyond that requirement.

Judge Phillips devoted more attention to the plaintiffs' equal protection claim, but not much more. He and Judge Britt were puzzled that the plaintiffs had nowhere identified themselves as members of a race different from the African Americans for whom the challenged districts were created, nor alleged any injury to their rights as members of a particular race, but instead had claimed injury to the constitutional rights of all voters, whatever their race. Only in alleging a violation of the Fifteenth Amendment bar against racial discrimination in voting, observed Phillips, "do they seem to confine [the challenged districting plan's] impact to members 'of the race or color of the plaintiffs.'" He realized that the plaintiffs' omission may have reflected "a deliberate (and humanly, if not legally, laudable) refusal" on their part "to inject their own race[s] into a claim whose essence is to deplore race-consciousness in voting-rights matters." But an asserted injury to "all" a state's voters could hardly "constitute invidious racial discrimination against some voters only, hence a denial of equal protection rights, and such a claim would therefore be self-defeating at the threshold." Although conceding that the court might be "doing plaintiffs' intentions (if not their legal cause) a disservice," Phillips characterized the case as a claim by white voters that North Carolina's majority-minority districts violated their equal protection and voting rights under the Fourteenth and Fifteenth Amendments.

So framing the plaintiffs' case, Judge Phillips relied primarily on *UJO* to reject their per se challenge to race-conscious districting. He also turned back the contention that the disputed plan had been adopted with the purpose or effect of discriminating against the plaintiffs and other white voters. "While it is sadly the case in contemporary society that such an intent might be judicially inferred were the state legislature controlled by a black majority," he observed, that obviously was not the case. Contrary to the plaintiffs' assumption, he added, it was not "enough [merely] to allege and prove an intent to favor black voters" in order to establish "an opposing intent to disfavor white voters in the required constitutional sense. . . . The one intent may exist without the other."

Nor, in the court's judgment, did the state's creation of "two 'grotesque' black-majority districts — however offensive it may be to [the plaintiffs'] general notions of good constitutional government — [operate] to 'fenc[e] out the white population of the [state, or either of the two challenged districts] from participation in the political process of the [state or districts], [or to] minimize or unfairly cancel out white voting strength.' . . . The plan demonstrably will not lead to proportional underrepresentation of white voters on a statewide basis. . . . Within the specifically challenged districts . . . , the mere fact that white voters (assuming the sad continuation for yet another season of racial bloc voting) will elect fewer candidates of their choice than if they were in white-majority districts is not a cognizable constitutional abridgement of their right to vote." The plaintiffs, Judge Phillips concluded, had questioned the "political and social wisdom" of the state's decision to create two "tortuously configured black-majority districts. The questions they have raised, however, are in the end political ones."

In his dissent, Judge Voorhees joined in much of the majority's opinion. He concurred, for example, in Judge Phillips's rejection of the plaintiffs' Article I, Sections 2 and 4, claims and their contention that race-conscious districting was per se unconstitutional. Voorhees thought that the plaintiffs were entitled to a trial, however, on their claim that North Carolina's First and Twelfth Districts violated equal protection. Had the North Carolina legislature simply yielded to the attorney general's suggestion that a second district be created, giving "effect to *black and Native-American* voting strength in" the south-central and southeastern portions of the state, he declared, the challenged plan would be entitled to the "presumption of constitutionality [that could] be properly inferred from the legitimacy and deference accorded the Attorney General's performance of his" preclearance duties. The district the attorney general had suggested, Voorhees noted, would also have adhered to the "sound districting principles such as compactness and population equality" that Justice White had required of majority-minority districts in his *UJO* plurality opinion. Instead, the General Assembly, "in purposeful disregard of the Attorney General's recommendations," had created "minority-leverage congressional districts so devoid of shape, . . . and so 'uncouth' and 'bizarre' in configuration, as to invite ridicule." Voorhees questioned, moreover, whether Congress could ever have intended "to permit elevation of the racial criterion to the point of exclusion of all other factors of constitutional dimension, such as contiguity, compactness, and communities of interest, which bear on the rights of these Plaintiffs."

By that point, North Carolina officials had already conducted party primaries and were preparing for the fall elections. Soon, however, Everett's suit and Voorhees's concerns would have a more sympathetic hearing.

CHAPTER 3

Shaw I in the Supreme Court

The district court's ruling naturally disappointed Robinson Everett. "I thought we might be thrown out as to the federal [defendants]," he later said, "because it wasn't their plan really, although they had [exerted] the underlying pressure. But I had thought we had some merit in our position [against the state] and would get along OK. That did not prove to be the case."

Everett was heartened, however, by the Supreme Court's current makeup, as well as Judge Voorhees's dissent, although Voorhees's "grounds . . . weren't as far-reaching as what we were suggesting." In theory, at least, the High Court would also be obligated to hear any appeal of the district court's ruling. Most litigants who are disappointed with a lower court decision are obliged to petition the Supreme Court for a writ of certiorari, a directive to the lower court to send up the case for review. But cert grants, as they are commonly called, lie entirely within the Court's discretion. If four or more justices consider a case worthy of review, a writ of certiorari is issued; otherwise, the Court declines review. The overwhelming majority of cert petitions are denied.

Losing parties in voting rights and certain other types of cases also have a right to file for a writ of appeal, which the Supreme Court is technically obligated to grant. Everett realized that the justices had a variety of means at their disposal for denying full review to such cases. For example, a majority could note "probable jurisdiction" — as a grant of review is formally termed — then summarily affirm the lower court's decision without full briefs and oral argument. Or the justices could grant a writ of appeal but later dismiss it on the ground that it raised no "substantial" legal issue. Everett also knew, though, that appeals had a substantially greater chance of receiving a full hearing before the Court than certiorari cases did. "The question was whether or not to go forward with an appeal," he later recalled, "and I thought, what the heck; it's not much of a job to do, and you don't have a whole lot of testimony. Let's . . . go up to the Supreme Court. We ought to get a ruling on this!"

———

That fall, a friend of Everett's son Greg was taking a political science course at UNC–Chapel Hill with Dick Richardson, a popular professor of judicial politics. Richardson invited Everett to visit the class and talk about the *Shaw* case. "I had agreed to do so. Well, [on December 7] the good news comes down that probable jurisdiction has been noted. So I get over to Chapel Hill and there are the TV people and so forth. . . . They wanted a press conference, and the professor decided the press conference could be held as a class. . . . That was an interesting moment."

Soon, too, "amicus briefs began flying in" supporting the plaintiffs' position. An "amicus curiae," or friend of the court, is an individual or organization with interests closely tied to those of a party in a case. With the consent of all parties or at the Supreme Court's request, a friend of the court can file a brief with the Court supporting one of the parties. "The Republicans were on our side. . . . They had had some change in philosophy. The guy that had sort of conjured up this [Bush administration encouragement of majority-minority districts], Ben Ginsberg, was no longer . . . counsel [to the Republican National Committee]. A guy named Michael Hess had become counsel. He was more inclined to the view that if the Republicans stress equal opportunity and not this sort of [majority-minority districting] stuff, it'd be better. They might lose a few places, but they'd be on sounder ground philosophically and otherwise. And so he had changed that policy, and they filed the amicus brief on our side."

Eddie Speas of the state attorney general's office had a more cynical explanation for the Republican Party's shift in position, at least in North Carolina. Speas readily embraced the thesis that the Bush administration hoped to pack African Americans into a few districts, not out of altruistic motives but simply to enhance the chances of white Republican candidates elsewhere. "I don't think there is any question that the agenda at least of the [Republican officialdom] was to dilute the Democratic vote by packing blacks into majority-minority districts.

I have absolutely no doubt that was their agenda." But Speas had a different explanation for the North Carolina GOP's change of heart on the issue. "I've heard it said that . . . the General Assembly trumped the Republican agenda. The Republicans [in North Carolina] had not foreseen the possibility that the Democratic legislature could comply with the Republican Department of Justice agenda and at the same time protect Democratic interests."

Whatever the motivation, the national Republican Party supported Everett in its amicus brief. The Washington Legal Foundation (WLF), a lawyers' group heavily involved in litigation in behalf of conservative causes, also supported the appellants. North Carolina Senator Jesse Helms, an icon of American conservatism, especially in racial contexts, signed the WLF brief. When the senator first won election in 1972 with the slogan "Elect Jesse Helms — He's One of Us," Everett had supported Helms's Democratic opponent, Durham congressman Nick Galifianakis, the son of Greek immigrant parents. Subsequently, Helms had been "very, very nice" to Everett. "He had been very kind when I became chief judge [of the Court of Military Appeals]. They had a hearing in the Senate when I was nominated. He made a nice statement, he and [North Carolina Democratic] Senator Robert Morgan. I had not had any philosophical battles with him, no contact with him for about ten years." Still, Helms's joining the WLF brief gave Everett "a strange feeling." The American Jewish Congress also filed an amicus brief for the appellants, "partly because," Everett assumed, "they had been very upset with that *UJO* case," and partly because of the organization's general distaste for affirmative action and related race-conscious policies.

Both Ben Ginsberg and Michael Hess signed the amicus brief filed by the Republican National Committee in the appellants' behalf, but Hess was listed as counsel of record. The Republican Party declined to take a position on Everett's claim that race-conscious districting was unconstitutional per se. Hess argued, however, that "at a minimum, the appellants' allegation of discriminatory intent and effect create[d] a presumption of unconstitutionality that [could] only be overcome by evidence of a legitimate and compelling state interest." He contended, moreover, that the justifications North Carolina had advanced in support of its disputed districts — compliance with the Voting Rights Act and the attorney general's recommendations —

were "mere pretexts for unconstitutional [racial] gerrymandering, the principal goal of which was incumbency protection."

Nor, declared Hess, should the political goal of incumbency protection be accepted as an adequate justification for the gerrymandering at issue. "The desire for incumbency protection, whether based on racial or political animus, led to the discriminatory districting challenged here. This confluence of political motive and discriminatory racial effect is an evident and continuing part of our system, and suggests that political and racial gerrymandering should be subject to similar analysis in order to achieve consistent, fair and effective representation for all citizens." In Hess's judgment, "there [was] no significant difference between a partisan gerrymander which has racial effects, and a racial gerrymander such as this one where race is the surrogate used to achieve the political goal of incumbency protection."

Hess assured the justices that they could find in favor of the appellants without disturbing their own precedents or the Voting Rights Act. While endorsing the "goal of fair representation for minorities," the *UJO* plurality had also suggested that minority districts adhere to "compactness" and other traditional redistricting principles, including "deference to existing 'residential patterns.'" Geographic compactness had been among the "necessary preconditions" announced in the *Gingles* case for establishing that multimember state legislative districts illegally impaired the ability of minority voters to elect representatives of their choice. A minority group challenging such districts was obliged to show that it was *"sufficiently large and geographically compact to constitute a majority in a single-member district,"* Hess stressed. North Carolina's disputed districts could meet no "common sense definition of [geographic] compactness." Yet in creating the House of Representatives, the framers of the Constitution intended "that representatives should be linked in some significant way to the interests of the community they represent."

In an affidavit filed for *Pope v. Blue*, the Republican Party's partisan gerrymandering challenge to North Carolina's majority-minority districts, election law expert Bernard Grofman had termed this relationship between representatives and their constituents "cognizability" — "the ability of a legislator to define, *in common sense terms, based on geographical referents*, the characteristics of his or her geographic constituency" — and stated that "the appropriate test . . . is not whether the voters do know the boundaries of the district in which they reside, but whether those boundaries could, in principle, be explained to them in simple, common sense terms." Were the disputed districts sustained, Hess declared, "the House of Representatives, the institution of our national government designed to be closest to the electorate, may cease to perform its intended constitutional function."

In the amicus brief for the appellants filed by the American Jewish Congress, Marc D. Stern emphasized his organization's historical commitment to legislation expanding the franchise and litigation attacking "racially exclusionary devices," including the poll tax, literacy tests, and segregated election districts. In all such efforts, the organization had assumed that "it was urging color-blind elections, where government above all would not insist on the relevance of racial matters." The organization recognized that government could not prevent people from voting along racial, religious, or related lines. "But under our constitutional system," wrote Stern, "it is one thing to tolerate such voting. It is quite another for government to design districts to reinforce racial, ethnic, religious or sexual voting patterns, and to make these factors the central organizing features of political affairs . . . to convert the principle of full, fair, and equal participation in the electoral process into a system of ethnic, religious, or racial fiefdoms."

To decide the *Shaw* case favorably for the appellants, however, the Court was not obliged to resolve questions about the ultimate scope and limits of Congress's power to protect voting rights. The Justice Department had interpreted the Voting Rights Act to require the creation of majority-minority districts. That, declared Stern, was "nothing less than a claim for proportional representation." Yet the Voting Rights Act's text "specifically repudiate[d]" such an interpretation by forbidding districts designed to ensure such representation in the House of Representatives and state deliberative bodies.

In noting probable jurisdiction in the case, the Supreme Court had directed the parties to brief and argue, as Stern phrased it, "the extent to which a state's purported compliance with the Voting Rights Act at the behest of the Attorney General immunizes its redistricting plan from attack as an unconstitutional racial gerrymander." In Stern's judgment, that question was grounded in a baseless assumption. "It assumes that the Attorney General acted pursuant to the Voting Rights Act" in objecting to North Carolina's original districting plan. "Whatever else may be said about the Attorney General's action, and North Carolina's response, it surely cannot be said to have been taken in compliance with the requirements of the Voting Rights Act."

The attorney general's objection had not rested, Stern reasoned, on a concern that the state's original districting plan would cause a regression in minority electoral strength, forbidden under Section 5's preclearance standards. Instead, the Justice Department appeared to have been concerned about "an absence of specific relation between the number of minorities and the number of persons belonging to the minority elected." But given Section 2's ban on districting adopted for the purpose of providing proportional representation, such concerns hardly established a Section 2 violation. The appellants were entitled to an opportunity to establish that the federal and state defendants had gone beyond the Voting Rights Act, or at least that the attorney general had failed to follow the *Gingles* standards in objecting to the state's initial districting plan. "We recognize," Stern concluded, "the importance of the Voting Rights Act, the persistence of subtle (and not so subtle) efforts to disenfranchise or dilute the political power of minorities, and the great power accorded Congress to address the lingering effects of past discrimination." But the American Jewish Congress was also convinced that a "single-minded focus on racial districting ha[d] a deleterious impact on the body politic" and violated the Voting Rights Act.

The brief filed for the appellants by the WLF was joined not only by Senator Helms but also by the Equal Opportunity Foundation, another conservative organization heavily financed by Richard Mellon Scaiffe, the wealthy Pittsburgh executive who would also fund a variety of efforts to discredit President and Mrs. Clinton. Unlike the Republican National Committee, these foundations and Helms embraced Everett's contention that all race-conscious policies are unconstitutional — undermining "the ideal," as they put it, "of a color-blind society in which the civil rights of all Americans are respected equally." Racial gerrymandering, their brief declared, "place[d] the state's stamp of approval on the [perverted] notion that people of different races are inherently different from one another." The Voting Rights Act did not require such gerrymandering. "More importantly, the Constitution prohibits a state from treating its citizens (as did North Carolina in this case) merely as members of a particular racial group rather than as individuals."

The brief also endorsed the appellants' suggestion that the critical language of the plurality opinion in the *UJO* case was inconsistent with the Supreme Court's other decisions and "not now good constitutional law, if it ever was." The Court's rulings in such cases as *Gomillion v. Lightfoot* (1960), striking down Alabama's racial gerrymander of a predominantly black community's boundaries, and *Wright v. Rockefeller* (1964), rejecting districts designed "to segregate on the basis of race or place of origin," as well as subsequent decisions, made it clear to the foundations and Helms "that the Fourteenth and Fifteenth Amendments protect *individual* rights, not group entitlements."

They also rested their support of the appellants, however, on narrower grounds. Answering North Carolina's assertion that it was merely attempting to comply with the attorney general's authoritative interpretations of the Voting Rights Act, they sought to minimize the attorney general's authority under the law. North Carolina could have sought preclearance of its first plan in the D.C. district court, bypassing the Justice Department altogether. "The face of [John Dunne's] letter" objecting to the state's first plan also "suggest[ed] that he would have been satisfied . . . if the General Assembly had provided a non-pretextual reason (such as, for example, a desire to create compact districts) for failing to create a second majority-minority district." Not even *UJO* had required states to act on every recommendation the attorney general made during preclearance negotiations. In *Beer v. United States* (1976), the Supreme Court had read Section 5 of the Voting Rights Act merely "to insure that no voting-procedure changes would be made that would lead to a retrogression in the position of racial minorities with respect to their effective exercise of the electoral franchise." Thus, *UJO* protected from constitutional challenge only those plans necessary, in the attorney general's judgment, to ensure compliance with that "nonretrogression principle." Justice Department denial of preclearance simply because alternative schemes might increase minority voting power was unwarranted "so long as the [initial] proposed change would not *decrease* existing levels of minority voting power." The North Carolina plans clearly were not necessary to protect against reductions in previously existing minority voting strength.

Eddie Speas was as disapppointed as Everett was heartened by the Supreme Court's decision to grant full review of the appellants' claims. "My sense was that the Supreme Court didn't take it to affirm it," he later said. "So we viewed with some trepidation the fact that they had taken this case." Even in appeals cases, which the Supreme Court is obligated to review, the justices often simply affirm the lower court summarily. "That's what we were hoping for. And when they didn't, and scheduled full briefing, that was a sign to us."

The Democratic National Committee (DNC) filed a friend of the court brief supporting the state. A number of civil rights organizations also filed a joint brief in the appellees' behalf. The Lawyers' Committee for Civil Rights under Law, organized in 1963 as part of President John F. Kennedy's effort to mobilize private lawyers in behalf of civil rights for all Americans, joined the brief, as did the ACLU, the Mexican American Legal Defense and Educational Fund (MALDEF), and the NAACP. The Lawyers' Committee had frequently represented blacks in voting rights cases before the Supreme Court. So had the ACLU, which since 1965 had maintained a southern regional office in Atlanta that focused mainly on barriers to minority political influence, such as at-large elections, discriminatory reapportionment devices, and preclearance-related issues. MALDEF concentrated its efforts on civil rights for Hispanic Americans and had frequently appeared before the Supreme Court in cases involving their voting rights. The NAACP, of course, had played a major role in civil rights litigation since the 1930s.

In their joint brief, the civil rights groups argued that North Carolina's attempt to comply with the Voting Rights Act was beyond constitutional challenge, whether or not its plan adhered to the attorney general's recommendations. The Supreme Court's rulings had repeatedly upheld race-conscious districting adopted to comply with the Voting Rights Act. So long as a state was attempting to conform to the statute's ban on dilution of minority voting rights and did not unfairly dilute the voting rights of the white majority, the brief's authors asserted, the legislature's action "is *per se* constitutional," not, as the appellants would characterize all race-conscious districting, inherently invalid. Nor did such districting deprive white voters of any rights: "white voters have no constitutionally protectible right to vote in a white majority district or to elect a white representative or to insist that legislative districts be compact or contiguous." White voters continued to vote under majority-minority districting plans; they simply were not in the districts they might have preferred.

Seeking to turn the Voting Rights Act to the state's advantage, the civil rights groups also emphasized that under Section 2, neither whites nor any other racial group had a right to elect representatives in proportion to their percentage of the overall population. As the *UJO* plurality had asserted, "so long as whites 'as a group, [are] provided with fair representation, we cannot conclude that there was a cognizable discrimination against whites or an abridgement of their right to vote on the grounds of race.'"

The joint brief also minimized any weight assigned to North Carolina's failure to adopt its second majority-minority district in the area the attorney general had suggested. The Justice Department's "imprimatur," counsel argued, did not immunize a districting plan from constitutional challenge; a state's plan was valid only because it did not deprive white voters of any rights. If a state legislature voluntarily adopted a plan that complied with the Voting Rights Act, the attorney general would have no opportunity to offer an alternative. He had no role whatever to play, moreover, in reviewing plans adopted by states not subject to Section 5's preclearance provisions. The authors of the joint brief thus could see no "principled constitutional or statutory basis to say that a voluntarily drawn plan is subject to constitutional challenge, while a plan drawn to comply with a suggestion by the Attorney General is not." Requiring the attorney general to "'suggest' any race-conscious district plan before it could be considered safe from constitutional challenge," they declared, "would both conflict with this Court's well-recognized deference to legislative judgments in redistricting and present an administrative nightmare for a Department of Justice that is already overburdened by its preclearance responsibilities."

In the judgment of the joint brief's authors, a constitutional requirement of "color-blind" redistricting would actually create "a double standard heavily weighted against minority voters." Since legislators invariably knew the racial compositions of the districts they drew, a court decision subjecting minority-dominated districts to strict judicial review, while presuming the constitutionality of predominantly white districts, would establish a "cruel and indefensible distinction." Indeed, forbidding consideration of a districting plan's impact on a racial group would itself be a race-conscious requirement — "one that disadvantage[d] precisely those whom the Voting Rights Act was designed to protect."

{ *Race and Redistricting* }

Not only did the Constitution *not* prohibit race-conscious redistricting, but such arrangements were particularly appropriate, the civil rights groups argued, in a state such as North Carolina, given its long history of racial discrimination at the polls. Even after the Voting Rights Act's adoption, North Carolina had lagged behind most other states in the protection of minority voting rights. By the end of 1965, the year the Voting Rights Act was adopted, thirty-four of the state's counties were subject to Section 5's preclearance requirements; by 1970, the number of counties covered by the act had jumped to thirtynine. In *Gingles*, the Supreme Court had recognized that certain legislative districts drawn after the 1980 census diluted minority voting rights in violation of Section 2. The *Gingles* Court had also found racially polarized voting, disproportionately lower black voter registration rates, statewide election campaigns marked by racial appeals, and white bloc voting against candidates that African American voters preferred. In light of that history, the joint brief concluded, race-conscious districting to comply with the Voting Rights Act was "a necessary, appropriate and minimally required response to past wrongs," and the appellants' criticisms of that effort rang "especially hollow."

Nor were the Lawyers' Committee and its allies impressed with the weight that the appellants and their amici had given the disputed districts' irregular shape. Federal law had required geographically compact districts early in the twentieth century, but that law had been allowed to expire, and later congressional apportionment statutes included no reference to compactness, contiguity, or related requirements. In a 1932 case, the Supreme Court had concluded that Congress no longer intended to require compact districts, and the state's amici thought that a judicially created mandate that districts meet such standards "would arguably fly in the face of Congress' expressed intent not to mandate [them]."

The various briefs filed in the Supreme Court by the appellants and appellees largely tracked their arguments before the district court. In one of his briefs, Everett underscored what he termed the DNC's "unconscious reliance on 'stereotypes'" in its amicus brief in behalf of the state. The DNC had insisted at one point that North Carolina's Twelfth District actually conformed to "rational redistricting principles" because, "despite its odd shape, [it] is still compact — the district recognizes a community of interest, mainly urban African-Americans with similar concerns and interests, is easily traversed and has less land area than any other North Carolina congressional district." The only "community of interest" that "serpentine" district embraced, Everett retorted, was "created by race" and embodied the stereotypical assumption of its creators "that any black in one end of the district would have a greater affinity with any black in another part than with a next-door neighbor of a different race."

Everett also took issue with any notion that the challenged plan could be justified as a remedy for past discrimination against North Carolina's minority population. "Whatever past sins of discrimination North Carolina may have committed against black voters by means of poll taxes, literacy tests, or otherwise, there has been no finding that these sins ever prevented the election of a black person to Congress." Instead, the failure of African Americans to win House seats reflected the relatively low percentage of the state's minority population and its distribution across North Carolina.

For their part, the state defendants relied heavily, as they had in the district court, on *UJO* and other precedents that, they claimed, supported North Carolina's majority-minority districts. They also challenged the appellants' use of Justice Harlan's *Plessy* dissent to oppose all race-conscious redistricting. Harlan's call for a "color-blind Constitution" in *Plessy*, they argued, was "not the clear endorsement of a *per se* ban on race-conscious state action that the Plaintiffs take it to be." Harlan opposed segregation laws, the appellees contended, drawing on passages from his dissent, because they were based on assumptions of black inferiority. Legislatures adopted such laws precisely "because of" their impact on black citizens. Unlike North Carolina's districts, they were based on "hostility to, and [were] enacted for the purpose of humiliating, citizens of the United States of a particular race." The disputed majority-minority districts obviously had no such invidious purpose.

The Supreme Court scheduled *Shaw* for oral argument April 20, 1993. Robinson Everett was to argue for the appellants, Jefferson Powell for the state, and Edwin Kneedler, an assistant in the U.S. solicitor general's office, for the federal government. Everett had been admitted to the Supreme Court bar thirty-nine years ago that month, while work-ing as a commissioner, or senior clerk, to Judge Paul W. Brosman of the Court of Military Appeals. In April 1954, his parents had gone to Washington for a meeting of the American Law Institute, and Robin-son suggested that they all use the occasion to become members of the Supreme Court bar. On April 26, North Carolina Senator Clyde Hoey, who had served many years earlier with Mrs. Everett's father in the North Carolina General Assembly, presented Robinson and his par-ents to the justices. The occasion of a father, mother, and son all being admitted to the Supreme Court bar attracted a good deal of press cov-erage, including an Associated Press wirephoto that ran in several newspapers. But Everett's parents never argued a case in the Court; nor would their son, until the *Shaw* litigation.

Oral argument before the Supreme Court is a relatively simple and typically brief affair. Counsel appearing before the justices stand at a lectern a few feet from the bench. Ordinarily, each side is allotted only half an hour for argument, but lawyers arguing first are obliged to save a few minutes of their time for any rebuttal they might wish to make to the contentions of opposing counsel. Justices can, and regularly do, interrupt attorneys with questions.

Since Everett's filing of an appeal in the case, President Bill Clinton had replaced George Bush in the White House and appointed Janet Reno to the post of attorney general. At 10:10 A.M. on April 20, Chief Justice William H. Rehnquist convened the justices to hear argument in Case No. 92-357, now entitled *Ruth O. Shaw v. Janet Reno.*

As counsel for the appellants, Everett had the dubious distinction of speaking first. To prepare for the occasion, he had written a twelve-page typescript summarizing his position. Not surprisingly, however, he would devote most of his time to fielding questions from the justices. Placing a large color map of the contested districting plan before the Court — a plan described by some, he said, as "political pornography"— he accused the Justice Department and state officials of inflicting "legal seg-regation of the congressional delegation of North Carolina." As a pre-condition for clearing the state's districting plan, he asserted, the attorney general had required the General Assembly to create "two seats which would be guaranteed for election of African Americans to Congress." Since North Carolina's minority population was relatively dispersed throughout the state, "the only way to achieve that [result] was to violate every one of the principles of redistricting and reapportionment which have heretofore been accepted by the Court."

Justice John Paul Stevens interrupted at that point with a question. "Mr. Everett, . . . you say that the district violates all the principles that have been established in the cases. Well, it doesn't violate the one person/one vote principle, does it?" Everett agreed. Stevens then wanted to know what principle the challenged plan did violate.

"Well, it violates the principles of compactness," Everett replied.

"But are they constitutional principles?" Stevens asked. "[And] do you include anything other than compactness?" When Everett responded that he included contiguousness among the redistricting principles required by the Constitution, Stevens weighed in again. "But this district is entirely contiguous, isn't it?"

Only "in a very marginal sense of the word," Everett answered. In certain places, portions of the Twelfth District were connected only at a single point. "We would view contiguousness as meaning more than a contact at a point," he asserted; "we would suggest that if there's any significance to contiguousness other than, say, . . . one point where there is an infinitesimal contact, that it violates contiguousness." The Twelfth District was also inconsistent, he added, with the principle that a district should encompass a community of interest.

"Well, Mr. Everett," Justice Sandra Day O'Connor interrupted, with a reference to *Pope v. Blue*, "I guess this Court summarily affirmed in a previous case that came before us raising just these points."

But that case, Everett hastily explained, was a challenge to political gerrymandering. "There was no assertion that this was done for the sole purpose of targeting two seats for persons of a particular race. That we think is the fatal flaw [in North Carolina's plan]."

Picking up on Justice Stevens's earlier questions, O'Connor then asked, "Isn't a State free to reject the idea of compactness if it chooses?"

"Perhaps," the appellants' counsel replied, "but not . . . in the context of seeking to assure the election of a person of a particular race, whatever that race may be."

The chief justice thought that this was the appellants' basic point— "that that sort of intent or motivation on the part of the legislature is subject to strict scrutiny?"

"Exactly, exactly," Everett responded.

At that point, Justice David Souter suggested that the appellants were not really contending that states were obligated, as a general matter, to adhere to the districting principles Everett had cited. Instead, said Souter, "your case really rests simply on the motivation by which this particular configuration supposedly was justified."

Everett agreed. The distortions in the districts' shape were "a reflection of [that] motivation, and the distortions show what happens once we start down the path to what might be termed segregating the electoral process." Boundaries with the "domina[nt]" purpose of assuring the election of candidates of a particular race, he added, were not merely subject to strict scrutiny; they were "invalid."

If the Voting Rights Act authorized or required such districting, Justice Byron White then asked, "Would you say . . . the Voting Rights Act is unconstitutional[?]"

So construed, Everett agreed, the statute would itself violate the Constitution. In response to further questions from White, Everett observed that sixty of North Carolina's hundred counties, including most of the counties in the Twelfth District, were not covered by the Voting Rights Act's preclearance provisions. "We have a situation where the . . . preclearance requirement is being used to affect adversely areas which have never been found guilty of any sort of [voting discrimination] . . . we've consistently taken the position that to manipulate the preclearance requirement for the [covered] counties, primarily in the northeast, as a basis for covering the entire State with a plan which is racially discriminatory, at least as we interpret it, is beyond the purview of the Voting Rights [Act] . . . but in addition and more fundamental[ly] we take the position that what was done is not authorized by the U.S. Constitution."

During questioning by Justice Souter, Everett appeared to concede that compactness and other traditional redistricting principles had no binding force as constitutional requirements. When Souter later suggested that Everett's problem was "not race consciousness as such in drawing lines; it's the specificity of the race consciousness in saying, in effect, that there must be a quota of two districts," the appellants' counsel "basically" concurred. However, Souter then asked how Everett would draw the line between permissible and impermissible uses of race consciousness, and in his reply, Everett referred once again to traditional redistricting standards. "But there again," Souter retorted, "we're getting back to . . . criteria which you conceded a while ago did not themselves have any independent constitutional significance. And I think you're now coming back to the argument that . . . when race is taken into account, although that may be permissible per se, it cannot be taken into account, in effect, without serving a series of other principles like compactness, community identification, and so on. And yet, you've conceded that these don't have independent constitutional significance. So, how do we derive your rule?"

When Everett responded that "you look at a number of factors and decide whether the paramount purpose was to achieve a particular [racial] result," Justice Antonin Scalia interrupted. Scalia had construed Everett's earlier remarks to mean "that race could be taken into consideration [only] if race had previously been taken into consideration in an adverse way" — in short, only as a remedy for past discrimination. "I wonder if you're wise," the justice observed, "in conceding that race . . . could be taken into consideration in any further extent."

Acknowledging that he "perhaps misspoke" earlier, Everett assured Scalia that he indeed had been thinking only of corrective action undertaken "where something has been done on racial grounds adverse to a minority group as, for example, breaking apart a community of minority persons into two districts and thereby basically diluting the vote. Then I think certainly some corrective action could be taken, and the corrective action would take race into account." He emphasized, however, that his reference to a black community meant a neighborhood, not one "predicated on the stereotype that one black. . . ."

Justice Souter interrupted at that point. "I think what you're objecting to is using race as a stereotype . . . assuming that all black people will vote for a black representative, and therefore drawing a district with a certain number of blacks in it on the assumption that since they're black, they will vote for a black representative. That's using race not for community, but for [a] stereotypical conclusion . . . , which is not very good for our society I assume."

"Justice Souter, that's exactly right," Everett responded. But Justice White was not convinced. White could see no difference between an assumption that black voters would vote for black candidates and the "assumption that an Irish Catholic will vote like another Irish Catholic and they're more apt to vote Democratic than Republican."

When legislatures engage in partisan gerrymandering, they make an assumption that most voters will not change their usual party preference before the next election. "Is that really different," White asked, "from any other kind of group interest?"

Justice Scalia next interjected a series of questions. "Does the Voting Rights Act apply to Republicans? Did we fight a civil war about Republicans? Does the Thirteenth and Fourteenth Amendment apply to Republicans? I didn't think so."

But Justice Souter had a ready response. "You don't think the Fourteenth Amendment applies to Republicans?" he asked his colleague. "You think it's okay for the sovereign to discriminate against Republicans? It's very interesting."

Once the laughter in the courtroom subsided, Everett conceded that, under *Davis v. Bandemer*, partisan gerrymandering would, under exceptional circumstances, violate the Constitution. "But the racial distinction," he added, was "something that a war was fought to get rid of. There are a line of opinions of this Court which in one way or the other have inveighed against racial classifications. We take that very seriously. We take the color-blind Constitution to be more than an idle aspiration, particularly under present conditions."

One justice was incredulous. "You're not resting [your case] on the principle of the color-blind Constitution, are you? I mean, you accept, for example, the *Gingles* analysis, and whatever that is, it isn't color-blind. . . . Is it fair to say that you accept the principle that redistricting can be done on the basis of trying to anticipate the possibility of a *Gingles* violation and to avoid it by drawing lines in such a way as to avoid voter dilution? You accept that principle, don't you? . . . That's not a principle of a color-blind Constitution, is it?"

Everett's reply was hardly reassuring to his questioner. "Well," he reluctantly conceded, "that may not be in one sense."

It was now Jefferson Powell's turn. Like Everett, Powell had barely begun his argument before being interrupted with a question from the bench. Chief Justice Rehnquist wanted to know Powell's stance, if any, on the statewide application of the Voting Rights Act in a state such as North Carolina, where only forty of its hundred counties were subject to the statute's preclearance requirements.

The state's counsel replied that statewide preclearance made "pragmatic sense," since state legislatures obviously drew up congressional district plans on a statewide basis. The authority for that approach, he added, was essentially administrative. "It's the way the act has been administered and interpreted."

"So," Rehnquist countered, "there isn't any authority in the act itself for that? It's just an administrative authority?"

Justice Souter came to Powell's defense. "I had just assumed that as long as any one covered county was going to be affected by the plan, that that would be enough to trigger the right to review."

Justice Scalia had a more fundamental question. "I'm not sure I understand your good faith defense"—what Everett had more bluntly termed the state's "Nuremberg" or "devil-made-me-do-it" defense. If the intent underlying a law was unconstitutional, Scalia asserted, surely the Justice Department's approval would make no difference. "I mean, suppose the Justice Department says it's okay to discriminate in appointments on the basis of race. That happens to be wrong, but if in good faith you follow that, that makes it okay?"

Assuring Scalia that that was "emphatically not" the state's position, Powell contended that the interpretation of the Voting Rights Act the attorney general embraced in his letter of objection to North Carolina's first districting plan "was well within the case law." The state, he conceded, obviously could not rely "on patently unconstitutional requests or demands from the Attorney General." But if the state's reliance on Justice Department interpretations of the law was "reasonable," its districting decisions were immune from judicial review.

Scalia was not persuaded. North Carolina had not been obliged to accept the attorney general's suggestion that a second majority-minority district was necessary to satisfy the Voting Rights Act's provisions relative to minority vote dilution. "You could," the justice observed, "have gone to the district court in the District of Columbia to say this is wrong. But you chose not to. Then I don't think you should rely on the Justice Department. You chose to do it. You took the easy way out I suppose you could say, but I'm not sure that gives you a good faith defense."

"What does a plaintiff have to prove," Justice White then asked, "to show that the State has violated the Voting Rights Act in redistricting?"

Under Section 5, Powell was not certain. But a constitutional challenge to North Carolina's majority-minority districts required a show-ing of invidious intent. "That's one of the things that's lacking in this case," declared Powell. "The plaintiffs have not alleged — indeed, the district court below said they could not plausibly allege — that the General Assembly chose this plan because it would impose an adverse impact on white voters or, indeed, any other racial group."

Citing *Croson* for illustrative purposes, Chief Justice Rehnquist observed that, under the Court's recent decisions, "an intent to clas-sify on the basis of race . . . [was] subject to strict scrutiny, not that it's automatically out, but that it's subject to strict scrutiny." But Powell insisted that such affirmative action cases were distinguishable from vote dilution precedents, in which a showing of "invidious" intent was required. Powell conceded Rehnquist's assertion that those cases pre-ceded *Croson*, but he argued that they remained valid law in the elec-tion field.

Justice Anthony Kennedy asked hypothetically whether a state not subject to the Voting Rights Act's preclearance provisions could engage in race-conscious districting. Powell responded by noting earlier cases in which members of the Court had suggested that under Section 2's vote dilution provisions, such districting might be appropriate in juris-dictions with a history of racially polarized voting. "So," Kennedy countered, "a State that has racially polarized voting under the Voting Rights Act, as you are interpreting it, is required to employ methods which will continue racially polarized voting . . . that's the logical con-clusion from your answer." But that would be true, Powell replied, only if the creation of majority-minority districts perpetuated racially polar-ized voting. Moreover, Section 2 of the statute, as amended in 1982, might require majority-minority districting to protect against minor-ity vote dilution.

At that point, Justice O'Connor raised a question that would as-sume major significance in the Court's decision. "Mr. Powell," O'Connor asked, "this District 12 is a highly irregular shape. . . . In places only as wide as a highway and stretching virtually the length of the State. Do you think that a district such as that could be in and of itself some evidence of an invidious intent?"

Powell argued that in a case in which plaintiffs claimed a discrep-ancy between a "State's purported purpose and its real purpose, . . . that might be probative of the existence of this covert intent." He insisted, however, that there was no dispute between the state and the plaintiffs over what the General Assembly had tried to do in adopting its disputed districts. "There's [merely] a dispute over how to characterize it legally." Later, Powell elaborated on his position. "The State did not have an independent policy of racial proportionality. The State's policy here was to meet the one person/one vote requirement, to satisfy the exigent requirements of the Federal Voting Rights Act, and otherwise to satisfy other State concerns. The State here was not pursuing an independent policy of racial balancing or anything of the sort."

Still later, Powell further developed the state's stance. "In the end this case is about the Voting Rights Act. At least up to this point, the plaintiffs' argument has been a pure argument that race consciousness is invidious and unconstitutional. [But] Section 5 and Section 2, as amended, both authorize and in appropriate circumstances require race consciousness in governmental decision making. Unless those provisions of the statute are unconstitutional, the plaintiffs' claim is incorrect. We believe this Court's decisions upholding the . . . act's constitutionality are correct, and that the district court should be affirmed."

Beginning his argument in behalf of the federal government, Assistant Solicitor General Kneedler stressed that several features of the Voting Rights Act would "effectively require" a state to take race into account when adopting a congressional districting plan. Section 5's effects test obliged states to ensure that a districting plan would have no "retrogressive effect" on minority voting rights. As construed in the *Gingles* case, the law required states to evaluate the racial composition of districts to guard against minority vote dilution. "Where a State is acting . . . in a good faith effort to comply with the Voting Rights Act," stated Kneedler, "the State does not, at the same time, violate the very [constitutional] amendments that the Voting Rights Act is designed to enforce and constitutionally designed to enforce under this Court's decisions."

When Kneedler cited *UJO* in defending his position, Chief Justice Rehnquist reminded the assistant solicitor general that "that was just a plurality opinion." Kneedler then reminded the chief justice that two additional members of the *UJO* Court had embraced an even broader reading of the Voting Rights Act than the plurality had, contending that a state's efforts to comply with even an unauthorized Justice Department interpretation of the act "would negate [a finding of] invidious intent."

Rehnquist next asked whether the challenged districts actually encouraged, and indeed were designed to encourage, racial bloc voting. Kneedler conceded as much, but he also emphasized that the minority vote dilution the Voting Rights Act prohibited was likely to occur "where you [already] have racially polarized voting and a minority is submerged in a majority white district. . . . We do not believe that the principle of the color-blind Constitution requires a State to be blind to the fact that its citizens regrettably may vote along racial lines."

Asked if he would find the challenged plan consistent with the Voting Rights Act even if enacted without Justice Department scrutiny, Kneedler readily agreed that he would. "Far from being a suspect, States should be encouraged to conduct their districting in a way that comes into compliance with the Voting Rights Act." But he also conceded that the attorney general's objections to North Carolina's first districting plan had "furnished the State with a pretty firm basis for doubt as to whether it could carry its burden [of justifying the first plan] if it chose, for example, the alternative to go to court. The State could legitimately believe it would have trouble carrying its burden of proving an absence of discriminatory purpose." The Voting Rights Act's requirements, as well as Congress's broad civil rights enforcement authority, he added, distinguished *Shaw* from cases in which the Court had required strict judicial scrutiny.

———

Everett had saved three minutes of his allotted time for rebuttal. Rejecting any suggestion on Kneedler's part that "if the Voting Rights Act authorizes something, then it is automatically valid," he once again accused the Justice Department and the state of misinterpreting the Voting Rights Act, which, he claimed, did not require or authorize majority-minority districts. The appellants objected, he declared, to a "quota system of . . . proportional representation . . . being forced upon the [North Carolina] congressional delegation. . . . That's exactly what it was, to have a quota of a certain number of members of Congress of a particular race. We find no authorization for that in any of the jurisprudence of the Court."

"Indeed," Justice Scalia helpfully interjected, "it's prohibited in the Voting Rights Act itself."

Justice Stevens wanted to know Everett's reaction if a city such as Chicago "create[d] a number of wards where the Polish vote would control? Would your standard be different?"

Everett thought it would be, adding, "I don't think race is in the same category."

"So," Stevens shot back, "in a city they could have one rule for the Polish Americans and a different rule for the African Americans[?]"

Everett then reminded the justice that race was "a much frowned upon" stereotype.

"Treating Polish Americans [as a group] is not a stereotype[?]" Stevens countered.

Polish Americans in Chicago, Everett replied, were "living in neighborhoods. It would probably be a situation of an actual community of interest."

"Well," answered the justice, "the blacks tend to live together. Polish Americans tend to live together in Chicago."

But Everett persisted. "I don't think anyone has ever said that one Polish American necessarily does [everything] like another Polish American. It's not the stereotype, which is what we're complaining of, the stereotype that one black thinks exactly like another and should be represented by another."

Leaving the courtroom after oral argument, Everett encountered his Duke law school colleague Walter Dellinger, later to be his adversary in the redistricting litigation. Dellinger, Everett later recalled, "seemed to think we might get two votes, maybe three. So he was not particularly encouraging of our viewpoint. I didn't know what to expect. I thought they had listened carefully. But I was not that tuned into Supreme Court jurisprudence. . . . We had a map and that was unusual; I thought they seemed to be impressed by the map. I was not a constitutionally skilled advocate of the Supreme Court. So it was a very different type argument, I suspect, than some they get otherwise. . . . I remember the Supreme Court recently heard argument when I was present, where one of the counsel, who was seventy-nine or eighty, had been a Nuremberg prosecutor. And [the justices] were just sort of interested in this particular guy. And they listened intently. [But] I had no idea how we came out."

On June 28, at the end of the Court's term, Everett was at Wrightville Beach with a cousin. "And we learn, lo and behold, that we've won. There is a cause of action!"

By a five-to-four vote, the Court had indeed overruled the district court's dismissal of the complaint, ordering a trial on the plaintiffs' allegations. When Walter Dellinger had predicted that Everett might win the votes of two or three justices, he no doubt had in mind Justices Scalia and Clarence Thomas, with the chief justice the third possibility, given those justices' well-known distaste for affirmative action and related race-conscious policies. The appellants, however, had also won the support of Justice Kennedy and the Court's most influential swing justice, Sandra Day O'Connor. Decidedly less predictable than the Court's most conservative members, O'Connor and Kennedy typically based their votes largely on the facts and circumstances of particular cases rather than sweeping philosophical convictions. The facts of *Shaw* pushed both into the plaintiffs' corner.

If he is in the majority, the chief justice traditionally has the prerogative of writing the Court's opinion in a case or assigning the task to another majority justice. In close cases, the chief often selects the member of the majority who is closest in thinking to the dissenters to write the Court's opinion. His hope is that such a choice will not only hold the majority together but perhaps even attract one or more dissenting justices, swelling the majority's ranks before a decision in the case is announced.

Chief Justice Rehnquist assigned Justice O'Connor the majority opinion in *Shaw*. Speaking for the Court, O'Connor affirmed, without elaboration, the district court's dismissal of the complaint against the attorney general and other federal officials. She concluded, however, that the appellants had stated a cause of action, or ground for judicial relief, against the state under the Fourteenth Amendment's equal protection clause. They were thus entitled to a trial of their allegations in the district court.

The justice began her explanation of the Court's decision by tracing the history of racial discrimination in voting, especially that portion relating to the drawing of legislative districts and other governmental boundaries. Despite adoption of the Reconstruction amendments, she observed, certain states had persisted in their efforts to circumvent the voting rights of the newly freed slaves. In the 1870s, for example, Mississippi concentrated most of its African American population in a "shoestring" congressional district running the length of the Mississippi River, leaving its other five districts under white control. Nearly a century later, southern states continued to resort to a variety of devices in excluding blacks from the polls. In the "exercise of geometry" struck down in *Gomillion v. Lightfoot* (1960), for example, Alabama had redefined Tuskegee's city boundaries "from a square to an uncouth twenty-eight-sided figure," excluding all but a few black voters from the city's elections and other residential benefits. Adoption of the Voting Rights Act had led to dramatic increases in black voter registration. The Court had soon recognized, however, that multimember districts and at-large election systems, among other arrangements, often had the impermissible purpose and effect of diluting minority voting strength. In its 1982 amendments to Section 2 of the Voting Rights Act, Congress went further, prohibiting election laws that resulted in the dilution of the minority vote, whatever the legislature's intent.

Against that background, the appellants' claim that North Carolina's majority-minority districts amounted to unconstitutional racial gerrymandering struck, declared Justice O'Connor, "a powerful historical chord," especially in view of the degree to which the challenged plan "resemble[d] the most egregious racial gerrymanders of the past." Even so, the appellants were not claiming an unconstitutional dilution of white voting strength; in fact, they had not even identified their race. Instead, they had argued that "the deliberate segregation of voters into separate districts on the basis of race violated their constitutional right to participate in a 'color-blind' electoral process."

The appellants also "appear[ed]" to concede, however, that race-conscious districting was not always unconstitutional. "That concession," O'Connor observed, "is wise: This Court never has held that race-conscious state decisionmaking is impermissible in *all* circumstances." As the Court construed their complaint, the appellants merely "object[ed] to . . . redistricting legislation that is so extremely irregular on its face that it rationally can be viewed only as an effort to segregate the races for purposes of voting, without regard for traditional districting principles and without sufficiently compelling justification." So framed, concluded O'Connor, the appellants had stated a claim for which judicial relief could be granted.

Elaborating on the Court's rationale, the justice asserted that reapportionment is "one area in which appearances do matter." The Fourteenth Amendment does not merely forbid laws that discriminate racially on their face; the equal protection guarantee also applies to laws that, although racially neutral on their face, are "unexplainable on grounds other than race." Districts with an extremely "bizarre" shape, such as North Carolina's Twelfth District, create such a presumption.

O'Connor agreed that compactness, contiguity, respect for the boundaries of political subdivisions, and other traditional districting principles are not constitutional requirements. But the concentration of a dispersed minority into a single district without regard for such principles, she added, has troubling implications. "A reapportionment plan that includes in one district individuals who belong to the same race, but who are otherwise widely separated by geographical and political boundaries, and who may have little in common with one another but the color of their skin, bears an uncomfortable resemblance to political apartheid. It reinforces the perception that members of the same racial group — regardless of their age, education, economic status, or the community in which they live — think alike, share the same political interests, and will prefer the same candidates at the polls. We have rejected such perceptions elsewhere as impermissible racial stereotypes. . . . By perpetuating such notions, a racial gerrymander may exacerbate the very patterns of racial bloc voting that majority-minority districting is sometimes said to counteract." She found "equally pernicious" the message such districting conveyed to politicians — the notion "that their primary obligation is to represent only the members of that group."

Justice O'Connor also gave short shrift to what she termed the Court's "highly fractured" *UJO* decision. *UJO*, she conceded, did uphold the creation of majority-minority districts. The *UJO* plaintiffs, however, had not claimed that the plan at issue there "was so highly irregular that it rationally could be understood only as an effort to segregate voters by race." As Everett had contended, the *UJO* plurality had found that plan consistent with traditional districting principles. "*UJO*'s framework simply does not apply," declared O'Connor, "where, as here, a reapportionment plan is alleged to be so irrational on its face that it immediately offends principles of racial equality. . . . Nothing in the decision precludes white voters (or voters of any other race) from bringing the analytically distinct claim that a reapportionment plan rationally cannot be understood as anything other than an effort to segregate citizens into separate voting districts on the basis of race without sufficient justification."

The Court declined to speculate on the constitutionality of a "reasonably compact" majority-minority district. Justice O'Connor merely concluded for the majority that a district "so irrational on its face" that it could be understood only as a racial gerrymander was subject to strict judicial scrutiny and would be struck down unless "narrowly tailored to further a compelling governmental interest." In concluding, however, she clearly stated the majority's general distaste for race-conscious laws, especially in the voting arena. "Racial classifications of any sort," she declared, "pose the risk of lasting harm to our society. They reinforce the belief, held by too many for too much of our history, that individuals should be judged by the color of their skin. Racial classifications with respect to voting carry particular dangers. Racial gerrymandering, even for remedial purposes, may balkanize us into competing racial factions; it threatens to carry us further from the goal of a political system in which race no longer matters — a goal that the Fourteenth and Fifteenth Amendments embody, and to which the Nation continues to aspire."

Each of the four *Shaw* dissenters registered their opposition to the majority's ruling and rationale. Justice White, joined by Justices Blackmun and Stevens, emphasized the absence of any substantial injury to the plaintiffs' voting rights. White noted that earlier cases had struck down only two types of election laws — those constituting a "direct and outright deprivation of the right to vote" through a poll tax, literacy test, or similar scheme; and those having "the intent and effect of unduly diminishing [a political or racial group's] influence on the political process." While conceding that this second standard imposed a "severe burden" on members of such groups, White found it "sound" and consistent with the very nature of the districting process. Unlike other state decision making that might provoke discrimination claims, districting regularly requires legislators to take race and other demographic factors into account. Whenever a district is created, legislatures invariably make an unavoidable choice about its racial composition. Redistricting plans, added White, not only affect group interests but also reflect the partisan aims of the majority party in the legislature. To allow judicial intervention whenever such decisions were made would "invite constant and unmanageable intrusion into the political process."

Under *Davis v. Bandemer,* which White wrote, members of a particular group were required to establish more than that a challenged districting plan had caused them to lose an election; they had to prove that they had been effectively excluded from the political process. The ultimate issue in cases of the *Shaw* variety, declared White, was "whether [a] classification based on race discriminates against *anyone* by denying equal access to the political process." In White's judgment, it "strain[ed] credulity to suggest" that the decision of North Carolina's white-dominated legislature to create majority-minority districts had the purpose of restricting white access to the political process. There was "no question" that the challenged plan did not have a racially discriminatory impact on white voters. After all, whereas they constituted 76 percent of North Carolina's total population and 79 percent of its voting-age population, whites retained a voting majority in ten (or 83 percent) of the state's congressional districts. White voters in the two districts in which members of their race did not have a voting majority might be disappointed "at the prospect of casting a vote for a losing candidate — a lot shared by many, including a disproportionate number of minority voters." But, asserted White, that "surely [did not constitute] . . . discriminatory treatment."

Nor was Justice White impressed with the majority's reading of purported precedents. The petitioners in *UJO* had contended, for example, that the majority-minority districting at issue there had no other reason but race, yet they lost their case. The Alabama law struck down in the *Gomillion* case had the effect of excluding most of Tuskegee's black voters from voting and other benefits of residence in that community. "In *Gomillion,* in short, the [white] group that formed the majority at the state level purportedly set out to manipulate city boundaries in order to remove members of the minority, thereby denying them valuable municipal services. No analogous purpose or effect has been alleged in this case."

The *Shaw* majority also relied on *Wright v. Rockefeller* (1964), in which the plaintiffs had alleged that a congressional districting plan excluded minorities from one of four districts, while concentrating them in the other three districts. As construed by Justice O'Connor, every member of the *Wright* Court had agreed that the plaintiffs' allegations that the statute at issue segregated voters on the basis of race and place of origin raised a valid constitutional claim. The *Wright* majority had merely joined the trial court's conclusion that the plaintiffs had failed to establish that the districts were based on race. "The boundary lines were somewhat irregular," as Justice O'Connor put it, "but not so bizarre as to permit of no other conclusion" than that they constituted racial gerrymandering. Justice White contended, however, that the *Wright* Court had simply affirmed the trial court's finding that the plaintiffs "had not met their burden of proving discriminatory intent," adding, "I fail to see how a decision based on a failure to establish discriminatory intent can support the inference [drawn by the *Shaw* majority] that it is unnecessary [in such cases] to prove discriminatory *effect*."

White did agree that, under *Wright*, "a complaint stating that a [districting] plan has carved out districts on the basis of race *can*, under certain circumstances, state a claim under the Fourteenth Amendment." But in such cases, he asserted, plaintiffs must allege both "discriminatory purpose and effect." In *Wright*, for example, it might have been established that the challenged districts were intended to, and in fact did, shield one district from any minority voter influence and pack minority voters in another district, "thereby invidiously minimizing their voting strength. In other words, the purposeful creation of a majority-minority district could have discriminatory effect if it is achieved by means of 'packing' — *i.e.*, over-concentration of minority voters." But *Shaw's* facts, White insisted, could establish no such claim.

To White, the majority's novel legal theory also made "no sense." In previous cases, the Court had placed the burden on plaintiffs to demonstrate that a districting plan had both the purpose and the effect of excluding an identifiable racial group from the political process. "Not so, apparently," he added, "when the districting 'segregates' by drawing odd-shaped lines. In that case, we are told, such proof no longer is needed. Instead, it is the *State* that must rebut the allegation that race was taken into account, a fact that . . . I had thought we practically took for granted."

{ *Race and Redistricting* }

Part of the reason for the majority's stance, White suggested, might lie with the emotional impact created by districts whose appearance seems to reflect "segregation" or "political apartheid." But White questioned such concerns. For one thing, the use of the term "segregate" appeared to him far afield from its historical context, and reference to a district 54.71 percent African American as segregated struck him as not "particularly accurate." More fundamentally, White saw no difference between a districting plan that "segregates" and other varieties of gerrymandering. In all cases, he thought, the challenger should be required to prove discriminatory purpose and effect.

The other element underlying the majority's rationale, White wryly observed, was the Court's "simultaneous discomfort and fascination with irregularly shaped districts." Like the appellees, he agreed that lack of compactness and contiguity suggested that something was "amiss" in a districting plan. But district "irregularities," he contended, were nothing more than "strong indicia" of a gerrymander; they had no bearing on a districting scheme's ultimate constitutionality. "Given two districts drawn on similar, race-based grounds, the one does not become more injurious than the other simply by virtue of being snake-like, at least so far as the Constitution is concerned and absent any evidence of differential impact." The majority's obsession with district shape, asserted White, was inconsistent with its concession that neither "compactness" nor "attractiveness" was an independent constitutional requirement. It also ignored the obvious fact that "a regularly shaped district can just as effectively effectuate racially discriminatory gerrymandering as an odd-shaped one." Finally, the majority's approach would hinder voluntary state efforts to ensure some degree of minority legislative representation in states with a dispersed minority population, as well as those in which concerns about incumbency protection or other districting considerations might prompt the creation of a majority-minority district in another location than the most "obvious" site.

Even if North Carolina's plan were properly subject to strict judicial scrutiny, Justice White thought that the state's interest in meeting the attorney general's objections to its first districting plan was clearly compelling and that the second plan was narrowly tailored to that interest. He thus saw no need for a remand of the case on that issue, but he cited numerous pitfalls in lower court efforts to follow the majority's directive. The fundamental difficulty, White concluded, lay with attempting to apply a constitutional standard "divorced from any [traditional] measure of constitutional harm. . . . State efforts to remedy minority vote dilution are wholly unlike what typically has been labeled 'affirmative action.' To the extent that no other racial group is injured, remedying a Voting Rights Act violation does not involve preferential treatment. . . . It involves, instead, an attempt to *equalize* treatment, and to provide minority voters with an effective voice in the political process."

Justice Blackmun filed a brief opinion joining Justice White's dissent. Blackmun found it "particularly ironic" that the majority had chosen as its opportunity for abandoning settled case law and announcing its "analytically distinct" constitutional claim a case in which white voters were challenging a districting "plan under which North Carolina has sent black representatives to Congress for the first time since Reconstruction."

Justice Stevens used his dissent largely to underscore two "undisputed facts" in the case that Justice O'Connor had devoted much of her opinion to proving — first, that the shape of North Carolina's Twelfth District was so "bizarre" that it must have been designed to help or harm a particular group of voters; and second, that it was drawn to facilitate the election of an African American to Congress. Those facts, observed Stevens, gave rise to three constitutional questions, to each of which he gave a negative response. On the issue whether the Constitution required compact or contiguous districts, he agreed with White that "bizarre and uncouth" districts could serve as "powerful evidence" of an ulterior legislative motive, especially in cases devoid of other evidence establishing invidious intent. But North Carolina's purpose for creating its majority-minority districts was obvious, and their irregular shape was thus, "for our purposes, irrelevant." He also agreed that irregular districts could violate equal protection, but only when adopted "for the sole purpose of making it more difficult for members of a minority group to win an election." No equal protection issue arose "when the majority acts to facilitate the election of a member of a group that lacks [political] power because it remains underrepresented." The difference between constitutional and unconstitutional gerrymandering has nothing to do with whether they are based on assumptions about the group affected, "but whether their purpose is to enhance the power of the group in control of the districting process at the expense of any minority group, and thereby to strengthen the unequal distribution of electoral power. When an assumption that people in a particular minority group (whether they are defined by the political party, religion, ethnic group, or race to which they belong) will vote in a particular way is used to *benefit* that group, no constitutional violation occurs. Politicians have always relied on assumptions that people in particular groups are likely to vote in a particular way when they draw new district lines, and I cannot believe that anything in today's opinion will stop them from doing so in the future."

Finally, Stevens, unlike the majority, would have reached no different conclusion when the minority group benefiting from such redistricting was defined on the basis of race. "If it is permissible," observed the justice, "to draw boundaries to provide adequate representation for rural voters, for union members, for Hasidic Jews, for Polish Americans, or for Republicans, it necessarily follows that it is permissible to do the same thing for members of the very minority group whose history in the United States gave birth to the Equal Protection Clause. . . . A contrary conclusion could only be described as perverse."

Although not joining White's opinion, Justice Souter also filed a dissent. Souter cited several reasons why the Court had traditionally subjected districting issues involving race to more deferential judicial scrutiny than equal protection challenges to other forms of governmental action. He lamented, moreover, the *Shaw* majority's decision to break with that pattern. First, wrote Souter, as Justice White and others had indicated, districting nearly always requires some legitimate consideration of race in areas with a racially diverse population. As long as members of different races share common interests and racial bloc voting persists, legislators are obliged, Souter reasoned, to consider race in ensuring that the districts they create do not lead to the dilution of minority voting strength. Second, in affirmative action and other nondistricting equal protection cases, the use of racial criteria works to the advantage of members of one race "at the obvious expense of a member of a different race." The same is true of voting schemes with the purpose of disenfranchising members of a particular race. "In districting, by contrast," observed Souter, "the mere placement of an individual in one district instead of another denies no one a right or benefit provided to others. All citizens may register, vote, and be represented. . . . One's constitutional rights are not violated merely because the candidate one supports loses the election or because a group (including a racial group) to which one belongs winds up with a representative from outside that group. . . . 'Vote dilution' thus refers to the effects of districting decisions not on an individual's political power viewed in isolation, but on the political power of a group. . . . The placement of given voters in a given district, even on the basis of race, does not, without more, diminish the effectiveness of the individual as a voter."

Under that categorical approach, Souter reasoned, there is no need for "searching" judicial scrutiny of a district plan found to dilute or abridge the right to participate in the electoral process on the basis of race. "There has never been a suggestion that such use of race could be justified under any type of scrutiny, since the [racial] dilution of the right to vote can not be said to serve any legitimate purpose." With such an approach, moreover, the Court could avoid the usual debate over "benign" as opposed to "invidious" racial discrimination, or "group entitlements as distinct from individual protection, or about the appropriateness of strict or other heightened scrutiny."

Given the majority's emphasis on the extremely bizarre shape of North Carolina's districts, Justice Souter assumed (or hoped) that *Shaw* might prove to be an aberration, invoked in few future cases as a basis for finding impermissible uses of race in the districting process. Whatever the ruling's impact, however, he was concerned that the majority had offered no adequate justification for treating "bizarrely shaped district claims differently from other districting claims." Regard for compactness and other "sound district principles" was the only justification Souter could imagine, but the Court had declined to consider them constitutional commands. Souter opposed, moreover, "respond[ing] to the seeming egregiousness of the redistricting now before us by untethering the concept of racial gerrymander in such a case from the concept of harm exemplified by dilution. In the absence of an allegation of such harm," the justice favored affirming the district court's dismissal of Everett's suit.

CHAPTER 4

The 1994 Trial

In its first *Shaw* opinion, the Supreme Court did not rule on the merits of the plaintiffs' claims. That is, the justices did not reach the issue of whether North Carolina's majority-minority districts violated the Constitution. Instead, Justice O'Connor simply held for the majority that the plaintiffs were entitled to a trial on their claims in the district court. In her obvious disdain for the challenged districts' bizarre shape and references to their resemblance to "apartheid," however, the justice appeared to send a clear signal to state officials and the trial court that the districts were in deep constitutional trouble. Everett thus assumed — "naively," he would later say — that "now the legislature would go ahead and do the redistricting." Everett asked for an audience with Mike Easley, the state's attorney general, hoping to convince him to go to the General Assembly and "tell the legislature, we're not in this to help Republicans or Democrats, blacks or whites; we couldn't care less who wins [elections]. We just want to have the right process, a fair process." "Huh," he later said, "that was a waste of time."

Initially, Everett did not know whether Easley and other state officials took him seriously or not. Later that summer, though, he got his answer. Everett had been invited to participate on an election panel at the Conference of State Legislatures' annual meeting in San Diego. Toby Fitch, one of the co-chairmen of the redistricting committee in the North Carolina house, was also scheduled to appear, but the General Assembly had recessed the day before, and Fitch was tied up with ending the session. Gerry Cohen, the state's chief mapmaker, was substituting for Fitch at the conference. At that point, Everett had heard nothing from his conference with Attorney General Easley. "And [Cohen] took great pleasure in explaining to me that [the General Assembly], before recessing, had appropriated half a million dollars to continue the litigation. And I was very naive. I thought, what are they going to spend a half million dollars for? But it turned out to be [an] easy [question]. They were going to fight to the hilt. And so that's what happened."

———

Counsel for neither the plaintiffs nor the state defendants would stand alone for the second round of proceedings in the district court. A number of Republicans won the right to intervene in the trial as plaintiffs. One of them was Arthur Pope, the chief plaintiff in *Pope v. Blue*, the unsuccessful partisan gerrymandering challenge to North Carolina's majority-minority districts. Raleigh lawyer Thomas Farr would serve as chief counsel to the plaintiff-intervenors.

Farr had impeccable conservative credentials. He grew up in Cincinnati, where his father was a conservative Republican and avid reader of William F. Buckley's *National Review*. One of Farr's high school teachers introduced him to the writings of Edmund Burke and other conservative philosophers, while also instilling in him an abiding interest in politics and government. Following two years at the University of Cincinnati, Farr completed an undergraduate degree at Hillsdale College, a small Michigan school with a commitment to conservative values. After obtaining a law degree at Emory, he went to Washington and earned a master's degree in labor law at Georgetown. While in Washington, he also worked for the National Right to Work Foundation, then became staff counsel to the U.S. Senate Committee on Labor and Human Resources. In that capacity, Farr was assigned to John P. East of North Carolina, a former university professor and protégé of Jesse Helms, whose National Congressional Club had largely funded and engineered East's successful 1980 Senate campaign. Following his stint with Senator East, Farr clerked for U.S. District Court Judge Frank Bullock, a Reagan appointee, in North Carolina. In November 1983, he joined Maupin, Taylor, a Raleigh law firm with close ties to the GOP. Among its senior partners was Tom Ellis, Senator Helms's principal adviser for many years.

One of the first cases Farr became involved with in North Carolina was a challenge to a state election regulation under which election officials discarded any crossover votes of voters who otherwise cast a straight party ballet. Woodrow Jones, the federal district court judge who declared the regulation unconstitutional, had been a member of the General Assembly when the law was enacted in the 1950s. The law, Jones acknowledged in ruling for the plaintiffs, had been adopted in the wake of Charlotte Republican Charles Jonas's election to Congress and was obviously intended to discourage votes for GOP candidates in the then heavily Democratic state. Farr had also served as general counsel to Senator Helms's campaign in a number of elections and would later be general counsel to the state GOP.

When the North Carolina Republican Party challenged North Carolina's majority-minority districts on partisan gerrymandering grounds in the *Pope* case, Farr had been chief counsel for the plaintiffs. In dismissing the suit, the district court had considered *Pope* an equal protection case governed by the Supreme Court's ruling in *Davis v. Bandemer*, which made it extremely difficult for the plaintiffs to establish a constitutional violation in challenges to gerrymanders designed to benefit one political party and disadvantage the other party's electoral chances. "I think that [the district court] really misunderstood the legal theory we were advocating," Farr later recalled. "What we were really trying to advocate in the *Pope* case was that [North Carolina's] districts were just so bizarre and crazily drawn. Not just the minority districts, but if you looked at the original congressional plan, there was just no rhyme or reason for why they did some of the things [they did] in the western part of the state [too]. And we thought [the legislature] had gone so far that the whole redistricting scheme had violated a due process concept. . . . And to that extent, at least as we understood the case, it wasn't really quite a straight *Bandemer* political gerrymandering case. But that's the way the court interpreted it. And we couldn't convince them that that really wasn't our primary theory, or that our theory was really worth anything. [The state's mapmaker] Gerry Cohen — he's a very, very bright guy and I've deposed him several times, and it's been both a challenge and a pleasure, because I like Gerry and he knows about ten times more about this stuff than I do. But one thing he said in some of the legislative discussion was that with the kind of computer technology that was becoming available, he could do a district from Murphy [on the western edge of the state] to Manteo [on the coast] that was ten feet wide. . . . And he's right. . . . And we were saying that the notion of congressional districts is based on the idea that there is a geographic area that represents a congressional district that has some sort of rational basis in its construction. And [state officials] were getting so extreme and so bizarre [with their districts] that . . . the voters were being deprived of due process in the different districts."

Consistent with the position Michael Hess had advanced in the amicus curiae brief he filed for the Republican National Committee (RNC) when the Supreme Court heard *Shaw I*, Farr also declined to embrace Everett's broad contention that all race-conscious districting is unconstitutional — a stance Justice O'Connor had flatly rejected for the *Shaw I* majority. "Judge Everett was arguing that you can never take race into account, and frankly I think he was also arguing that the Voting Rights Act is unconstitutional. We said the Voting Rights Act is not unconstitutional. . . . It's a compelling interest for the state to take race into account to protect itself from a potential Section 2 violation. But to do that, you need to put the remedial district[s] in the part of the state where blacks have had their votes diluted. . . . We said . . . that if the state could show a section in the state where the [*Gingles* compactness and related] conditions were met, it could serve a compelling interest to create essentially a pre-remedial minority district in order to protect the state from a Section 2 violation. . . . We never argued for a minute that the Voting Rights Act was unconstitutional or that there could not be circumstances where the state could legitimately take race into account in drawing districts."

Privately, Farr would insist, too, that he had no connection to, and did not support, any Republican strategy to pack minorities into a few southern districts in order to improve the chances of white Republican candidates in other districts. Michael Hess, "the guy who was my client, not [previous RNC counsel] Ben Ginsberg, [had] the correct interpretation of the Voting Rights Act. . . . I can assure you I didn't advocate going all over the place and packing minorities into districts. I had no role in that and would not think that would be a good thing to do. . . . What did I know about the Bush administration and the Republican Party? Well, what I knew was that the Bush administration Justice Department objected to the first [North Carolina] plan because [the state] didn't put a second, *compact* minority district in the only place in the state where they could do that" — the southeastern district combining African Americans and Native Americans that the Justice Department had proposed. "The Democrats fought like heck and would have gone to court as opposed to agreeing to that district. Instead, they came up with this bizarre I-85 district idea" borrowed from Republican representative David Balmer. "I think David Balmer was up too late one night, and on about the fifteenth [plan] he did, he came up with this I-85 thing." That plan allowed the Democrats to gain a district without jeopardizing incumbent Democrats in other districts, but it did not satisfy precedents preferring geographically compact districts.

Everett was elated at the GOP's decision to intervene in the case on the plaintiffs' side. "I guess obviously they thought they were going to help their political organization," he later remarked, "although I think their counsel Michael Hess . . . thought as we did. . . . The Republicans were able to bring in top-flight experts. . . . So, as a result, we were able to generate good witnesses; we had the money to bring the evidence out."

Everett also attempted to include as an intervenor the Americans for the Defense of Constitutional Rights (ADCR), a nonprofit corporation he and the other plaintiffs had created to raise funds and provide other support for the litigation. The organization was housed in Everett's law office, its presence indicated by a simple paper sign taped to the office door. Because the ADCR's founding members and the sole members of its board of directors were the five *Shaw* plaintiffs, the state argued that the plaintiffs would adequately represent the ADCR's interests, and the district court denied the organization's motion to intervene in the suit. Although granting intervenor status to several of the *Pope* plaintiffs and other Republicans, the three-judge panel also rejected the motions of the state GOP and its chairman, Jack Hawke, to participate in the case as plaintiff-intervenors.

———

Ralph Gingles, chief plaintiff in the *Gingles* case, and more than twenty other African American and white voters were permitted to participate in the suit as defendant-intervenors. Anita Hodgkiss of Ferguson, Stein, the state's principal civil rights law firm, would be their chief counsel at the trial, and Adam Stein, one of the firm's senior partners, would also play an active role in the case. Stein, like Tom Farr, was not a native southerner, but that was the extent of any similarity in their backgrounds. A Brooklyn native, Stein had spent most of his childhood in Washington, where his father was "sort of a professional deputy director" with a number of New Deal agencies. "[My father] didn't want to be in Washington under the Republicans after Eisenhower won [in 1952]. So we moved to Princeton," where the elder Stein held a number of posts with the university and Adam's mother played an active role in Democratic precinct politics. "She would get 95 percent turnout of the Democrats in our precinct," Stein remembered. "And [veteran] Congressman Frank Thompson knew that. He said she was the best 'ward heeler' in that part of New Jersey."

After several false starts at college, marriage to his high school sweetheart, and a tour with the army in Germany, Stein took an undergraduate degree at New York University, then attended law school at George Washington, completing a degree in 1967. During his youth in Washington, family friends included prominent liberals of the day, such as Joseph Rauh, the controversial founder of the Americans for Democratic Action and lead counsel in many civil liberties lawsuits. "Rauh was a role model. I thought it would be wonderful to do the things he was doing. I admired him and the work he did, his courage, perseverance, and skill."

Stein followed Rauh's example. In the summer after his first year in law school, he became active in the work of the Law Students Civil Rights Research Council — a group providing help to lawyers handling civil rights and related cases, especially in the South. Stein was assigned to Charlotte and the firm of Julius Chambers, the African American founder and senior partner for many years of Ferguson, Stein. "Chambers and I got on well, and I loved the work he was doing. [After law school,] we moved to Charlotte."

Both as an intern and as a member of Chambers's firm, Stein would be involved in many civil rights suits, including a public accommodations challenge to a New Bern barbecue restaurant that limited service to blacks to a take-out window at the rear of the building, a suit desegregating Raleigh's YMCA, and the protracted Charlotte desegregation case, as well as suits in forty other school districts and a variety of employment discrimination cases. His clients also included black youths accused of firebombing white-owned buildings, Vietnam draft dodgers, a topless dancer, and the operators of Adam and Eve, an Orange County mail-order sex-products distributor. For the last client he won a not-guilty jury verdict in a federal obscenity trial after "the Christian somebodies or another raised a big ruckus" about the business's operations and its plans to expand into another county. When a district attorney banned a rock group's sexually explicit album, Stein was among the critics who persuaded the official to reverse his position.

He also played a major role in efforts to improve appellate representation for death-row inmates and other indigent defendants. In 1980, Stein took a leave from his firm to establish and head North Carolina's first Appellate Defender's Office, which now handles roughly a third of all indigent appeals and has greatly improved the quality of appellate advocacy for poor defendants in the state.

After five years with the Appellate Defender's Office, Stein returned to his firm. Julius Chambers, who would become head of the NAACP Legal Defense Fund's national office and then chancellor of North Carolina Central University, eventually severed his ties with the practice, leaving Stein and James Ferguson, an African American who had joined the firm the same year Stein had, as the firm's senior partners.

When Stein crossed the professional color line, joining one of North Carolina's first racially integrated law firms, he provoked whispers and slurs. Some referred to him as "that 'nigger lawyer.'" "It was a pretty segregated world then," he later told a reporter. "As I would move about the state with Chambers or Jim Ferguson or Charles Becton [another African American in the firm], you could feel the electricity — in courthouses, in restaurants, and motels." The racial context of many of their cases only aggravated the situation. During the Anson County desegregation suit, Stein later recalled, "every school board member's house was bombed. Things were rough there. A lawyer from the Legal Defense Fund [in New York] was working for us, and we were in Anson for depositions. . . . There was a strip motel [there]. We stayed there one night, and cars just kept driving through the parking lot [throughout the night] and shining their headlights in the windows. And the lawyer from New York felt it would be better to commute from Charlotte [in the future]. Our lead plaintiff . . . had her house shot into a few times. She was on the highway, too. So it was a fear with some basis."

But the most common reaction to the racially mixed group, Stein later noted, was "awkward politeness. The people we came in contact with were uncomfortable with an integrated party. They could have more [easily] accepted an all-black group." Over time, however, tensions eased. Stein's work in civil liberties cases and with the Appellate

Defender's Office also earned him the admiration of civil libertarians. In 1990, for example, the North Carolina Civil Liberties Union conferred on Stein its Frank Porter Graham Award in recognition of his efforts to promote racial equality and civil liberties.

Stein's firm was an obvious choice to represent the defendant-intervenors in the *Shaw* case. He had done some legal work for Howard Lee when the African American former mayor of Chapel Hill had campaigned unsuccessfully for a congressional seat. He had also represented the plaintiffs in a case that resulted in a North Carolina supreme court decision establishing the right of college students to vote in their college community. That had been the extent of Stein's voting rights work until *Shaw*. But Leslie Winner, another partner in the firm, had been chief counsel for the *Gingles* plaintiffs; Lani Gunier, who once clerked for the firm, had been involved in *Gingles* as a member of the NAACP's legal staff; North Carolina house speaker Dan Blue had clerked for Julius Chambers while in law school; and Twelfth District congressman Mel Watt was a partner in the firm. In the redistricting that followed the 1990 census, Winner had been Blue's special counsel, playing a major role in the districting process. After the Supreme Court's decision in *Shaw I*, Stein later said, "we decided together with various civil rights people that we were talking to that it was important that there be a voice [in the suit] for those benefited by it. . . . So we talked to people we thought would be interested and rounded up some [clients]."

In the North Carolina attorney general's office, Eddie Speas and Tiare Smiley were pleased that Stein's firm was entering the case. The intervenors' lawyers would, of course, bring considerable expertise and resources to the state's defense, but the state's counsel welcomed them for another reason as well. Legally, a defense of North Carolina's majority-minority districts, Smiley later explained, would require presentation of "a full record of North Carolina's [very painful] racial history." Politically, however, the state's attorney general and his staff hardly relished such an assignment. "Obviously, in an equal protection case, the state has to 'slash its wrists,' . . . to show how bad we are. . . . The defendant-intervenors took care of that for us. . . . The really nasty stuff we could let them say. . . . We're not wanting to castigate the state for its past history and as the attorney general's office go around accusing the state, the legislators, and all the various government agencies. . . . So in a lot of ways, it was very useful that the defendant-intervenors could do that. And of course they had a richer detail in terms of witnesses."

The three-judge panel scheduled the trial to begin March 28, 1994. As that date approached, Everett urged members of the court to issue an injunction halting the upcoming party primaries pending the outcome of the trial. Citing the "needless confusion and expense" an injunction would create for congressional candidates, the panel denied the motion, with Judge Voorhees again dissenting, albeit on this occasion without opinion. Everett assured reporters that the court's decision would have no effect on the forthcoming trial, adding, "We're very optimistic that the activities in the primary will become irrelevant because there will be different districts" after the trial. But in a brief supporting its petition to appear as a friend of the court in the case, the Justice Department claimed substantial evidence in support of the defendants' contention that North Carolina's majority-minority districts served state interests that were sufficiently compelling to withstand the plaintiffs' challenge.

On the eve of the trial, newspapers carried the comments of principals in the suit. "A quota system works against everybody, white or black," Everett told one reporter. "It works against the whites in the 12th and 1st districts and the blacks in the other 10 districts. It creates districts where voters are polarized on the basis of race." But Speas contended for the state, as he would at trial, that "beauty is only skin deep. Rather than the visual appearance, the focus ought to be on who we have in the district and what interests they might have." Arguing that the state had merely followed the directives of the Justice Department, the state's attorney also insisted that "federal law requires that race be taken into account" in the redistricting process of a state with a history of racial discrimination at the polls. "Our position," he added, "is that taking federal law into account is not a violation of federal law." Twelfth District congressman Mel Watt was equally adamant. "My position is that minorities have not been able to be elected — because of the racially polarized history of elections — in ninety years. Anybody who would suggest that that kind of tradition is more important than democratic representation doesn't understand the principles on which democracy is based."

The trial began with opening statements by counsel in which they summarized and drew inferences from the evidence they would present in support of their clients. Everett pointed out, for example, that compactness was not included among the criteria adopted by the legislature in designing North Carolina's congressional districts, even though earlier decisions upholding majority-minority districts arguably had required that they be geographically compact. The plaintiffs would also establish, he said, that the socioeconomic data the state planned to use in arguing that one of the challenged districts (the First) reflected rural communities of interest, and the other (the Twelfth) urban interests, had not even been available when the districts were drawn. "In short," Everett declared, "we will seek . . . to show exactly how the racial gerrymandering took place; to show the over-riding purpose was to draw [a] racial classification and racial lines, and thereby [produce] the very type of injury that Justice O'Connor had in mind in her opinion" in *Shaw v. Reno.*

Drawing on the statements of legislators and other state officials, Tom Farr devoted his opening statement primarily to whether the state could establish a compelling interest to justify the racial gerrymandering the challenged districts allegedly embodied. Toby Fitch, observed Farr, had asserted during the General Assembly's deliberations that the districts went far beyond the Voting Rights Act's requirements. Speaker Dan Blue had stated that the act did not require stringing black voters together "to create districts to help political parties." And Dennis Winner, chairman of the senate redistricting committee, had argued that the Voting Rights Act obliged the state to create a majority-minority First District in the northeastern part of North Carolina, where the African American voting population was relatively concentrated, but he found it "totally unreasonable and not within the Voting Rights Act to combine a little piece of a black community in Gastonia with a little piece of a black community in Charlotte and run it up I-85 like a string of pearls." "That's," added Farr, "not our argument. That's statements by Dennis Winner, chairman of the redistricting committee, made at the time this plan was adopted."

Like Everett, Farr also underscored the absence in the legislative record relating to the creation of the challenged districts of "anything close to the type of analysis that is called for by the *Gingles* case. In particular, . . . there wasn't anyone associated with this at any time who

would dare to make the suggestion any of these districts we're challenging today were geographically compact or . . . geographically compact in the black population centers that came out of these districts."

Along the same lines, Farr was equally disdainful of the defendants'
"functional compactness" defense, under which they had claimed in
pretrial papers filed with the court that the challenged districts were
compact in terms of the similar interests of their voting populations,
whatever their geographic shape. Farr conceded that their theory was
"very creative and novel" but declared, "if the court takes [the *Gingles*
Court] for its word and decides that geographical compactness is
what's really required, I think you have to rule for the plaintiffs."

To prevail, the state was obliged to prove that the challenged districts did not constitute racial gerrymandering or, if they did, that they
were narrowly tailored to promote a legitimate and compelling state
interest. In his opening statement for the defendants, Eddie Speas
focused on the racial gerrymander issue. On that question, as he interpreted *Shaw v. Reno*, the plaintiffs were obliged to prove that there was
no other reason than race for the districts' odd shape. In challenging
the plaintiffs' contention, Speas asserted, the state would first review
the legislative history surrounding the districts' creation. That history,
he assured the panel, would demonstrate that the General Assembly
had been motivated by a variety of considerations in its districting decisions. "You will find that the legislature was concerned with communities of interest, the legislature was concerned about politics, the
legislature was concerned about [protecting] incumbents and you will
find significantly that the legislature was concerned about creating an
urban 12th District and rural 1st District." As evidence of those concerns, the defendants would place into evidence the legislative record
as well as the testimony of legislative mapmaker Gerry Cohen and
Representative Toby Fitch. Next, observed Speas, he would present
data and expert testimony reflecting the degree to which each of the
challenged districts embodied distinct communities of interest — one
urban, the other rural. Finally, an expert would show that though not
geographically compact, the challenged districts were functionally
compact in terms of the communities of interest they represented.

Emphasizing that the redistricting had resulted in increased voter
turnout in the 1992 elections, despite the plaintiffs' claim that the contested districts were confusing to voters, Speas urged the panel not to

attach undue weight to the districts' bizarre shape. "Turn-out is what this case is about . . . not . . . appearances. Beauty is only skin deep. This case is about whether or not this plan achieves the end of providing fair and effective representation for North Carolina citizens; geographic compactness was not in this. In its place communities of interest was emphasized and that emphasis on communities of interest created a plan that provides all . . . citizens, black and white alike, a fair plan for fair and effective representation of their interests."

Adam Stein and Anita Hodgkiss left opening statements for the defendant-intervenors to Dayna Cunningham, an NAACP attorney from New York. The compelling justification for the challenged districts, Cunningham declared, was the state's interest in "including African-Americans in the congressional process in a meaningful way for the first time in this century." Consideration of race in the creation of North Carolina's congressional districts had hardly begun with the latest round of redistricting, Cunningham reminded the court. "If you go back to the turn of the century with the dismemberment of the historic [majority black] 2d Congressional District," she asserted, "you will see racial considerations have long played a role in congressional districting in North Carolina. Throughout this century, and particularly in the last three decades, racial considerations have been an implicit and, indeed, explicit part of the redistricting process. In particular, one question [was] asked over and over again in the redistricting process. And that is, how to manage or how to handle the black influence, the strong black influence in the eastern part of the state, particularly around Durham. . . . The result [of such maneuvering] has been that since the turn of the century, since 1901, North Carolina's congressional delegation has been completely racially segregated."

The challenged districts were necessary, Cunningham added, to end that pattern and bring North Carolina into full compliance with the Voting Rights Act. Evidence presented to establish that need would include data confirming the continued problem of racially polarized voting in the state. In the 1992 Democratic primary in the First District, for example, black candidates had received 89 percent of the African American vote but only 5 percent of the white vote.

Turning to another factor justifying the creation of majority-minority districts, Cunningham drew on the 1990 Helms-Gantt Senate race in summarizing evidence to be used to demonstrate continued reliance on racial appeals as a "constant and prevalent feature" of North Carolina's congressional elections. The "most infamous" incident from that race, she declared, was the Helms campaign's "White Hands Advertisement," in which "a pair of white hands [was] seen [in the TV spot] crumpling a rejection notice [while] the voice-over explains this is due to minority quotas." During the same contest, she reminded the panel, the Republicans had also mailed "intimidating and misleading" postcards about voter eligibility to 40,000 recently moved African American voters, but not to 220,000 white voters who also had recently changed their residence.

Continuing her depiction of North Carolina's unfortunate racial record, the defendant-intervenors' counsel next cited common barriers to minority voting, including threats to livelihood, fear of violence, harassment of poll watchers seeking to assist black voters, and lack of access to financial and political resources. Given such a climate, she declared, the challenged districts' configurations should have no bearing on the court's decision. "Here, despite the shape of the districts, the evidence will show all the traditional redistricting factors, communities of interest, . . . supporting communication between legislators and voters, and fairness, inclusiveness in the process are advanced by these districts; not harmed by these districts. And finally, the evidence will show that far from a racial gerrymander, [the contested plan] is a deliberate attempt at racial integration . . . and bi-racial cooperation and attempts, for the first time in this century, to include African-Americans in a meaningful way in the congressional process."

Following the opening statements, Judge Phillips invited Robinson Everett to proceed with presentation of the plaintiffs' case, but counsel for the Republican plaintiff-intervenors called the first witness. Thomas Hofeller was a redistricting specialist with a Falls Church, Virginia, polling and consulting firm. During the 1990 redistricting cycle, he had participated in the development of redistricting plans in between twenty and twenty-five states. Under questioning by RNC chief counsel Michael Hess, and assisted by a number of maps and related exhibits, Hofeller led the court through a county-by-county examination of the Twelfth District and the considerations that had guided state legislative committees in the redistricting process.

Asked by Hess to define contiguity, one of those considerations, Hofeller responded, "In the general sense, I would say [a] district is [contiguous if it] is all in one piece functionally. . . . One could put a pencil down at any point in the district and trace around the . . . outer boundary of the district, including portions of water that are in the district, and come around the entire perimeter of the district all the way back to the point of beginning without having to lift the pencil off the page, and without touching or crossing any line or portion of the line previously drawn." North Carolina conformed to that traditional districting criterion, he asserted, only by resorting to two relatively novel conceptions — "point contiguity" and "double crossover contiguity." Point contiguity was a redistricting concept under which a district remained contiguous with itself only at a single point in space (a crossover point), and double crossover contiguity referred to a situation in which two districts bisected each other at a single point, yet each remained contiguous with itself at that point. When Hess asked about these notions of contiguity, Hofeller replied, "I wouldn't define them as contiguity." He added that he had never seen a double crossover in his nearly thirty years of involvement with congressional districting. "So," asked Hess, "those cross-overs and point contiguity would not satisfy your definitions of contiguity?"

"They certainly wouldn't . . . , no," Hofeller answered.

Hess next questioned his witness about the sort of majority-minority districts that might legitimately have been enacted. When Hofeller responded that such districts should be placed in areas in which minority voting populations were geographically concentrated, as required by the *Gingles* decision, the RNC counsel asked the witness where he would have placed North Carolina's districts. Not surprisingly, Hofeller recommended, as had the Bush Justice Department, one district in the northeastern part of the state and another combining African American and Native American voters in the south-central and southeastern sections. And how, Hess asked, would the challenged plan compare with others in the nation in terms of geographic compactness? "This," the witness responded, "will probably be the textbook example for the decade for non-compactness." Hofeller readily acknowledged that the relationship of Interstate 85 to the Twelfth District was "not quite as has been advertised before in the press. . . . I know there's an anecdote [that] says if you open your car doors and drive down the length of I-85, you will kill half the people in the district. Obviously, you won't kill any people in the district." He added, however, that a person driving on the interstate from the west end of the district to its east end would cross in and out of the district twenty-one times.

At the conclusion of his questions, Hess asked Hofeller to summarize the significance of the maps and other data covered in his testimony. "Number One," the witness replied, "the minority districts that are created in the current plan are not geographically compact or are not comprised of geographically compact minority concentrations. Two, that the minority districts in the current plan presented by themselves would not support a Section 2 geographic compact[ness] finding [under the Voting Rights Act]. At least I would not recommend that they would to somebody if I were advising them. Three, that . . . there exists a more tailored or more compact [approach to] the minority districts in North Carolina which is more in line with traditional redistricting criteria. . . . Four . . . , that . . . the [legislative redistricting] committee adopting criteria for the creation of districts, really had no independent policy of its own. . . . Lastly, that the shapes and configurations of the North Carolina districts will probably be the textbook example of redistricting in terms of bizarre districts and . . . disputes over the shape and nature of the districts."

In his few questions to the witness, Everett quickly got to what for him was the crux of the case. "Would you state," Everett asked, "what conclusion you formed as to the separation in terms of race in the plans that are currently effective in North Carolina?"

"The overriding criteri[on] which was used in the creation of the minority districts," Hofeller replied, "was the black population percentage and . . . race, and that was the purpose for which the districts were drawn. . . . It's very difficult for me to see, from the shape of the districts and looking at the [census] block by block configurations, that there would be any other reason." Adam Stein moved to strike that testimony as unresponsive, but Judge Phillips overruled the objection.

Now it was Eddie Speas's turn. The state's deputy attorney general quickly raised Hofeller's extensive ties with the Republican Party and partisan interest in the design of North Carolina's congressional districts. As a paid party consultant, the witness had drafted majority-minority districting plans for the GOP. "You testified at your deposition they were your bosses in drawing the earlier plans, didn't you?" Speas asked. When Hofeller acknowledged his previous testimony, Speas inquired whether he had made adjustments in the plans to suit Republican political interests. "I made some adjustments because they wanted them made," the witness replied; "I made other adjustments for other reasons." Speas then got Hofeller to concede that one of the GOP plans had grouped three incumbent Democratic congressmen into the same district and that the principal Republican proposal included a "non-contiguity," as well as deviations from the sort of geographic compactness Hofeller had extolled during Hess's direct examination.

After obtaining a further concession from Hofeller that congressional districts nationally had become progressively less geographically compact over the past two decades, Speas turned to the witness's earlier pronouncements on the issue. Since obtaining a Ph.D. in 1980, Hofeller had published one article with three co-authors in a political science journal. Among other things, that 1990 publication had quoted approvingly a study by an academic who described geographically compact congressional districts as "out-dated, irrelevant or even a positive nuisance." Hofeller replied that the author was a Democratic consultant who had participated in the creation of a notorious example of congressional gerrymandering in California during the 1980s. "I don't subscribe necessarily to his viewpoint, no," he added.

"I don't believe you are employed by a university, are you?" Speas countered, then noted the quoted scholar's excellent academic credentials.

To greater effect, Speas next quoted a passage from the article Hofeller had co-authored. "In the modern age," the witness and his colleagues had written, "geographic compactness is not as important as it once was." The compactness argument, they suggested, "was perhaps especially significant in the past, but loses some of its strength in an age of telephone, computers, superhighways and airplanes."

"If we had anticipated the kind of compactness abuses that have been perpetrated in the 1990 cycle," Hofeller rejoined, "we perhaps would have phrased this somewhat differently." At that point, Judge Phillips called a brief recess in the proceedings.

When Hofeller's testimony resumed, Speas probed the witness about the value of geographically compact districts relative to particular legislative bodies, suggesting that compactness was less important for full-time representatives with large staffs, such as members of Congress.

Referring to Twelfth District maps, he also underscored the ease with which a member of Congress could cross the district on Interstate 85 and other area highways.

Then Speas returned to Hofeller's journal article, specifically the following passage: "Whether districts should be homogenous or combine different types of areas, whether urban and rural, rich and poor, etc., is another matter entirely and should not be determined merely as a side effect of a compactness measure." "Based on that statement," observed Speas, "I take it you would agree that it is legitimate for a state to determine that it wants to create a district where most of the citizens are urban or reside in urban areas" (such as the Twelfth District, it was unncecessary for him to add). Hofeller declined a blanket response, testifying instead that the legitimacy of a particular district would depend on a variety of considerations. When Speas attempted, again referring to maps, to establish that the Twelfth District was truly an urban district, the witness only partially agreed, noting that "there's an awful lot of empty space even between those citizens of relatively dense areas."

Adam Stein began his cross-examination of Hofeller for the defendant-intervenors by tying the witness to *Pope v. Blue*, the suit in which Republican plaintiffs had complained that the challenged districts amounted to unconstitutional partisan gerrymandering rather than the race-based districting the *Shaw* plaintiffs were claiming. The "principal thrust" of an affidavit Hofeller had filed in *Pope*, Stein declared, "was to say that what North Carolina did in its 1990's redistricting was to do a political gerrymander; isn't that so?" When the witness claimed that he could not recall the specifics of his affidavit, Stein persisted. "Do you recall stating in the affidavit, complaining in the affidavit about the placement of the 12th District going along the Piedmont [crescent] instead of going from Charlotte towards Wilmington [on the southeastern coast] as being political to protect [Democratic] representative Charlie Rose and others?"

"I don't know specifically what I said in that [affidavit]," Hofeller replied. "But at that time I think my impression was the effect of the district being where it's placed now [was that it] had more of an effect on the Republican districts than it did on the Democrat districts. . . . I knew a lot less [then] about what had gone on through the [redistricting] process."

Stein was hardly satisfied. "Do you recall that in your affidavit you charged that this Democratic dominated legislature made decisions to enhance the prospects of [Democratic] representative [Steve] Neal and to protect Representative Neal?" he asked Hofeller at one point. Later, Stein referred to another passage from Hofeller's *Pope* affidavit in which the witness claimed that part of the districting plan was designed to enhance the electoral strength of three Republican congressmen. Stein's point was clear: in the *Pope* suit, Hofeller had claimed that "this was all a political gerrymander," not the race-based district he was portraying in his *Shaw* testimony. But Hofeller continued to profess little recollection of his affidavit and emphasized, when given the opportunity, what he now considered the racial motivation underlying the contested redistricting. He scorned, moreover, the defendants' contention that districts could be "functionally" rather than geographically compact, declaring at one point during Stein's cross-examination that "some of the definitions that I have heard of compactness fashioned by the defense in this case have been the most bizarre interpretations I have heard." Stein also raised further questions about Hofeller's objectivity, observing, for example, that the witness had testified as an expert witness for both plaintiffs and defendants in redistricting suits.

———

The next morning, the judges and counsel visited the General Assembly for a demonstration of the way in which congressional districts were constructed. When the trial resumed, attorneys for both sides subjected Hofeller to additional questioning. Attempting to point up inconsistencies between Hofeller's statements in *Shaw* and his statements in other suits, Stein drew on Hofeller's testimony in a Florida case "to the effect that compactness should give way to equal opportunities for minorities to elect representatives of their choice." Stein also questioned Hofeller about the boundaries of a majority-minority district the witness had endorsed in the Florida case — a district longer than North Carolina's Twelfth District. "Didn't you also tell the court in Florida . . . [that] Section 2 [of the Voting Rights Act] required that there be three majority black districts drawn" there?

"I don't remember what my exact testimony was," Hofeller answered. "If you have it and you would like to read it, I would be glad to verify it."

The plaintiffs' next expert witness was Timothy O'Rourke, a Clemson political science professor. Under questioning by Tom Farr, O'Rourke, like Hofeller, concluded that North Carolina's majority-minority districts were racially motivated and defended his preference for geographically compact districts to ensure voter access to representatives and allow representatives the opportunity for regular contact with their constituents. Referring to the work of Bernard Grofman, a leading political scientist in the redistricting field, O'Rourke spoke of the principle of "cognizability," which Grofman had defined as "the ability to characterize . . . district boundaries in a manner that can be readily communicated to ordinary citizens of the district in common sense terms based on geographic reference[s]." Representation based on geography, the witness declared, was "central to American politics" and to legislators' ability to be truly representative of voter interests. Districts thus should be contiguous and geographically compact. Identifying compact districts as "nicely shaped" and drawing on the recent research of other scholars, O'Rourke further observed that four of the twenty-eight least compact congressional districts in the nation were in North Carolina — the Fifth and Seventh Districts, as well as the two at issue in *Shaw*. According to that study, he added, the Twelfth District was "the worst in the nation."

O'Rourke also commented on the relationship between a district's cognizability and the degree to which districting plans split counties and voting precincts. "Most citizens," he testified, "have some general familiarity with the boundaries of political units, city boundaries, county boundaries. So the extent to which a district follows long-identified political subdivision boundaries will make it a district that a citizen is, in effect, better able to recognize." The congressional districting plan in effect in the 1980s, he understood, had split only four counties, and that had been necessary to satisfy the Supreme Court's one-person, one-vote formula. In contrast, "the current plan, by my count, splits 44 counties; 37 counties are split in two, and seven counties that are split three ways."

Districts could be organized around various functional communities of interest, O'Rourke conceded, but he favored the traditional geographical approach to districting. "To the extent [the functional approach] leads to the creation of districts that sort of cross over geographic regions or [carry] districts from one area of the state to another in ways that breach this [geographic] notion of political community, it will undermine cognizability. And if it undermines cognizability, I think ultimately it will undermine representation. I might add that this is, in my view, . . . not idle speculation. . . . There are some studies by political scientists that would indicate that where congressional districts are congruent with what I call a political community, that citizens are better able to identify either congressmen or . . . candidates in a congressional contest."

To bolster his assertions, O'Rourke cited a 1986 study indicating that voters in a city wholly contained within a single district were better able to identify their congressperson than were voters in a city divided among several districts. One reason for this, the witness added, was that a city contained within a single district would constitute a single media market in which the media would focus on the member of Congress representing that market rather than on a number of representatives. It was thus hardly surprising, he suggested, that only 6 percent of respondents in a survey of the Twelfth District, which covered several media markets and regions of the state, could identify Mel Watt as their congressman.

Everett would later say that he had been very impressed with O'Rourke as a witness, including his willingness to testify without compensation other than travel expenses. Speas, in contrast, "thought [O'Rourke] had just done a terrible job and that his testimony had been slanted and biased. I think I was able to establish that. And there is nothing that gives a lawyer — at least this lawyer — any greater pleasure than cross-examining an expert witness."

Speas began his interrogation of O'Rourke with pointed questions about his professional credentials and qualifications as an expert witness in racial redistricting litigation. The witness, who had received his Ph.D. in 1977, conceded that he had published only one article in a refereed journal, although a book he had authored on reapportionment had of course been refereed by its publisher. "That refereed article does not relate to the subject matter of your testimony here today, does it?" Speas asked.

"No, not directly," O'Rourke replied. O'Rourke also acknowledged that his teaching responsibilities at Clemson included state and local government and constitutional law, but that he had taught a voting rights course while on the faculty of the University of Virginia early in his career.

"Did you apply for tenure at the University of Virginia?" Speas asked.
"Yes," O'Rourke responded.

"Did you receive tenure?"

"No," the witness answered.

Speas next turned to O'Rourke's extensive testimony regarding cognizability. The state's attorney wanted to know if the witness had ever seen that term other than in the law review article on which he had based part of his direct testimony. O'Rourke acknowledged that he had not and that he knew of no empirical study of the principle other than another article cited in his testimony and works cited in that research. Under questioning by Speas, he also agreed that the latter article had not actually mentioned the term "cognizability."

Earlier that year, O'Rourke had delivered a paper at a meeting of the Western Political Science Association in which he had suggested that the shape of districts and the splitting of counties in district plans affected voter roll-off, that is, the degree to which voter participation drops from a presidential race to a congressional contest on the same ballot. In the paper, he had reported that ballot roll-off in Mecklenburg County, which was split between two congressional districts, was the sixth highest among North Carolina counties, and under questioning, he agreed that his paper had provided the basis for his testimony about the relationship between the configuration of districts and voter turnout. Had the witness intended to imply, asked Speas, that "the division of counties somehow causes low turn-out, causes roll off [?]"

"That was a notion that I had," O'Rourke answered, "but as I looked at that I was not persuaded that the division, per se, of counties, connected to roll off."

"Have you come to the conclusion that, in fact, there's absolutely no relationship between divided counties and roll off in North Carolina?" Speas asked. When the witness responded that he had reached no conclusion on the matter, Speas began to develop his own case for that proposition. Using one of O'Rourke's own exhibits, the state's counsel got the witness to acknowledge that Cumberland County (Fayetteville) was split among three districts, yet had the fourth *lowest* roll-off rate in the state. "In fact," pressed Speas, "more people voted in congressional elections in Cumberland County [did they not] than voted in the presidential election [a race in which cognizability presumably would not have been an issue]?" The witness agreed and further conceded that approximately 97 percent of presidential voters in Rowan County, which was also split among three congressional districts, voted in the congressional election as well.

After running through a long litany of split counties with highly variable degrees of voter roll-off, Speas again raised his basic question: "Wouldn't you have to conclude, Dr. O'Rourke, that there's absolutely no relationship between dividing counties and voters participating in congressional elections?" O'Rourke agreed but contended that the division of counties was less important than the division of geographic communities, which, according to earlier research, did relate to roll-off. But Speas then got the witness to concede that he had not taken into account other factors related to turnout, such as education, income, age, and the competitiveness of an election contest — factors O'Rourke had also termed significantly related to turnout in a deposition he had filed in the case.

During her brief cross-examination of O'Rourke for the defendant-intervenors, Anita Hodgkiss recalled the witness's earlier testimony that the creation of two majority black districts in North Carolina would weaken minority electoral influence in other districts. She focused particularly on O'Rourke's preference for a larger number of "opportunity" districts with substantial minority populations over one or two districts in which African Americans constituted a voting majority. Given the extensive racially polarized voting still evident in North Carolina, she wanted to know whether the witness had conducted empirical research into the percentage of minority voters needed to establish an opportunity district. After a lengthy exchange, O'Rourke responded, "My answer is I have not undertaken independent analysis of racial . . . polarization. My answer is, further, that no analysis could tell you exactly what percentage is necessary."

Hodgkiss also used the witness to underscore the defendants' contention that there was no statutory requirement for compact districts. In that line of questioning, however, she may have gone too far. "Given the history of the U.S. Congress not requiring compactness of congressional districts, and I'm recognizing that there may be policy arguments one way or the other as to why compactness should be required in congressional districts, . . . is there any reason why the North Carolina legislature can't decide not to have compactness as a criteri[on] in congressional redistricting?"

"The answer," O'Rourke rejoined, "is *Shaw v. Reno* . . . to the extent that lack of compactness becomes a vehicle for effecting an unconstitutional racial classification, yes. The legislature must give some attention to compactness. That's how I understand the Supreme Court's ruling."

O'Rourke was the last of the plaintiffs' witnesses. Both sets of parties, however, had previously introduced documentary exhibits, such as the maps referred to earlier. Counsel had also deposed a number of principals in the case. One of those questioned in a deposition session was Melvin Shimm, Everett's Duke colleague and *Shaw* co-plaintiff. In response to questions by Speas and Hodgkiss, Shimm emphasized that his concept of a compact district was "a geometric one" and termed other notions of compactness "senseless" in the redistricting context. He conceded, however, that he had no difficulty contacting his congressman or knowing in what district he resided. He also acknowledged that he had little basis, other than the Twelfth District's shape, for his assertion that the challenged districts were designed to ensure the election of African American candidates. When Hodgkiss suggested that the districts were designed to allow blacks to elect candidates of their choice rather than black candidates per se, Shimm disagreed. Black voters, he asserted, were overwhelmingly likely to favor black candidates. When he ran for an at-large seat on the Durham city council, he recalled, he had received a "fairly firm" assurance that he would get the endorsement of the city's Committee on Negro Affairs. But when a black minister filed for the seat, the committee's chair told Shimm, "You know we are going to have to bullet vote for him."

Although not so intended, the Duke professor's concerns tended to support the state's contention that the continued presence of racially polarized voting in a predominantly white state helped justify North Carolina's majority black districts. Everett's questioning of his colleague, however, gave Shimm the opportunity to stress his empathy, as a Jew, for African Americans and the mistreatment to which they had been subjected historically. Not one of his father's family, he testified, survived the Holocaust; only one of his wife's father's siblings had escaped death at the hands of the Nazi regime. "She now walks around with a tattoo on her arm and she tells me how she was used as a draft animal in building factories." Shimm himself had suffered discrimination at various points in his life. When he was four, neighborhood bullies, calling Jews "Christ killers," had dragged him from his "little trike" and given him a real "going over." He had also been beaten up in school and in the army. He got "rejection after rejection" from New York law firms despite his excellent academic record, and his Yale law school placement officer had remarked of one firm he had applied to, "they never hire any Jews." About 40 percent of Shimm's law class had been Jewish; only two, including Shimm, got offers from Wall Street firms. "I know what it feels like," he said, "to be rejected for reasons that one considers to be completely irrelevant to one's competence, one's abilities. And for this reason, I think in a personal way I feel for blacks in a way that someone who hasn't gone through a similar sort of experience can not feel. I think that is enough, enough of spilling my guts."

Despite such empathy, Everett interjected, he assumed that the witness was still convinced that the challenged plan was unconstitutional. "Not only do I think it is unconstitutional," Shimm vigorously responded, "not only do I think it is a denial of equal protection, but the thing that really . . . exacerbates the problem is I think it is an ineffectual kind of program. That is to say, I think in many ways it is counterproductive. . . . To the extent that you segregate blacks in a particular district and diminish their representation in other districts, you diminish the incentive of congressmen who could otherwise have them in their district to respond to whatever particular needs they had. But even more objectionable, it seems to me, is this notion that blacks can only represent blacks because the corollary of that is if blacks can only represent blacks, then [whites] can only represent [whites]. And this supplies, I think, a very good basis for anybody who is so inclined to say, 'I am not going to vote for a black.' And in the long run, I think it is a far more pernicious consequence."

Under questioning from Everett, Shimm also itemized the electoral successes of blacks in predominantly white areas, including a majority of the Durham city council; speaker Dan Blue, the witness's former law student, in the General Assembly; an African American state auditor; and Harvey Gantt, who had beaten a popular white candidate for the Democratic senatorial nomination but lost to Senator Jesse Helms in the general election. But "I don't think," said Shimm, "any Democrat could have beaten Helms. . . . I think [he] is unbeatable as long as he wants to run." Shimm conceded that "there are whites who won't vote for blacks. There are whites who won't vote for Jews either. And there are blacks who won't vote for Jews. But this doesn't mean that this is a universal kind of phenomenon. I think the tendency is the other way. I think there is more and more acceptance or recognition that one's race, one's religion doesn't have any bearing on one's ability to do the job properly."

CHAPTER 5

The 1994 Trial — The Defense Responds

After asking for and being denied a directed verdict in their favor, counsel for the state called their first witness, Gerry Cohen, director of bill drafting for the General Assembly and the state's chief redistricting mapmaker. Cohen had worked in several campaigns of African American candidates, including Howard Lee's winning mayoral bid in Chapel Hill and his unsuccessful congressional campaign. A candidate for office himself on four occasions, Cohen had won election to the Chapel Hill town council while in law school there. He served on the council six years but lost mayoral races in 1975 and 1979. He had been with the legislature seventeen years, thirteen years as director of bill drafting.

Tiare Smiley, who had worked closely with Cohen during the Justice Department preclearance negotiations, led the questioning for the defendants. Guided by Smiley, Cohen discussed in exhaustive detail the process by which the contested congressional districts had been created, but with special emphasis on the degree to which political considerations had trumped race in the deliberations. Among many other examples, Cohen pointed out that the voting precinct of Henson Barnes, then president pro tem of the state senate, had been placed in the Third District rather than the majority-black First District, in the event that Barnes, who was white, decided to run for Congress. A tiny strip of one precinct was included in the Third District so that an aide to Martin Lancaster, the district's incumbent Democratic congressman, could reside in the district, and Sampson County was placed in Lancaster's Third District in an effort to enhance his reelection prospects. The Eighth District was redrawn to improve the reelection chances of Democratic incumbent Bill Hefner in part because, as chairman of the House Appropriations Committee's subcommittee on military construction, Hefner could protect North Carolina's sizable interest in military bases located in the state. Several other districts were also shaped with an eye toward protecting Democratic incumbents, including the Seventh District's Charlie Rose and Tim Valentine in the Second District.

During questioning, Smiley asked Cohen about point contiguity — the connecting of parts of a district by a single point — especially whether it had been "unknown" to the state legislature, as the plaintiffs suggested, before the adoption of the contested redistricting plan. When Cohen responded that point contiguity had been used in redistricting at least since 1966, Judge Phillips interjected a question about "this weighty matter of point contiguity." The judge asked whether it would be possible for legislators to simply make a corridor across such points at least a hundred yards wide. When the witness agreed that it was feasible, Phillips noted that the state in that way could "avoid whatever odium" the plaintiffs wanted to attach to point contiguity.

Smiley had Cohen summarize the criteria adopted by the General Assembly's redistricting committees for use in the congressional districting process — substantially equal populations, avoidance of minority vote dilution, single-member districts of contiguous territory, and refusal to split precincts and census blocks except where necessary to comply with other criteria. "Why was compactness not included?" asked Smiley.

"Because," the witness answered, "with . . . especially the first four criteria, to carry those out, . . . equal population, creating majority-minority districts, keeping single member districts, having them contiguous, it's very difficult to have districts that were geographically compact."

Smiley also asked Cohen about his contacts with John Merritt, the congressional staffer who had given him districting plans designed to protect the electoral interests of Representative Charlie Rose. During a meeting with legislative counsel Leslie Winner and Cohen at the General Assembly, Merritt had displayed a plan providing for the creation of two majority-black districts. "I looked at that plan," Cohen testified, "and immediately recognized that it had, to my recollection, three Republican members of Congress in the same district. And I said to him that . . . I wasn't instructed to screw Republicans, and I handed it back to him and said I wasn't interested in it."

A second plan that Merritt proposed to Cohen a day or two later closely resembled one that Republican legislator David Balmer had circulated and another suggested by Mary Peeler of the state NAACP. Each of those proposals included a district running along the piedmont crescent, similar to the one ultimately adopted as the Twelfth District. The Peeler plan, in particular, provided for a majority-black district that ran from Durham to Charlotte without disadvantaging Democrats. "Having a congressional district running from Charlotte to Durham," Cohen testified, "[took] black concentrations out of counties such as Mecklenburg, Rowan, Cabarrus, Davidson, Guilford, Alamance, which are themselves all in Republican congressional districts. . . . Taking black populations out of Republican congressional districts . . . does not disadvantage Democratic candidates as opposed to taking black population concentrations out of Democratic counties," as the Balmer plan did.

While the redistricting plans were taking shape, Cohen had also attended a public hearing on the issue in the state legislative auditorium. One speaker at that hearing, a Greensboro attorney, noted that the Peeler plan did not treat all urban communities alike. "He thought," Cohen testified, that "all the urban communities in the Piedmont Crescent area should be included" in a single district. "At that point," claimed Cohen, "we began to look at the urban and rural nature of the district[s]. . . . We looked back at the plans and looked at how much was urban and rural in the proposed 1st and 12th Districts."

The next morning, Wednesday, March 30, Cohen continued his testimony, including references to changes in the Peeler plan designed to ensure the creation of an urban Twelfth District and a rural First District. When Smiley asked whether he looked only at statistics relating to black populations in that effort, the witness responded, "No, I wasn't looking at them at all. I was looking at the report of the total population of the 12th and 1st Districts, not at the racial classification of any of the populations."

"All right. Did this urban/rural concept guide your efforts, your later efforts on the plan?"

"Yes," Cohen replied over Tom Farr's objection, which Judge Phillips overruled, "it was a central part of the plans for finishing the redistricting plan from that point forward." Under questioning from Smiley, Cohen also indicated that he had shared the concept with the legislative leadership. He then summarized the commonalities of interests separating the two contested districts. The rural counties of the First District, for example, had in common poverty, high unemployment, poor housing, and low levels of education.

As Smiley moved toward the conclusion of her questioning, she gave Cohen an opportunity to further discuss incumbency protection and other political considerations allegedly motivating the redistricting, with the witness providing detailed examples in each instance. "Was race a factor in drawing those districts?" she then asked. When Cohen replied affirmatively, she continued, "Was race the sole factor?"

"No, it was not. There were a number of other factors that I discussed [with legislative leaders], [cores] of existing districts, presuming the opportunities of incumbent congressmen to be reelected, accommodating concerns of individual legislators, members of Congress, committee chairs . . . and . . . keeping the 1st and 12th District, one very urban in nature and the other very rural in nature."

Adam Stein devoted his brief examination of Cohen to the lack of cohesion between Native Americans and African Americans in Robeson County as an obstacle to the creation of a minority district comprising those two population groups, as the Justice Department had suggested. The two groups, the witness said, had similar voting patterns in general elections but not in primaries. In the 1990 Democratic senatorial primary, Cohen testified, blacks voted overwhelmingly for Harvey Gantt, while Native Americans strongly favored a white candidate for the Democratic nomination.

Tom Farr began his cross-examination of Cohen somewhat surprisingly, given the racial gerrymander claim the plaintiffs were making and the district court's rejection of the partisan gerrymandering claim raised in the *Pope* case. Farr focused initially on what he termed "a little bit of political gerrymandering going on" when the challenged districts were being created. Cohen readily conceded again that a number of changes in the shape of the districts were made to protect incumbent Democrats. "I don't believe you testified," asked Farr, "as to any changes that you made from the Peeler plan to the enacted plan that [were] suggested by any Republican aides of Republican congressmen; is that correct?" When Cohen agreed, Farr exclaimed, "Where were you when I needed you in *Pope v. Blue?*"

Recalling Cohen's earlier testimony that it was not his job "to screw

Republicans," Farr asked him whether one of the state mapmaker's assignments was to protect incumbent Democrats, adding, "if the Republicans ended up getting screwed a little along the way, you wouldn't lose your job; is that correct?" Cohen replied that his objective was to preserve the existing partisan balance in North Carolina's congressional delegation, "not shift it dramatically one way or the other, as various different alternatives might have done."

Farr then began probing Cohen about recent partisan voting patterns in the state, suggesting that Republicans were perhaps entitled to more congressional seats than the General Assembly's latest districting might allow. At that point, however, Judge Phillips intervened, asking whether such questions went beyond the scope of the suit. "It is the plaintiff-intervenor's theory," Farr attempted to explain, "that all of the lines drawn on the congressional map that was ultimately enacted were driven by politics, and voting rights issues [played] a very secondary role. Therefore, we believe it's relevant testimony to . . ."

Judge Phillips interrupted. "I will remind you that a condition of intervention here by your clients was that they adopted the theory of the original plaintiffs in this case, which was not one of partisan gerrymandering. I'm going to let you continue with your line of questioning. But I'm going to tell you that, in assessing the evidence, I'm going to consider that anything that gets outside the scope of the issues as defined when you came in it, are irrelevant."

Despite Phillips's admonition, Farr persisted with questions designed to underscore the partisan nature of the redistricting process. In response to the attorney's questions, Cohen agreed that he was a registered Democrat; that he served at the pleasure of the Democratic leadership in the General Assembly; that all the candidates for whom he had campaigned in the past were Democrats; that Leslie Winner, special counsel to the house redistricting committee and a member of Stein's law firm, was the sister of Dennis Winner, a Democrat and chair of the senate redistricting committee; and that Leslie Winner had later been elected to the state senate from a district she had been involved in creating.

Later, Farr pointed out apparent inconsistencies between Cohen's testimony and assertions he and other state officials had made during preclearance negotiations with the Justice Department. Did the witness not agree, he asked, that under the *Gingles* decision, the Voting

Rights Act did not require majority-minority districts unless the African American population was sufficiently concentrated to allow the creation of geographically compact districts? Cohen responded that his definition of geography included not simply maps but "the entire totality of the political process." The challenged districts were compact, he added, "because they put together persons with commonalities of interest with common history, common factors, tying different parts of the districts together."

Farr then cited statements Cohen had prepared for submission to the Justice Department during the preclearance process. In them, Cohen defended North Carolina's initial creation of one rather than two majority-black districts and attacked one of Balmer's proposals for two majority-minority districts. The Twelfth District in Balmer's plan, Cohen had observed, "defies imagination, stretching for 125 miles . . . [and] never being more than five miles wide." He thought it "preposterous to say that this district is compact." Since the district ultimately adopted ran 150 to 160 miles, Farr asked whether Cohen thought it would be equally "preposterous" to consider it compact. Naturally, the witness disagreed, contending that the Twelfth District, unlike the one in Balmer's plan, was compact in the sense that it reflected commonalities of interests among its constituents. "None of those alternative plans had districts," Cohen testified, "that were compact in the nature of having an urban and rural district with carefully defined urban and rural natures and communities of interest."

Farr persisted, citing a preclearance submission in which Cohen declared that a district "would not be sufficiently compact if it was so spread out there was no sense of community. That is, if its members and representatives could not effectively and efficiently stay in touch with each other or was so convoluted that there was no sense of community, . . . if its members could not easily tell who actually lived within the district." But Cohen insisted that in the context in which he had used the term, "including commonalities of interest and communities of interest," the two contested districts and North Carolina's Fourth District were "the most compact in the state."

In an effort to impeach Cohen's credibility, Farr also branded a mere "pretext" the state's claim that the challenged districts were configured so that the First District would encompass a rural, and the Twelfth an urban, population. "It was an after the fact," he charged, "just fiction brought up by the state to attempt to justify these districts." Citing data that cast doubt on the state's characterization of the districts as urban and rural, Farr added that "there was no hard data upon which any such conclusion could be based."

At that point, Judge Phillips interrupted. "Seems to me," he admonished Farr, "that the data you are now producing [are] not data that would have impeached [state officials'] belief at the time. That data only became available to you and them later. I don't see how that draws [into] question what may have been a wrong perception on their part at the time."

"We don't think they made a wrong perception," Farr countered; "we think they understood this [rural-urban] dichotomy was not exactly as they are explaining it to the court, and that's the purpose for this information."

But Judge Phillips was not persuaded. "Evidence of this kind, which by your own statement only becomes available later, might tend to prove that they were wrong in their perception because they didn't have the right data. But I don't see how it could impeach anything [Cohen] said about his understanding of the legislative leadership at the time." Farr withdrew the question that had provoked the exchange.

For the rest of that afternoon and part of the next morning, Robinson Everett cross-examined Cohen. In seeking to undermine the state's contention that the challenged districts were designed to reflect rural and urban interests rather than simply to ensure the election of African Americans to Congress, Everett got the witness to concede that there was nothing in the legislative history of their adoption "which purports to adopt or to define communities of interest as a criterion [for] the establishment of congressional districts in North Carolina." Cohen also acknowledged that the one majority-minority district the state had originally created was more compact than the First and Twelfth Districts ultimately adopted after the Justice Department's rejection of the first redistricting plan.

In seeking to underscore the weaknesses of districts that are contiguous at only one point in certain areas, Everett questioned Cohen about the relationship of Congresswoman Eva Clayton's First District to Martin Lancaster's Third District. "Mr. Lancaster . . . being a human being, . . . a person occupying some finite space in the three-dimensional world," the plaintiffs' counsel asked, "it would be impossible for him to go from the eastern part of his district to the western part without going through Ms. Clayton's district?"

"While he would remain in his district," Cohen responded, "part of his body would be in the 1st District as well, that's correct." Cohen also agreed that it would take about three hours to drive from one end of the Twelfth District to the other, thirty to forty-five minutes longer if one remained within the district for the entire trip.

During his questioning, Everett asked Cohen about changes the General Assembly had made in the First District's shape to accommodate the interests of Clayton and other African Americans interested in seeking the seat. On redirect examination of Cohen in behalf of the defendant-intervenors, Stein asked whether modifications had also been made for white candidates. Cohen responded that the original First District plan had not included the residence of state representative Walter B. Jones, Jr., but had been revised to put Jones, who planned to campaign for the First District seat from which his father was retiring, back in the district. Stein also gave Cohen the chance to repeat his previous assertions that the shape of the challenged districts was driven by a desire to have each district reflect communities of interest, while the plan in general embodied the legislature's interest in protecting incumbents. During recross-examination by Everett, the witness emphasized that although representation of communities of interest had not been among the stated criteria guiding the General Assembly's redistricting committees, those criteria were "a floor, not a ceiling, on what the legislature was doing." Speaker Blue and other leaders in the redistricting process, he added, had also instructed him to consider communities of interest, and the notices about public hearings on redistricting had invited the public to comment on issues relating to that factor.

———

Toby Fitch, the African American representative who had co-chaired the house redistricting committee, was the defendants' next witness. When Eddie Speas began with questions about the witness's eastern North Carolina background, Everett objected on grounds of relevance. "The plaintiffs in this case believe that the legislator comes to the legislature as [a] blank slate," Speas rejoined. "I believe I'm entitled to demonstrate to the court the kinds of information that they bring with them to the legislature." Judge Phillips allowed the question, and Fitch briefly described his life and career, particularly his law practice and involvement in politics. He had first been elected to the state house in 1984 from a majority-black district created as a result of the *Gingles* case. When speaker Dan Blue appointed him and two "rednecks," as he put it, from Sampson and Alamance Counties to co-chair the redistricting process, Fitch "didn't know how we were going to all three fit in to be co-chairs together to talk about what I had understood and seen grown men cry over in the past, and that was redistricting turf and who blacks belonged to and who blacks didn't belong to." He had been pleased to find, however, that the three "were able to sit together as very understanding men and work through redistricting."

During further questioning, Fitch described the districting process and the major role of politics and compromise in the creation of districts. He also testified that he and the other co-chairs had favored the creation of two majority-black districts from the beginning but had been willing to settle for the one produced in the 1991 legislative session. Fitch thought that if Justice Department officials "did their job in the fashion I thought they would do, they would reject the first plan and send it back and instruct us to do a second. And that's exactly what they did."

Fitch also recalled his developing interest in the notion of one majority-minority district representing an essentially urban population and the other a rural population. "I take it," said Speas, "you think there's some difference between Durham and eastern North Carolina."

The witness readily agreed. "I don't think that all black folks are the same." When Durham's urbane representative Mickey Michaux "came down in [the] tobacco area with water in the fields," Fitch remembered, he arrived "in patent leather shoes and silk shirt and driving a black El Dorado Cadillac. He's distinct" from the people of the state's rural east. With urban and rural districts, said Fitch, "those who wore suits and didn't work in the fields . . . could be with those who wore suits[,] and those who wore bib overalls could kind of be together with us who wore bib overalls." During the redistricting process, he and his co-chairs decided that North Carolina should have two such distinct districts and instructed the General Assembly's map-maker Gerry Cohen "to move forward with that proposition."

Dayna Cunningham of the NAACP questioned Fitch for the

defendant-intervenors. In response to her questions, the legislator asserted that he did not believe that the majority-minority district the Justice Department had proposed — combining African Americans with Native Americans of Robeson County — would serve the same urban-rural purpose as the districts ultimately adopted. Durham and Charlotte would have dominated that district, he said, while its rural minority populations would "basically [have been] stepchildren."

Everett was the first lawyer for the plaintiffs and their intervenors to examine Fitch. He began by asking the witness whether he believed "the end justifies the means."

The witness responded, "No, sir, I do not believe that the ends justify the means, because I don't believe that it's 100 percent right to step on somebody just because somebody stepped on you."

"Are you answering no or yes?" Everett countered.

"To make the broad categorical statement do I believe that the ends justify the means," Fitch shot back, "what are you talking about? . . . I don't exactly know what you mean."

Fitch, Everett persisted, had acknowledged in earlier testimony his awareness of the *Gingles* decision. Was the witness aware of *Gingles*'s requirement that majority-minority districts embody "some type of geographical compactness"?

Fitch responded that he was not aware of "any constitutional requirements . . . that said I had to have a geographical[ly] compact district that ran for a certain period; that it was round or that it was square, or that it looked nice and pretty to the whole wide world."

When Everett explained that he had asked the witness "about geographical compactness, not prettiness," Judge Phillips sustained Cunningham's objection, adding, "It seems to me he gave an answer to the question put to him."

Everett then asked whether the majority-minority district the state originally proposed to the Justice Department was more geographically compact than the two districts ultimately adopted. "I don't mean to beg the question," Fitch replied, "but I think that's in the eyes of the beholder. And to the degree that it allowed people whom I felt had been left out and locked out to elect, it's a beautiful, ugly, compact situation." But to others, he conceded, "it may not be that."

A few minutes later, Everett turned to a statement in the districting preclearance documents filed with the Justice Department about which Gerry Cohen had been asked previously — a statement criticizing any district "so spread out in shape" it offered constituents and representatives "no sense of community" and made it difficult for them to know who actually resided in the district. Fitch acknowledged that the statement carried his name but not his authorship. He also conceded that geographical compactness was not among the criteria used in the districting process. When Everett suggested, however, that "community of interest" — the crux of the defendants' urban-rural district argument — was not a criterion either, the witness said that he did not know, but pointed out that such concerns had been raised during the public hearings on redistricting.

Tom Farr devoted his cross-examination primarily to seeking concessions from Fitch that racial considerations had driven the districting process. He suggested, for example, that state officials had decided on two majority-minority districts — rather than three or four — because two was roughly proportionate to the minority percentage of North Carolina's population. He questioned, moreover, whether Fitch had initially favored two majority-black districts, as he had testified earlier. Along that line, he quoted a statement the witness had made in opposition to plans for two majority-minority districts that GOP legislators had proposed. Did the witness recall stating, asked Farr, that those plans "would actually have the effect of weakening the political influence of the black population in North Carolina by packing them in two districts?"

"That sounds like something I might have said politically," Fitch acknowledged. Plans drawn by his colleagues of the "Republican persuasion," he added, were intended "not to help minorities, but to help" the GOP. Asked by Farr whether he recalled stating during floor debate on the redistricting plan finally enacted that it exceeded the requirements of the Voting Rights Act, Fitch said that he remembered making no such statement but added, "Politically, I might have said that."

––––––

The defendants next called Allan Lichtman, a political historian at American University. Drawing on 1980 and 1990 census data as well as a telephone survey, Lichtman had prepared a report examining the degree to which the challenged districts could be explained on grounds other than race, the demographic composition of the districts, and the political opinions of constituents as a measure of communities of interest. He had also reached conclusions regarding whether nonracial explanations for the districts reflected the intent of North Carolina legislators, as well as the effect of the contested plan on voter participation, especially voter roll-off from presidential to congressional elections.

The First and Twelfth Districts, Lichtman testified in response to Eddie Speas's questions, were relatively homogeneous in socioeconomic status and political opinion, despite their irregular geographic shapes. In terms of economic status, the First District was the fourth most homogeneous in the state, and the Twelfth ranked second in homogeneity, even though the challenged districts were also clearly the most racially mixed in North Carolina, and blacks and whites differed sharply in socioeconomic level. Even when compared with all the relatively compact districts created after the 1980 census, the First and Twelfth Districts were relatively homogeneous. Their residents also shared similar political views on such issues as the economy, unemployment, health care, poverty, homelessness, the federal budget deficit, crime, education, ethics, and drugs. In fact, compared with the Fourth District, the most geographically compact in the state, the Twelfth District was more homogeneous in terms of resident political opinion on issues, and the First District was nearly as homogeneous as the Fourth District.

"There's no indication," said Lichtman, "that the apparent geographic non-compactness of Districts 1 and 12 compared to District 4 has meant that with respect to commonalities of interest on political opinion, . . . Districts 1 and . . . 12 emerge as heterogeneous. To the contrary, they emerge as about as homogeneous or, if anything, a shade more so than District 4." All three districts, he added, were about equally homogeneous, and although there were greater opinion differences among whites, they were relatively homogeneous in their views also. "I'm certainly not going to say," the witness observed, that "this analysis shows that non-compactness translates here into greater homogeneity; but certainly the analysis does show there's no indication whatsoever that Districts 1 and 12, relative to compact District 4, are heterogeneous. If anything, [they] come out about the same or maybe even slightly more homogeneous than District 4." Nor did the findings of his research show that the contested districts had combined persons purely on the basis of race, without regard to their "material conditions or . . . political opinions."

In response to further questions, Lichtman applauded the First and Twelfth Districts as "distinctive" districts. "The value of creating [such] districts in terms of the whole [redistricting] plan is that you are having a set of districts that do reflect the various interests within the state. . . . And you have, then, a congressional delegation sitting in Washington that likewise reflects the differing interests across the state as a whole." The First District was predominantly rural, with "far and away the poorest" black population in North Carolina; it was also next to last among districts in terms of the socioeconomic standing of its white population. The Twelfth District, in constrast, was urban, and its black population was about average in socioeconomic status relative to the entire state. In contrast with the First District's white population, the Twelfth ranked in the middle among all districts in terms of white socioeconomic standing. Noting that the challenged districting plan created more distinctive districts than had its counterpart enacted after the 1980 census, the witness also agreed that race helped account for that difference, adding, "as we already indicated, race is correlated with socioeconomic factors."

Everett and other counsel for the plaintiffs vigorously objected when Lichtman relied on 1990 census data in his testimony; the legislature, they argued, obviously had not had access to that material when the challenged districts were adopted. Judge Phillips, however, allowed the witness to continue. Later, Speas asked Lichtman how, without that data, the General Assembly would have possessed the information necessary to include socioeconomic distinctions in its redistricting deliberations. "Legislators," the political historian replied, again over the protests of the plaintiffs' lawyers, "by the very nature of their jobs, and even more pointedly by the very nature of their political survival, have detailed knowledge, particularly within their own districts, of the basic socioeconomic, demographic, and political characteristics of their district." Census data, he asserted, were "not necessary to construct districts with a concern for commonality of interest. You don't have to refine it to that level. You basically have to know what are the areas that share socioeconomic, demographic, and political characteristics."

To satisfy himself that a concern for communities of interest had influenced the General Assembly's districting decisions, Lichtman also examined the legislative record, which convinced him that such concerns had indeed been an element of the process. He offered support as well for the defendants' assertion that bizarrely shaped districts had no meaningful effect on voter turnout, particularly drop-off from participation in presidential elections to participation in congressional races. Roll-off in North Carolina was only about 3 percent, he said, reiterating previous testimony, while the national rate was around 8 percent. The state's congressional districts ranked last in geographic compactness, he added, but North Carolina also had a lower roll-off rate than all its neighboring states. Lack of geographic compactness not only did not undermine voter participation; "to the extent the results show any relationship, they're showing a relationship in the opposite direction." Nor, apparently, did the shape of the challenged districts or the race of constituents affect voter contact with representatives.

Guided by Speas, Lichtman further asserted that an alternative districting plan suggested by the plaintiffs would not reflect the urban-rural dichotomy to the extent the challenged districts did. The First Districts in the two plans were about equally rural, but the urban district in the alternative plan was 20 percent less urban than that in the contested plan.

During his cross-examination of Lichtman for the plaintiff-intervenors, RNC counsel Michael Hess brought up Mel Watt's 6 percent recognition rate among citizens of his district. Did not, Hess asked, such a low level of recognition — derived from a poll conducted nearly a year after the congressman took office — have significance for the representational issues the challenged districts raised? Lichtman countered that nearly a third of Eva Clayton's constituents knew her — "an extraordinary recognition level for a first-term congressperson in a brand new district" that also lacked geographic compactness. Watt's recognition level was lower than one might expect, and Clayton's was higher. One possible reason for the difference, the witness suggested, was that Clayton had gone through two tightly contested primary campaigns, while Watt had faced no meaningful primary competition. But Hess also got in a shot at Lichtman's use of census data that were not available to the General Assembly at the time the First and Twelfth Districts were created. When the witness relied on the same sort of data in a Louisiana majority-minority redistricting case, asked Hess, "isn't it true that the court called your use of that data spurious?" When Speas and Stein objected, Judge Phillips ruled that Hess could probe the witness about similarities in his testimony in the Louisiana suit and that in *Shaw* but could not "try to get [Lichtman] to comment upon his awareness of what the court may have thought of him," which the judge characterized as "completely aimless examination."

Everett began his cross-examination with a question about Lichtman's explanation for the different levels of recognition Watt and Clayton enjoyed among their constituents. Everett thought that Watt, like Clayton, had also run in two primaries and a general election campaign. Lichtman was now uncertain, but Congressman Watt happened to be in the courtroom. "Mr. Watt is sitting back there shaking his head no," Judge Britt interjected, "so apparently. . . ."

"No," the witness asserted, "as I thought, he did not."

Even so, Everett persisted with questions about Watt's low recognition rate and suggested that "this inability to correctly identify the congressional representative indicate[s] some confusion on the part of the respondents." Lichtman agreed but noted that the survey in question required respondents to recall their congressperson's name, rather than select it from a list of choices. Everett also probed the witness about the failure of legislative committees to include homogeneity among the redistricting criteria. Lichtman pointed out, however, that the public hearings on redistricting had included attention to communities of interest, which, he asserted, "certainly is a way of talking about homogeneity and in a way the public can understand. If they talked about homogeneity, no one would have understood."

Everett further suggested that ballot format and the opportunity for voters to cast a straight-ticket ballot with a single vote might influence the degree of voter fall-off between presidential and congressional elections. "My purpose," the witness replied, "was not to try to discover what factors, other than non-compactness, drive fall-off. My study was simply to show there's no relationship whatever between fall-off and . . . compactness, including the double-contiguities and point contiguities that are in North Carolina, and not in these other states."

Lichtman was no more cooperative when Everett suggested that a representative in a homogeneous district would tend to focus on the needs of the dominant population group, giving little attention to other constituents. "I wouldn't say they do it any less [for all constituents]," the witness observed, "because legislators are always paranoid and always believe no matter what, their elections are in great jeopardy and maximize their [constituency] service. When [districts] are more heterogeneous, they can't rely on the issues as much as they can when the districts are relatively more homogeneous. It's a more challenging task of representation with respect to issues."

Lichtman was Speas's last oral witness. Stein would be calling only one witness for the defendant-intervenors, Twelfth District congressman Mel Watt, who would also be a witness for the state. The plaintiffs indicated that they also planned to call several rebuttal witnesses. Before adjourning for the weekend, Judge Phillips expressed the hope that the trial could be completed in one more day. "I may unleash one of these district judges altogether on Monday," he added, only half jokingly. "I have been very tender and they have been both squirming about the length of the examinations I have permitted to go on, particularly Judge Britt. And we want to get through on Monday without jeopardizing anybody's rights in the case."

Counsel and their witnesses undoubtedly shared the judge's hope. At one point during his testimony, Lichtman had been asked whether he had heard Cohen's lengthy testimony about point contiguity and double crossover contiguity. "More than I ever want to remember," the witness had wearily replied.

––––––

On Monday, April 4, Judge Phillips convened the trial's final session, and Anita Hodgkiss began questioning Mel Watt. Of humble Mecklenburg County roots, Watt had been raised in a house with a tin roof and no running water, no electricity, and no inside toilet. But he was also a Phi Beta Kappa graduate in business administration of UNC–Chapel Hill and had received his law degree at Yale, where he was on the law journal staff. A member from 1971 to 1992 of the law firm Julius Chambers had founded and in which Adam Stein was a senior partner, he had also served one term (1985–1986) in the North Carolina senate — the choice of the Democratic Party when the original candidate died before the election.

Watt had not sought election to a second senate term but had served as campaign manager in several of Charlotte architect Harvey Gantt's election bids. Contrary to press reports, the two were not married to sisters, but they were next-door neighbors as well as frequent tennis partners, and Gantt had designed Watt's home. When Gantt first ran for a seat on Charlotte's city council, Watt agreed to manage his friend's campaign. With Watt managing his races, Gantt won elections in 1975 and 1977, lost his first bid for the Democratic nomination as Charlotte mayor in 1979, won a council seat again in 1981, and was elected mayor in 1983. Watt was in the state senate and did not manage Gantt's successful 1985 reelection bid. But Watt was back as campaign manager when Gantt won his party's U.S. senatorial nomination in 1990 and then lost to Jesse Helms in the general election.

Watt appeared as a witness in *Shaw* for essentially two purposes. First, he could provide testimony from personal experience about the continuing role of racial appeals in North Carolina's political campaigns — a factor that helped justify the creation of majority-minority districts. Responding to Hodgkiss's questions, he claimed that white backlash had prevented Harvey Gantt from getting the most votes among city council candidates, and thus designation as Charlotte's mayor pro tem, until 1981, when "white community guilt" over Gantt's loss of an earlier mayoral race to a less qualified white opponent resulted in his amassing the largest council vote that year. In none of his Charlotte races, moreover, had his friend ever won 50 percent of the white vote.

Watt focused, however, on the use of race in Gantt's 1990 senatorial bid against Helms — from hate mail and telephone calls, to Klan threats to blow up a restaurant at which Gantt was speaking, to the use of a postcard mailing designed to intimidate black voters who had recently changed their residences, to the white hands–black hands advertisement and other racially charged television spots. "They did one commercial," Watt recalled on the witness stand, "that focused on me as the campaign manager and distorted my appearance and distorted my voice and implicitly was saying to the public that this was a black operation; the campaign manager was black, the candidate was black and everybody else in the campaign was black, so to speak."

The congressman's second function as a witness was to convince the court that the Twelfth District's odd, elongated shape had adversely affected neither his ability to campaign and represent his constituents nor their access to him. With Interstate 85 running through the district, and with the hub of one major airline in Charlotte and the hub of another at Raleigh-Durham, Watt had no trouble, he testified, reaching or crossing his district. By establishing offices in every major city in the district and providing regular office hours for staff to meet with citizens in other communities, he had ensured his constituents easy access to him and his staff. But how, Hodgkiss asked, would constituents know they lived in the congressman's district? The election boards of all but two counties, Watt answered, "have sent out cards to everybody telling them what congressional district they vote in." The common interests of the constituents in his urban district, he added, made it easier for him to represent their concerns in Washington. Watt even considered it an advantage that residents of the same general geographic region now had two or three congresspersons, rather than one, representing them or their neighbors. And when Everett questioned the wisdom of such thinking during cross-examination, the witness was unpersuaded. "As my Mama used to tell me, two heads are better than one, all the time."

The plaintiffs had offered in evidence a number of written declarations from residents of the Twelfth District who claimed that Watt had little contact with their communities. Jake Froelich, a longtime friend of Everett's who was prominent in the High Point furniture industry, had filed one of the statements. Watt testified that in fact he had attempted to contact Froelich during several visits to High Point, had made several appearances there, and had both a telephone number and an office in nearby Greensboro.

On beginning his cross-examination, Everett questioned the congressman's assurances with respect to the ease and speed with which he could cover his lengthy district. The plaintiffs' lawyer expressed doubt, moreover, whether a member of Congress in a sprawling district would be clearly recognizable to his constituents, particularly in a district covered by several newspaper and broadcast markets. Through questions drawn from testimony reflecting Watt's preference for homogeneous districts, Everett also suggested that a congressperson in such an area might be inclined to represent only the interests of the dominant population group, while neglecting other constituents.

At one point, too, Everett implied that the Twelfth District might have been configured especially for Watt. After all, the congressman and Leslie Winner, Blue's special counsel in the redistricting process, were members of the same law firm. And Winner later won election in a state senate district created in that redistricting cycle, just as Watt had won the new Twelfth District seat. "Would it be true, basically," asked Everett, that "you [and Winner] had no closer relationship [in the redistricting process] than just an average citizen in Mecklenburg County?"

"That might be going a little bit far," Watt replied, a slight edge in his voice. "I mean, I had a law partner who was working on the plan. . . . But . . . if the question you are asking is did I have any impact on the drawing of this plan, the answer is absolutely not; and if the question you are asking is did I have it drawn for my benefit, the answer is absolutely not. And if the question is did I have it drawn for Harvey Gantt's benefit, the answer is absolutely not."

But Everett persisted, asking whether certain changes in the proposed Twelfth District would have benefited a Charlotte candidate for the seat. Emphasizing Watt's ties to Gantt and relying on erroneous media reports, he even asked whether Watt and Gantt were married to two sisters. "I'm not related to that guy," Watt jokingly answered; "don't you accuse me of that."

Watt's responses to other questions were more pointed. Asked whether he considered it "appropriate" to create majority-minority districts, even if they were not geographically compact, Watt replied, "Against a more than 90-year history of racially polarized voting that makes it impossible for a black candidate to be elected, I think as a temporary measure, this is something that is both desirable and legally required and constitutional. . . . In the absence of majority black districts, no black person is going to be elected to Congress from North Carolina. . . . I think that [it] would be unacceptable if South Africa, for example, came forward with a plan that excluded or made it impossible for whites to be represented in their democratic process, and I think it should be unacceptable in this country."

Did Watt think, asked Everett, that geographical compactness and other traditional redistricting principles "should be discarded if necessary, in order to create majority black districts?"

"Well, my tradition, Mr. Everett," the witness shot back, "is the tradition of democratic representation, and I value that over the traditional principles that you have articulated. . . . That's what the Voting

Rights Act is about, and to some extent, that's what the Constitution, hopefully, is about."

A few minutes earlier, Everett had inquired into the congressman's recent appearance on a PBS news program, during which he had complained that some of the Supreme Court's opinion in *Shaw v. Reno* was based on "racist assumptions." Watt emphasized to Everett that he was not accusing *Shaw*'s author, Justice O'Connor, or any other member of the majority of being racist. On the program, however, he had asserted that "the logical extension of what she was saying is that a 55 [percent] black district which happens to be 45 percent white is racial gerrymandering, is racial apartheid, yet a 90 percent white district which is 10 percent black is somehow integrated. . . . I would characterize that as racist."

Following Watt's testimony, the panel heard briefly from two rebuttal witnesses called by the plaintiffs and their intervenors. In an effort to challenge portions of the testimony of Toby Fitch and Gerry Cohen, Tom Farr examined Arthur Pope, the former GOP legislator who had been a plaintiff in the unsuccessful partisan gerrymandering suit contesting the state's redistricting plan. Not surprisingly, the witness concurred with the plaintiffs' contention that the state's defense of the challenged districts as embodying urban and rural communities of interest was an "after-the-fact justification" of the plan. Moreover, although he agreed that an interest in protecting Democratic incumbents had significantly influenced redistricting, Pope considered that a "concealed" rather than overtly recognized factor in the legislature's deliberations, noting, for example, that a number of redistricting leaders had denied that incumbency protection had anything to do with their decisions.

Responding to questions by Everett, Pope also agreed that the overriding purpose of the redistricting was to ensure the election of two African Americans to Congress. During Smiley's cross-examination, Pope conceded that he and other Republicans had favored two or more majority-minority districts as well, but he insisted that they favored far more compact districts than those created by the General Assembly. As he had in his own suit, the witness stressed again that the legislature "only drew the black majority districts when it did not endanger a white, incumbent Democrat. And that was not a proper consideration." By drawing such statements from Pope, Smiley bolstered the state's contention that politics, rather than race, had driven the redistricting process. During his cross-examination of Pope, Stein pursued essentially the same course for the defendant-intervenors.

Over the objections of the defendants and Judge Britt, Everett was permitted to call his Duke colleague and fellow *Shaw* plaintiff Melvin Shimm as a rebuttal witness. As a resident of a split precinct in the Twelfth District, Shimm testified about the confusion the district's configuration had created for his neighbors, some of whom were uncertain what district they resided in and who represented them in Congress. Opining that Watt remained "a very, very faint presence" in Durham, Shimm further asserted that "the local media ignored him, not completely, but comparatively ignored him." He noted, for example, that when the local press urged readers to contact their representatives in Congress on a matter of public interest, Watt's name was omitted from the list. Watt's own testimony in the suit had convinced Shimm that the congressman perceived African Americans as his "paramount constituency" and "relegates non-black members of his district to a second class status. [It] seems to me that this effectively . . . disenfranchises me, and to that extent I do believe that he is unable to represent me as I think my representative should." During cross-examination by Cunningham, however, Shimm conceded that he had never attempted to contact Watt and had contacted a member of Congress only twice during his forty-one years in Durham. One reason he had not attempted to contact Watt, said Shimm, was his "belief [that he] would [not] get a full, impartial, disinterested hearing."

"Your belief was not based on any effort to actually contact him or based on any response you received?" asked Cunningham.

"No," Shimm answered, "it was based on statements that he made that he perceived his role to be the representative of certain elements of the constituency."

At the close of the trial, Judge Phillips announced that the panel would reconvene for final arguments on April 18. On August 2, the judges upheld the defendants two to one, with the two Democrats on the court again forming the majority and the Republican in dissent.

On August 22, Judge Phillips issued a lengthy opinion for the court, and Judge Voorhees filed a dissenting opinion.

Phillips's opinion clearly reflected the majority's discomfort with Justice O'Connor's opinion for the Supreme Court in *Shaw v. Reno*. Until *Shaw*, he wrote, the Court had recognized only two grounds for an equal protection challenge to congressional redistricting plans: a state's failure to comply with the one-person, one-vote principle of the reapportionment decisions, and the adoption of districts with the purpose and effect of "'diluting' or canceling out the voting strength of an identified group of voters — that is, of so diminishing their ability to influence the political process as essentially to shut them out of it, as opposed to merely making it more difficult for them to elect representatives of their choice in particular districts." *Shaw*, however, recognized a third, "analytically distinct" way, as Justice O'Connor put it, in which a districting plan might violate equal protection. Under *Shaw*, a districting plan designed to separate voters into different districts based on their race was subject to strict scrutiny because it, like all race-based legislation, "threatened 'to stigmatize individuals by reason of their membership in a racial group,' 'to incite racial hostilit[ies],' and 'to stimulate our society's latent race-consciousness.'" Such districting was subject to strict judicial review whether its alleged purpose was "benign" or invidious and, even "though race-neutral on its face," if "rationally" it could not "be understood as anything other than an effort to separate voters into different districts on the basis of race, . . . [without] sufficient justification."

Such a claim, Phillips observed, was essentially the same one the Supreme Court had recognized in suits brought by members of the majority race in attacking race-based affirmative action programs as "reverse discrimination." But transposing it to the redistricting context raised significant problems about which the parties were "in flat disagreement." First, noted Phillips, there was the issue of standing. The defendant-intervenors had argued that the plaintiffs and their intervenors lacked standing to sue, that is, that their case should be dismissed based on their failure to assert concrete injury to their own legal rights. *Shaw v. Reno*, they conceded, had held that plaintiffs, as a general proposition, had standing to challenge a districting scheme without alleging that it had the purpose and effect of diluting their voting strength. The defendant-intervenors also read *Shaw*, however, as requiring a showing by particular plaintiffs that the plan at issue had caused a member of Congress to represent only the interests of a racial group to which they did not belong or had exacerbated racial bloc voting by members of that group. The *Shaw* plaintiffs, the defendant-intervenors argued, had not surmounted that hurdle.

Judge Phillips acknowledged the force of their argument. Citing Supreme Court precedents requiring litigants to allege direct and substantial "injury in fact" to their personal legal rights, the judge conceded that, "at first blush," the *Shaw* plaintiffs did not appear to have "even alleged, much less proved," such injury. Ruth Shaw and Melvin Shimm, the two plaintiffs who resided in the Twelfth District, had contended, for example, that living in such a bizarrely shaped district had caused them to doubt the quality of their representation and feel "disenfranchised." Such "abstract, theoretical, and merely speculative" harms, asserted Phillips, bore the "marks of the sort of 'injury in perception' rather than 'in fact'" about which Justice Scalia — a member of the *Shaw v. Reno* majority — had complained in a recent dissent.

The judge concluded, nevertheless, that the Supreme Court would recognize the plaintiffs' claim to standing, just as it had recognized in affirmative action cases that a state's use of racial classifications "necessarily inflicts 'stigmatic injury.'" His acceptance of that interpretation of *Shaw*, though, was reluctant at best. In the affirmative action cases, after all, such classifications worked to advantage members of a particular racial group relative to others in the allocation of benefits. "But laws that assign voters to particular districts on the basis of race, unlike racial set-asides, do not appear to subject members of any racial group to 'unequal treatment' vis-a-vis any other. So long as all citizens may vote, all individual votes receive the same weight, and no racial group's voting strength is unduly diluted, all racial groups are by definition given a fair opportunity to participate in the electoral process, even if some are better positioned than others to elect representatives of their choice in particular districts."

Shaw v. Reno had also left unclear, in Phillips's judgment, the showing necessary to trigger strict scrutiny in a majority-minority districting case. The plaintiffs and their allies had argued for strict review of any districting in which race played a "substantial" or "motivating" role, even if other factors also had a substantial influence on the shape

{ *Race and Redistricting* }

of districts. In contrast, the state and its intervenors read *Shaw* as requiring strict scrutiny of a districting plan only when the districts at issue had a "highly irregular" shape, concentrated racial groups in numbers disproportionate to their percentage of the state's entire population, and had a shape and location explainable only in racial terms. And even if the first two conditions were met, a plan would escape strict scrutiny if district shape and location could "rationally be explained by reference to some districting principle other than race." In such cases, the defendants argued, a state should be required to show only a rational basis for the configuration of its districts.

Refusing to give *Shaw* such a narrow construction, Judge Phillips declared that "the language and structure of the Court's opinion, if not its actual holding, strongly suggest that the Court intended . . . to place race-based redistricting legislation into the same category as all other forms of race-based state action," subjecting it to strict scrutiny on "the basis of proof . . . that racial considerations played a 'substantial' or 'motivating' role in the line-drawing process, even if they were not the only factor that influenced that process." Nor did he think that *Shaw*, despite language in Justice O'Connor's majority opinion, required "aesthetically 'ugly'" districts to trigger strict scrutiny. The bizarre shape of a district with a disproportionate minority population was only circumstantial evidence that race, rather than other factors, drove the redistricting process. At the same time, he attempted to assure the defendants that the court's conclusion on the point would not subject all districting plans to strict review simply because legislators were inevitably aware of the racial consequences of their decisions. "There is a critical distinction," he declared, "between 'race-conscious' action and 'race-based' action."

Phillips handed the state a victory when he turned to application of the strict scrutiny standard in the redistricting context. The plaintiffs and their allies had conceded that they had the burden of proving that the challenged districting plan was racially motivated and thus subject to rigorous review. But they had also argued that once the requisite racial motivation was established, the burden should shift to the state to establish that the plan was narrowly tailored to serve a compelling governmental interest. The court disagreed, citing Supreme Court precedents holding that plaintiffs have the burden of proof throughout such litigation.

Moving to the issue of whether race-based districting served a compelling governmental need, Phillips also rejected the plaintiffs' suggestion that the state must show that it had a compelling reason for enacting "the *particular* race-based redistricting plan under challenge, with all its twists and turns." The defendants had to show, the panel concluded, only that they had a compelling interest justifying some sort of race-based districting plan; whether particular districts, such as those at issue in *Shaw*, passed constitutional muster would depend on whether they were narrowly tailored to serve the compelling interests that race-based districting was said to serve. In the court's judgment, a state's interests in complying with the Voting Rights Act and eradicating the effects of past and present racial discrimination in its political processes were sufficiently compelling to justify such districting.

In deciding whether a particular districting plan was narrowly tailored to serve such interests, Judge Phillips drew on Supreme Court rulings in related fields to declare that the court's finding on that issue had depended essentially on five factors: the efficacy of alternative non-race-based remedies; whether the plan at issue imposed a rigid racial "quota" or a flexible "goal"; the duration of the plan; the relationship between the plan's goal and the percentage of minorities in the districts at issue; and the plan's impact on the rights of innocent third parties. With respect to the first factor, Phillips concluded that a state with a compelling interest in race-based redistricting for the purpose of complying with the Voting Rights Act "obviously [had] no *completely* race-neutral alternative means of accomplishing that end." The questions, rather, were whether a challenged plan "creates more majority-minority districts than is reasonably necessary to comply with the Act, and whether the majority-minority districts it creates contain substantially larger concentrations of minority voters than is reasonably necessary to give minority voters a realistic opportunity to elect representatives of their choice in those districts." On the second factor, Phillips found that since race-based districts did not guarantee minority candidates a fixed percentage of congressional seats, such plans would seldom be struck down as establishing fixed quotas rather than flexible racial goals. With respect to the third factor, the constitutional requirement for a census and redistricting every ten years ensured that race-based districting plans would by nature be temporary, with legislatures obliged to evaluate the continuing need for such districts during every redistricting cycle. The fourth factor would be satisfied, added Phillips, so long as the percentage of majority-black districts in a plan did not substantially exceed the portion of minority voters in the state as a whole.

With respect to the final factor relating to whether a districting plan served the narrow tailoring requirement, the plaintiffs and their allies had argued that race-based districts imposed an undue burden on innocent persons if they deviated from traditional districting principles such as geographic compactness, contiguity, and respect for counties, voting precincts, and other political subdivisions to a greater degree than necessary to accomplish a compelling state interest. If the legislature could have drafted a districting plan that furthered such a goal without sacrificing such traditional districting principles, only that plan would conform to the narrow tailoring standard.

Judge Phillips agreed, however, only that such plans must conform to *constitutionally mandated* principles, such as one person, one vote and the ban on the undue dilution of a group's voting strength. Even the *Shaw* Court had recognized that compactness, contiguity, and other such principles were not constitutional mandates. And equal protection, the judge asserted, did not forbid states to disregard such principles in pursuing "other legitimate redistricting objectives, such as protecting incumbents, preserving the integrity of established neighborhoods, and recognizing the voting strength of various political parties." The *Shaw* Court, he added, had not mandated "wise or aesthetically-pleasing districts" but simply wanted to ensure that legislatures did not covertly pursue forbidden ends in the redistricting process.

Undue concern for compactness and related considerations, in Phillips's judgment, also made little practical sense. Professor O'Rourke, one of the plaintiffs' own experts, had testified that there was no consensus or empirical evidence establishing that adherence to such criteria ensured fair and effective representation. Nor was there a manageable judicial standard for determining the degree to which districting plans must conform to such principles in order to satisfy constitutional requirements. Judicial insistence on such principles, added Phillips, would also constitute undue interference in the districting process — a matter "long . . . thought to be the primary province of the state legislatures." Only, he concluded, if a districting plan failed to give equal weight to all votes, diluted a particular group's vote, or was not grounded in "rational districting principles" ensuring all citizens "fair and effective representation" did it impose an undue burden on innocent third parties. A race-based plan that complied with those standards might still cause "stigmatic" or "dignitary" harm to minority and nonminority voters that it classified by race, but that was not sufficient to establish an undue burden warranting judicial intervention.

Against the backdrop of such considerations, Judge Phillips concluded that North Carolina's General Assembly had deliberately created the challenged districts with narrow majorities of African Americans, thereby giving them a reasonable opportunity to elect representatives of their choice; that the legislature's action was taken in an effort to ensure state compliance with the Voting Rights Act; that the desire of some legislators to create majority-black districts as a remedy for North Carolina's long and continuing history of racial discrimination in voting would not have been sufficient to justify the adoption of such districts independent of the state's effort to comply with the federal law; that the two districts were highly irregular in shape and extremely lacking in geographic compactness relative to other districts in the state and nation; and that North Carolina had subordinated compactness and respect for political subdivisions to a variety of other considerations, including one person, one vote, the need for effective black voting majorities, the desire to create urban and rural majority-minority districts with distinct and homogeneous commonalities of interest, an effort to protect incumbents, and "the maintenance of technical territorial contiguity." Based on these and related factual findings, the panel held that the plaintiffs and their intervenors had standing to challenge the contested districts as violations of equal protection, that the plan constituted a deliberate racial gerrymander subject to strict judicial scrutiny, that the plaintiffs had the burden of establishing that the districts were not narrowly tailored to promote one or more compelling state interests, that North Carolina had a compelling interest in complying with the Voting Rights Act, and that the disputed districts were narrowly tailored to promote that interest.

Particularly in view of the Justice Department's authoritative insistence that North Carolina adopt two majority-minority districts as a condition of preclearance, Phillips added, the state had a strong reason for concluding that two districts were required by federal law. Moreover, the plan did not pack minority voters into majority-black districts in percentages much greater than those reasonably necessary to give them a reasonable chance to elect representatives of their choice, did not impose a rigid electoral quota, would be of limited duration, and did not unduly burden the voting rights of innocent persons. Instead, the challenged plan had created districts that, though "relatively non-compact," were based on rational districting principles. It thus satisfied the narrow tailoring requirement.

The plaintiffs, Phillips observed, had "characterized the plan as 'a constitutional crime.'" But he and Judge Britt had a different view. "We have concluded instead that, under controlling law, it is a justifiable invocation of a concededly drastic, historically conditioned remedy in order to continue the laborious struggle to break free of a legacy of official discrimination and racial bloc voting in North Carolina's electoral processes that has played a significant part in the ability of any African-American citizen of North Carolina, despite repeated responsible efforts, to be elected to Congress in a century. We decline in this case to put a halt to the effort by declaring the plan unconstitutional."

———

Judge Voorhees vigorously objected to the ruling and much of the majority's rationale. Voorhees naturally concurred with the court's finding that the challenged districts amounted to a racial gerrymander subject to strict judicial review. "The constitutional injury here," he declared, "derives not only from the nature of the State's ultimate objective — namely, to classify citizens on the basis of their race — but also from the means employed to achieve that objective — namely, voting districts so grossly misshapen as necessarily to divide and stigmatize their citizenry along racial lines. As the legislature must go to greater and greater lengths of disfigurement to achieve a racially preconceived result because of the dispersion of minority voters among the population, the districts at last become so bizarre in shape that they can only be perceived as racially designated districts."

Unlike the majority, however, Voorhees could find no "compelling justification for the means employed as well as the ends served." In his judgment, the challenged districts were "inherently defective, by characterization not sufficiently 'narrowly tailored' to survive strict scrutiny." Emphasizing the *Gingles* opinion's suggestion that majority-minority districts be geographically compact, Voorhees could find no justification for the state's assertion that the noncompact districts at issue were necessary to ensure compliance with the Voting Rights Act. The legislative history surrounding adoption of the disputed plan contained no evidence of concern that it was required by the vote dilution provisions of Section 2 of the Voting Rights Act, and only the Justice Department's objection to the state's first districting plan suggested that the challenged districts were necessary to conform to Section 5's preclearance provisions. But "blind deference" to the attorney general's interpretation of the Voting Rights Act, Voorhees declared, did not immunize the state's plan from constitutional scrutiny, and the majority's reliance on the Justice Department's stance to justify the state's action "vest[s] the Department . . . with unbridled and unprecedented discretion." The defendants' claims that the challenged districts were necessary to protect the state from possible vote dilution claims under Section 2, moreover, were "only weak post-hoc rationalizations." Since only parts of two counties in the Twelfth District were even subject to preclearance requirements, Voorhees also found it contrary to "common sense" that the state would defend the disputed districts as necessary for compliance with Section 5.

Even on the assumption that North Carolina had a compelling interest in creating majority-minority districts to comply with the Voting Rights Act, Voorhees disputed the defendants' contention that the challenged districts were narrowly tailored to further that objective. First, he argued, district shape was at least relevant to whether the state had adopted the least restrictive means available to ensure its compliance with federal law without offending the demands of equal protection. But the districts at issue "lack[ed] all inherent integrity, . . . ceas[ing] being districts at all, instead merely patching together islands of voters with only a legislative intent to group predetermined numbers of voters by race." Contrary to the majority, he also declared that the challenged plan more closely resembled the "strict" quota struck down in a recent Supreme Court affirmative action case than the "flexible goal" the majority saw. Given the stigma associated with race-based districting and the burden it imposed on all minorities as well as nonminorities, Voorhees contended that the contested districts could hardly be deemed the least restrictive means available for compliance with federal law when more compact districts could have been adopted. He challenged, too, the majority's conclusion that states need honor only constitutionally mandated redistricting requirements, particularly in view of the emphasis on compactness and contiguity in *Shaw v. Reno*. Contrary to the majority, he further contended that the bizarre shapes of the First and Twelfth Districts made "fair representation virtually impossible" there.

Judge Voorhees concluded his dissent with Justice Kennedy's "acute observation" in a recent affirmative action case. "I regret," the justice had written, "that after a century of judicial opinions we interpret the Constitution to do no more than move us from 'separate but equal' to 'unequal but benign.'" The panel's opinion meant, Voorhees feared, that "North Carolinians must live for an indefinite period of time with congressional districts in which the races are intentionally made 'separate but equal' without sufficient justification."

When the panel had announced its ruling earlier that month, North Carolina political leaders expressed relief that the state's fall congressional elections could go forward without the turbulence of last-minute redistricting. Frank Parker, a black law professor and election law specialist in Washington, D.C., saw the ruling as perhaps signaling a judicial shift toward support of such districts. Although a recent district court decision had overturned majority-minority districting in Louisiana, *Shaw* made Parker think that "people are giving this a second thought." He asked, "What would be the impact on our democratic system to cut back on the number of minority representatives? Wouldn't that parallel the results of the first Reconstruction? Even the Supreme Court itself will have second thoughts about de facto kicking black representatives out of Congress." Laughlin McDonald of the ACLU hoped that the evidence presented at the trial would overwhelm the emotional appeals the plaintiffs had made on *Shaw*'s first visit to the Supreme Court. "In *Shaw* [I]," he said, "the plaintiffs played up the shock value of their case with talk about political pornography and political obscenity." But the trial had shown that "these plans are not like apartheid or segregation. They are biracial districts, the most integrated districts in the state."

Other observers saw the irony in the GOP's alliance with the *Shaw* plaintiffs. Ted Arrington, a Republican political scientist at the University of North Carolina's Charlotte campus, suggested that the Republicans who intervened on the side of Everett and the other plaintiffs "should be grateful that they lost." Like many other election law experts, Arrington predicted — accurately, it turned out — that, given the high rate of minority voting for Democratic candidates, the state's creation of two majority-black districts would improve the 1994 chances for GOP contenders in other districts.

But neither the Republican intervenors nor, of course, the *Shaw* plaintiffs were about to abandon their cause. Everett declined to comment, but his co-plaintiff Melvin Shimm was not so reticent. The case, he told a reporter, was almost certainly headed to the Supreme Court for the second time.

CHAPTER 6

A Predominantly Racial Purpose

The *Shaw* plaintiffs filed notice they were appealing the district court's decision on August 29, 1994, a week after the panel issued its opinions in the case. The Supreme Court would not announce its decision in *Shaw v. Hunt*, or *Shaw II*, until June 13, 1996. Prior to that date, however, the justices issued a number of rulings elaborating their position in majority-minority districting disputes.

The most important of those decisions was *Miller v. Johnson* (1995). Georgia had adopted a congressional districting plan with three majority-black districts after the Justice Department denied preclearance to two earlier proposals containing only two majority-minority districts. Voters challenged the state's new Eleventh District, which joined African American Atlanta neighborhoods with poor black populations in coastal Chatham County, 260 miles away. By a two-one vote, a federal trial court held the district invalid under *Shaw v. Reno*. Sharply criticizing the Justice Department for its close cooperation with the ACLU in attempting to maximize the number of majority-black districts, the majority construed *Shaw I* to require strict scrutiny of any redistricting plan in which race had an "overriding, predominant" influence. Based on the district's irregular shape and evidence of the state legislature's racial purpose and intent, the judges held the challenged district subject to strict review. And though agreeing that Georgia had a compelling interest in compliance with the Voting Rights Act, the district court majority concluded that the statute did not require the creation of three majority-black districts.

On appeal to the Supreme Court, the *Miller* appellants did not contest the district panel's finding of predominantly racial gerrymandering. Instead, they argued that under *Shaw I* a racially motivated district was subject to strict scrutiny only if its shape was so bizarre that it was unexplainable on any basis other than race. The plaintiffs, they contended, had not surmounted that hurdle.

Speaking through Justice Anthony Kennedy, a five-four Supreme Court majority disagreed. "The essence of the equal protection claim recognized in *Shaw*," observed Kennedy, quoting extensively from the Court's opinion there, "is that the State has used race for separating voters into districts. Just as the State may not, absent extraordinary justification, segregate citizens on the basis of race in public [facilities] . . . , so did we recognize in *Shaw* that it may not separate its citizens into different voting districts on the basis of race. . . . When the State assigns voters on the basis of race, it engages in the offensive and demeaning assumption that voters of a particular race, because of their race, 'think alike, share the same political interests, and will prefer the same candidates at the polls.' . . . Race-based assignments 'embody stereotypes that treat individuals as the product of their race, evaluating their thoughts and efforts — their very worth as citizens — according to a criterion barred to the Government by history and the Constitution.' . . . They also cause society serious harm. . . . 'Racial gerrymandering, even for remedial purposes, may balkanize us into competing racial factions; it threatens to carry us further from the goal of a political system in which race no longer matters — a goal that the Fourteenth and Fifteenth Amendments embody, and to which the Nation continues to aspire.'"

In *Shaw v. Reno*, of course, Justice Sandra Day O'Connor had emphasized the importance of appearance in districting suits generally and the particularly bizarre shapes of North Carolina's disputed districts. Justice Kennedy refused to read *Shaw I*, however, as "suggest[ing] that a district must be bizarre on its face before there is a constitutional violation." Nor, he insisted, had the *Shaw I* majority concluded "that in certain instances a district's appearance (or, to be more precise, its appearance in combination with certain demographic evidence) can give rise to an equal protection claim, . . . a holding that bizarreness was a threshold showing, as appellants believe it to be." *Shaw I* had not barred equal protection analysis in challenges to districts that lacked an extremely bizarre shape. "Shape is relevant," concluded Kennedy, "not because bizarreness is a necessary element of the constitutional wrong or a threshold requirement of proof, but because it may be persuasive circumstantial evidence that race for its own sake, and not other districting principles, was the legislature's dominant and controlling rationale in drawing its district lines. The logical implication . . . is that parties may rely on evidence other than bizarreness to establish race-based districting." A racial gerrymander would be more easily established in cases involving districts of highly irregular form, but other evidence could be used to expose an overriding racial purpose.

Kennedy conceded that legislatures were inevitably aware of racial demographics in the redistricting process, but the issue, as the district court had concluded, was whether race "predominates in the . . . process." Plaintiffs challenging majority-minority districts had the burden, he declared, "to show, either through circumstantial evidence of a district's shape and demographics or more direct evidence going to legislative purpose, that race was the predominant factor motivating the legislature's decision to place a significant number of voters within or without a particular district" and that legislators "subordinated traditional race-neutral districting principles, including but not limited to compactness, contiguity, respect for political subdivisions or communities defined by actual shared interests, to racial considerations." Once that burden had been met, a challenged plan would be declared unconstitutional unless it was found to be narrowly tailored to further a compelling governmental interest.

In the Court's judgment, Georgia's "predominant, overriding" motivation had been racial, and the disputed district was not narrowly tailored to serve the state's compelling interest in complying with the Voting Right Act. The legislature clearly had adopted a third majority-minority district merely to satisfy the Justice Department's "black-maximization" policy under its Section 5 preclearance powers. But Kennedy rejected the notion that a "State has a compelling interest in complying with whatever preclearance mandates the Justice Department issues." Courts have an obligation to make independent determinations whether particular race-based districts are necessary to accommodate the Voting Rights Act, and the majority found no "reasonable basis" for concluding that Georgia's two early two-district plans violated Section 5. The earlier plans had increased the number of majority-black districts in the state from one of ten to two of eleven. Thus, they had not violated Section 5's nonretrogression principle against redistricting that further reduced minority voting strength. By pressuring the state to create an additional majority-minority district, the Justice Department had gone beyond what the Voting Rights Act required, resulting in Georgia's violation of the equal protection guarantee.

————

While considering *Miller*, the Supreme Court put Everett's case in "cold storage," as he put it. When the justices struck down Georgia's redistricting plan on June 29, 1995, however, they also announced that they would again review North Carolina's disputed districts. Briefs were to be filed at the Court in September, with oral argument to follow in early December.

The *Miller* Court's conclusion that districts drawn with a predominantly racial purpose, whether bizarre in appearance or not, were subject to strict judicial review naturally heartened Everett and the other *Shaw* appellants, who were confident that they could convince the High Court that North Carolina's districts were both highly irregular in shape and overwhelmingly racial in motivation. In the wake of a nationwide GOP sweep in the 1994 elections, the Republicans had taken control of North Carolina's house of representatives. The new house majority leader, Leo Daughtry of Johnston County, was also elated at the *Miller* decision, predicting that the Supreme Court would reject his state's contention that the challenged districts reflected urban and rural communities of interest rather than race. "The 12th [District] is absolutely, unqualified[ly] based on race," said Daughtry. "Anybody that says differently should not be in business because they'd lose all they had."

Twelfth District congressman Mel Watt conceded that the Court had set the "standard . . . higher than we hoped it would be. Especially when you take in[to] account the lack of representation of African-Americans in North Carolina in the past — in that sense it's a step backwards." But both Watt and Eva Clayton of the First District cautiously predicted that their districts would satisfy the High Court. "Through the Voting Rights Act," Clayton declared in a press release, "this nation recognized that special efforts were needed to ensure that minorities have an opportunity to meaningfully participate in the voting process and to elect candidates of their choice. The people of this nation have sacrificed, waged war and shed blood in defense of the right to vote and to participate in government. Surely the creation of so-called 'irregular districts' to promote regular voting by all citizens is no less and no more than a commitment in defense of democracy."

———

The briefs filed in the Supreme Court by the appellants and their intervenors largely tracked arguments made during the 1994 trial, as well as the *Miller* majority's rationale. Attacking the reasoning and holding of the district court majority, Everett challenged, for example, the panel's conclusion that North Carolina's plan was narrowly tailored to promote a compelling governmental interest. Both the bizarre shape of the disputed districts and the state's "unparalleled flouting of traditional districting principles," he declared, "reveal unmistakenly the 'overriding' race-based purpose of the General Assembly," as did the legislative history underlying the plan's adoption. Such districts sent voters and representatives the clear message that legislators were to represent only the interests of the dominant racial group in a district. They also "constantly reinforce racial stereotypes and remind voters that race is being used by the government as the basis for allocating rights and responsibilities." Like the Supreme Court in *Miller*, Everett also contended that North Carolina's two majority-minority districts were unnecessary to ensure the state's compliance with the Voting Rights Act and were simply the General Assembly's response to a Justice Department "'max-black,' 'if-you-can-you-must' policy" that exceeded the requirements of federal law and the Constitution.

As he had before the district court, Everett ridiculed the state's defense of the contested districts as motivated primarily not by race but by such nonracial considerations as incumbency protection and the desire to reflect distinctly urban and rural communities of interest in the districting process. The latter defense, he charged, was based on demographic data unavailable to the legislature until after its adoption of the challenged plan. Such "post hoc" and "fictitious interpretations of legislative intent" were designed to cloud the legislators' dominant concern — "their fervent desire that two African-Americans from North Carolina serve in Congress for the first time since 1901. This end — however laudable — does not justify 'balkanizing' the State with racial gerrymanders, which aggravate, rather than remedy, 'racial polarization.'"

In response to a question during oral argument from Justice O'Connor, Everett would suggest again that districts drawn for a racial purpose "can't survive," that race is an "impermissible" basis for districting. But that remark drew a sharp rebuke from O'Connor, who declared, "I thought this Court said it was O.K." And in his brief and argument, Everett generally avoided any emphasis on his personal commitment to a "color-blind" Constitution.

A friend of the Court in the cases was not so inhibited. The Pacific Legal Foundation, a libertarian organization favoring limited congressional regulatory power over the states, broad immunity of states from lawsuit, and the protection of private property against federal or state control, filed an amicus curiae brief in behalf of the appellants and their intervenors. In it, Pacific's counsel contended that "racial segregation in redistricting [was] per se" unconstitutional, adding, "there are no codicils or clauses in [the Fifteenth] Amendment with respect to a particular race — it is wholly color-blind and forbids *all* discrimination in voting, not merely discrimination that social engineers anoint as 'invidious.'"

Noting that caste systems in India and elsewhere were often defended on the ground that particular religious groups constituted distinct communities with interests of their own that were not shared by other communities, the foundation saw such arguments as "remarkably similar to the current justification for racial gerrymandering in America" — and both were equally unacceptable. "A caste system might allow racial clans to be organized into a tribal federation, but it can never result in an indivisible nation of independent and free-thinking men and women." Only when seeking to remedy "the present efforts of identified past illegal discrimination by a particular government entity" could a racial classification withstand strict scrutiny. In Pacific's judgment, however, such a rationale could never support race-conscious districting. "Each time a governmental entity redistricts its jurisdiction, the slate is cleaned. The fact that a previous group of legislators invidiously gerrymandered by race after a previous census has absolutely nothing to do with the present redistricting process — either the new plan is race-neutral and must be deferred to, or it segregates individuals by race and must be struck down as unconstitutional. There simply is no grey area in redistricting."

In their brief, counsel for North Carolina argued that the Court should uphold the state's districting plan primarily on three grounds. First, they contended again that the plaintiffs could not show direct and substantial injury to their legal rights and thus lacked standing to contest the districts in court. None of the plaintiffs resided in the First District, and although two (Shaw and Shimm) did live in the Twelfth District, they also lacked standing because the challenged plan provided fair and effective representation for all citizens and did not cause stigmatic or representational harms to any of the plaintiffs. As they had during the trial, for example, they noted that North Carolina's rate of voter drop-off from presidential to congressional election participation was among the lowest in the nation, casting doubt on the appellants' argument that bizarrely shaped districts were confusing to voters and inhibited their interest in the electoral process.

Next, the state defendants maintained that the district court had applied an inappropriate standard in declaring the challenged districts a racial gerrymander and subjecting them to strict review. The district court panel had concluded that strict scrutiny was necessary whenever racial considerations played a "substantial" or "motivating" role in the districting process. But under the Supreme Court's *Miller* ruling, race, the state maintained, had to be the "predominant" consideration in a district's configuration. And evidence presented at the 1994 trial, the defendants argued, had clearly demonstrated that the disputed districts were based not primarily on race but on six race-neutral factors — North Carolina's interests in complying with one person, one vote and with the provisions of the Voting Rights Act, its desire to reflect an urban community of interest in the Twelfth District and a distinct rural community in the First District, incumbency protection, and promotion of the political interests of Democratic candidates.

The ACLU was among organizations filing amicus curiae briefs in behalf of the appellees. Its brief, among other things, disputed the appellants' characterization of the challenged districts as exercises in racial segregation. "The majority-minority congressional districts in the South," the organization's counsel declared, "are in fact the most *racially integrated* districts in the country. They contain substantial numbers of white voters, an average of 45%. . . . Moreover, blacks in the South continue to be represented more often by white than by black members of Congress, 58% versus 42%. . . . No one who has lived through it could ever confuse existing redistricting plans, with their highly integrated districts, with racial segregation under which blacks were not allowed to vote or run for office. Segregation more accurately describes the systems that existed in states such as North Carolina, South Carolina, and Virginia, where all the congressional districts were majority white and no blacks in modern times had ever been elected to Congress prior to the creation of meaningfully integrated districts." Frequently, the brief writer added, voters in majority-minority districts elected white candidates. Contending that such districts actually promoted biracial coalitions and reduced racial bloc voting, the brief cited the experience of an African American congressman in Mississippi who was initially elected in a majority-black district with only 11 percent of the white vote and 52 percent overall, yet won reelection in 1988 with 66 percent of the total ballot.

On December 5, the same day *Shaw* was argued for the second time before the Supreme Court, the justices also heard argument in *Bush v. Vera*, a Texas case in which six voters contended that twenty-four of the thirty congressional districts constituted racial gerrymanders. A three-judge district court had found three of the districts unconstitutional. The justices heard *Vera* first, and when Javier Aguilar of the Texas attorney general's office, only a minute into his argument, referred to his state's majority-minority districts as "opportunity districts," Justice Antonin Scalia, one of the Court's harshest critics of race-conscious policies, promptly interrupted, his voice dripping with sarcasm. "What is this opportunity district?" the justice exclaimed. "We've never used this term. You can call them motherhood and apple pie districts if you want, but that will be insulting my intelligence." Aguilar apologized, promising not to use the offensive term again.

Lawyers for both sides in the North Carolina litigation would receive their share of rough treatment as well. On this occasion, Everett spoke for the plaintiffs. Michael Hess had been scheduled to argue the case for the plaintiff-intervenors, but the RNC counsel had died of AIDS earlier that year, and Tom Farr took his friend's place. "It was an incredible honor for me," Farr would later say. "I worked very hard to get ready for that argument." Farr's law partners were very helpful, especially Jim Dever, who had been editor of the law journal at

Duke and later clerked for the chief judge of the U.S. Court of Appeals for the Ninth Circuit. "I felt I was as prepared to argue something as I ever have been in my life . . . , and I enjoyed the repartee" with the justices. But Farr also recalled a friend's comparison of a lawyer before the Supreme Court with "the dead mouse between the paws of a cat," adding, "I think there was some of that going on while I was arguing."

Eddie Speas argued for the state before the Court, and Paul Bender, deputy U.S. solicitor general, was allotted oral argument time as a friend of the Court in behalf of the state and its intervenors. Also arguing for the intervenors was veteran civil rights lawyer Julius Chambers. The North Carolina Central University chancellor had told a reporter several days earlier that he had worked nights and weekends for the past two months preparing for his appearance before the Court. "The whole question to me is, 'How do we ensure that African-Americans in North Carolina will have an equal access to the electoral process?' And I trust everyone is interested in that happening." Adam Stein — Chambers's former law partner and co-counsel in many civil rights cases, as well as chief counsel for the *Shaw* defendant-intervenors — underscored what he hoped would be the tremendous symbolic impact of Chambers's presence in the case. "Part of our case is to show there remains persistent discrimination in many walks of life, including voting. Nobody knows that history and knows all the cases that have been brought to prevent that discrimination better than Julius Chambers."

Opening for the appellees, Everett was again equipped with a large map of his state's congressional districts. He also sought at the outset, as he put it, "to maintain the honor of North Carolina." He had been present for the oral argument in the Texas case. "There was a question [there]," he told the justices, "about two of the districts in Texas being, I believe, the least compact in the country, and I have here perfect evidence that we have four of the least compact."

Of the *Shaw* plaintiffs, only Ruth Shaw and Melvin Shimm resided in the Twelfth District. Everett and the remaining two plaintiffs were in North Carolina's Second District; none resided in the First District, the other district at issue. Asked about the plaintiffs' standing in the case, the appellants' counsel argued that, due to the "ripple effect" of the redistricting process, all the plaintiffs had standing with respect to all the state's congressional districts. Although reminded that in

United States v. Hays, a 1995 Louisiana redistricting case, the Court had denied standing to litigants who did not live in the district they were challenging, Everett persisted, emphasizing that two of his clients lived in the Twelfth District and that its configuration obviously affected the shape of other districts in North Carolina, including the First District. But certain members of the Court hardly appeared convinced.

At one point, Everett seemed to argue again that majority-minority districts could never survive strict scrutiny, a position the Court had obviously rejected in *Shaw v. Reno*. Perhaps for that reason, Farr began his argument by stressing that the Republican intervenors were not questioning the constitutionality of the Voting Rights Act and were readily conceding that a state's interest in complying with Section 2 of the act might, under certain circumstances, satisfy the compelling interest standard. But Farr insisted that North Carolina could not have created two majority-black districts that satisfied the *Gingles* requirement that such districts be geographically compact. He argued, moreover, that North Carolina had created its two majority-black districts not to comply with Section 2's safeguards against minority vote dilution but purely "to respond to the dictates of the Justice Department." At the very least, he added, districts created to overcome past discrimination in the districting process must be confined to the area where a constitutional violation had been established; a state was not free to establish such districts wherever its officials wished.

Farr would later recall that Justice David Souter asked him more questions than anyone else but "was very respectful." During a lengthy exchange, Souter probed the lawyer about his assertion that a state's interest in protecting the electoral chances of incumbents would never be sufficiently compelling to satisfy strict scrutiny. Citing *Miller*'s holding that majority-black districts constituted a racial gerrymander and were subject to strict review only if race was the predominant factor in their adoption, Souter suggested to Farr that incumbency protection and other traditional, nonracial districting criteria could be used to establish that considerations other than race dominated the districting process and that a particular plan was thus not vulnerable to strict review. The justice readily agreed that incumbency protection was not in itself sufficiently compelling to justify a predominantly racial districting plan. "But it is a relevant consideration, as I under-

stand it, under *Miller*, in determining the extent to which race predominates, because one of the things you ask, the principal question
you ask, I guess, is, has race subordinated traditional districting principles? Now, if one districting principle is incumbency protection, if that
as a matter of historical fact is true, . . . then do you not concede that
the boundary can vary from the compact boundary that could satisfy
Gingles without flunking the narrow tailoring test?" When Farr refused
to yield that point, Souter suggested that the appellant-intervenors'
counsel was really asking for a modification of *Miller*.

But Farr's treatment was mild in comparison with the grilling Speas
received from the bench. The veteran state's attorney began with the
assertion that the Twelfth District constituted an urban district composed of voters with similar interests and that it was tied together by
interstate highways and accessible to both voters and their representatives. For that reason, the district court had concluded that the
Twelfth District, like others in the state, "provided fair and effective
representation for North Carolina citizens."

"That's what a district court is supposed to sit in judgment of," a
justice interrupted, "of whether a particular redistricting scheme provides fair and effective representation? . . . Where do you get this test?
I mean, I don't see it in any of our cases. . . . We just don't sit in the
abstract and decide whether there's fair and effective representation."

Asked what compelling interest the challenged districts served,
Speas gave the by now familiar response that they were designed to
comply with Sections 2 and 5 of the Voting Rights Act. Once it had
been established that majority-minority districts could be drawn for
that purpose, he observed, "principles of federalism and the discretion the States must have in this area give to the States discretion as
to where they will place that district so long as it provides fair and effective representation."

"So then the remedy has nothing to do with the initial violation," a
justice asserted at that point. "That's a very strange doctrine of law."
When the state's attorney attempted to explain that the persistence of
racially polarized voting in the areas where the disputed districts were
located justified their creation, he was promptly reminded that, under
the *Gingles* decision, majority-minority districts also had to be compact
and cohesive. "Is there any evidence that two compact districts, black
majority, not minority majority [including Native as well as African

Americans], but black majority districts could have been created? . . . Could two have been created? Is there testimony and evidence, and I'd like you to cite it to me, because your opponent contends . . . that you could have had a justification for creating one majority black and one majority minority [district], but that there is no justification on the *Gingles* standards, even if you're not going to use the *Gingles* standards in the districts where you apply them, for two black majority districts. . . . Under *Gingles* . . . there have to be two creatable, compact black majority districts."

"Of course, your Honor," Speas replied, "to a large extent, compactness is in the eye of the beholder."

"Can you create two or not?" the justice shot back. "Well, . . . if you don't know, don't bother answering that."

A major theme of the state's defense was the argument that, under *Miller*, majority-minority districts could be subjected to strict scrutiny only if a predominantly racial purpose underlay their creation. Acting without the benefit of *Miller*, the district court had invoked strict review on a finding that race was merely a substantial motivating force in the districting process. If the district court had applied the standard adopted in *Miller* rather than the lenient formula it did apply, the state contended, the trial court majority would have found no basis for subjecting the challenged districts to strict scrutiny.

Toward the end of his argument, Speas was finally given an opportunity to elaborate on that portion of North Carolina's case. Disputing the appellants' assertion to the contrary, he argued that the district court should not have characterized the disputed districts as racial gerrymanders subject to strict review. "The district court did not have the benefit of this Court's decision in *Miller* when it decided this case. It applied a test that's too lenient. It said, the test is whether race was one of several substantial and motivating factors in the redistricting process . . . and [it] found, that race was used in combination with five other [nonracial] factors." He no doubt intended to add that the district court itself had found that race was not the *predominant* consideration behind the creation of the challenged districts, as required for strict scrutiny under *Miller*. By that point, however, Speas had exhausted his allotted time.

Julius Chambers followed the state's attorney to the lectern. Chambers began his case for the defendant-intervenors by emphasizing that *Shaw* was not *Gomillion v. Lightfoot*, the 1960 case rejecting Alabama's attempt to gerrymander all but a few black voters from a municipality, thereby denying them further participation in the community's elections. "Nobody has excluded any citizen of North Carolina from participating in the electoral process. Black and white citizens are, through this legislation, provided for the first time in over 90 years an opportunity to now have a voice . . . in the election of Congresspeople in North Carolina. We have gone through a period in North Carolina where we have purposely discriminated against black people. We've then moved, only through the urging of legislation and this Court, to periods where we have permitted blacks to register and vote. We've moved to the Voting Rights Act. We now for the first time have gotten to a point where black people will have a voice, or an opportunity to have a voice in the election of Congresspeople, and I hope in the Court's review of this case it appreciates that we're operating not in a vacuum, but in a situation where we've had a history of purposely excluding black people. And now we're trying to devise a remedy, and that remedy is one, I submit, this Court has approved where we say it is necessary to have a majority black district in order to give black people an opportunity to have a choice in who represents them in the legislature. Nobody is guaranteeing any black representative. We are only giving people a voice, and we know from the decision in *Gingles* that this Court, and that the Congress in enacting Section 2, felt it imperative that we create districts where people would have a real voice and not a farce."

Much of Chambers's time before the bench, however, was consumed in an exchange with Justice Kennedy over the compactness issue. Challenging the notion that majority-minority districts must always be geographically compact, Chambers maintained that "compactness ought to be viewed in terms of what's meaningful, functional, what works." He also reminded the justices that the *Gingles* decision involved state legislative districts, which were easier to make geographically compact than were congressional districts, covering a much greater population. Chambers read *Gingles*, moreover, as permitting states "to ensure that we bring people together with a community of interest" in the districting process. To Kennedy, however, that smacked of proportional representation. "It seems to me," he added, "proportional representation is the last thing that you should argue for, that it's ultimately very, very dangerous and divisive."

"We're not talking about proportional representation," countered Chambers. "What we're talking about is ensuring . . . , at least for once, . . . a chance to have a voice in the election of your representatives."

During his brief appearance as an amicus curiae in behalf of the defendants and their intervenors, Deputy Solicitor General Paul Bender emphasized that the United States did not take the position that a state had the discretion to place majority-minority districts wherever it wished in order to comply with the Voting Rights Act. Bender further argued that North Carolina had not taken that route in creating the Twelfth District. Instead, two portions of the district — Charlotte and Durham — had substantial black populations that had been victims of the sort of racially polarized voting that triggered vote dilution claims under Section 2. Those populations, moreover, were politically cohesive with other minorities in the state who had been the victims of polarization.

Bender also asserted that the Court, in his judgment, could not force a state to abandon nonracial redistricting principles such as incumbency protection and the erection of urban and rural communities of interest merely because they were not among those the Court considered "historically justified." When a justice interjected that the Court had referred to "traditional" principles because, the justice assumed, "they are less manipulable," the deputy solicitor general agreed but went on to observe, "Tradition is a very good way of showing that they weren't done here for racial reasons, but if you are convinced, as the [district] court was in this case, that [the drawing of districts is] not done for racial reasons, I don't think the fact that this is the first time [state officials] decided that they needed to have an urban district because of urban problems that had recently arisen and they think that it's important for those people to vote together . . . should disqualify them from doing it."

Ruth Shaw had been present for the first Supreme Court oral arguments in *Shaw v. Reno.* "In my wildest dreams," she later said, "I would never have thought that someday I would sit up in the Supreme Court and hear the marshal say, 'Ruth Olson Shaw versus Janet Reno, the Attorney General of the United States.' That's something you don't think about." The case's first visit to the High Court, she recalled, had attracted little attention. "Nobody thought we were very important; no one paid attention. . . . Scalia was quite sarcastic. . . . O'Connor was a little bit hard to peg. I think sometimes they play devil's advocate. . . . [Chief] Justice Rehnquist sometimes seemed to help Robinson a little bit in that he would say, 'Isn't what you mean . . . ?' "

Shaw found the oral arguments in *Shaw v. Hunt*, the case's second visit to the Court, somewhat disconcerting. "I was a bit uncomfortable the second time, because there were people from Durham there from the black community and a few of them were quite aggressive. Some of them were shaking their fists at me. . . . I can understand why they did it, if it made them feel better. . . . [But] I had worked with them politically in Durham, so it was a bit uncomfortable. It took some of the fun away. It brought back the fact that this was a controversial thing."

———

Whatever unpleasantness the experience caused Ruth Shaw, she was no doubt pleased with the Court's decision in *Shaw v. Hunt*. On June 13, 1996, a five-four majority, speaking through the chief justice, handed the plaintiffs another victory. Since none of the plaintiffs resided in North Carolina's First District, the Court dismissed that portion of the suit on the ground that no plaintiff had standing to challenge the First District's constitutionality. But Ruth Shaw and Melvin Shimm lived in the Twelfth District, and Chief Justice William Rehnquist concluded for the majority not only that their district was a racial gerrymander subject to strict scrutiny but also that it was not narrowly tailored to further a compelling state interest.

Rehnquist conceded that the district court had not had the benefit of the racial predominance standard announced in *Miller* when it decided *Shaw II*. He also concluded for the Court, however, that although "it would have been preferable for the [trial] court to have" decided the case according to *Miller*, its findings, "read in the light of the evidence that it had before it, comport with the *Miller* standard." In determining that the challenged district was a racial gerrymander, the lower court had evidence of the Twelfth District's highly irregular and noncompact shape, as well as evidence of the legislature's objective. That evidence, the Court concluded, established the state's predominantly racial purpose. "We do not quarrel," Rehnquist declared, "with the dissent's claims that, in shaping District 12, the State effectuated its interest in creating one rural and one urban district, and that partisan politicking was actively at work in the districting process. That the legislature addressed those interests does not in any way refute the fact that race was the legislature's predominant consideration. Race was the criterion that, in the State's view, could not be compromised; respecting communities of interest and protecting Democratic incumbents came into play only after the race-based decision had been made."

In a dissent, Justice John Paul Stevens argued that states could avoid strict scrutiny if they actually applied nonracial districting principles rather than merely using them as a pretext for race-based line drawing. Rehnquist disagreed. "*Miller* plainly states that although 'compliance with "traditional districting principles such as compactness, contiguity, and respect for political subdivisions" may well suffice to refute a claim of racial gerrymandering,' a State cannot make such a refutation where 'those factors *were subordinated to racial objectives.*'"

Nor did the majority agree that the Twelfth District was narrowly tailored to further compelling governmental interests. Rehnquist acknowledged that a state's interest in remedying the effects of past or current discrimination could justify racial districting under certain circumstances. Drawing on affirmative action decisions, however, he emphasized that such discrimination must be specifically identified, not simply a general assertion, and that a legislature must have a "strong basis in evidence" for making such a determination. The district court had rejected the defendants' contention that the challenged district was actually designed to ameliorate past discrimination. Although several legislators had raised such concerns, they did not command the votes necessary to ensure adoption of the challenged plan solely on that basis. Moreover, although the appellees had relied on two reports by a historian and a social scientist in defending their claim, both reports were dated *after* the plan's adoption. A district court's findings of fact were to be overturned, Rehnquist asserted, only if they were "clearly erroneous." Under that standard, the Court could not reject the trial court's refusal to consider the disputed districts a remedy for past racial discrimination in the electoral process.

The state and its intervenors had defended the districting primarily on the ground that it was necessary to ensure compliance with the Voting Rights Act. But the *Shaw II* majority rejected that argument as well. As in *Miller*, the Court denied the contention that the Twelfth District was necessary to ensure that the state complied with Section 5's preclearance provisions. A state's decision to adhere to other districting principles rather than adopt as many majority-minority districts as possible did not in itself, declared Rehnquist, justify an inference that a districting plan was race-based and unconstitutional. "It appears," he observed, "that the Justice Department was pursuing in North Carolina the same policy of maximizing the number of majority-black districts that it pursued in Georgia [in the *Miller* case]. . . . We again reject the Department's expansive interpretation of [Section] 5."

The appellees had also argued that adoption of the Twelfth District was necessary to protect the state from a vote dilution lawsuit under Section 2 of the Voting Rights Act. The chief justice conceded that plaintiffs could allege a Section 2 violation in a single-member congressional district drawn in such a way as to fragment politically cohesive minority voters among several districts or pack them into one or a few districts, thereby diluting minority voting strength. Citing *Gingles*, however, Rehnquist also emphasized that the minority group in question must be "sufficiently large and geographically compact to constitute a majority in a single-member district," be "politically cohesive," and face a white majority that "votes sufficiently as a bloc to enable it . . . usually to defeat the minority's preferred candidate." Based on the totality of the circumstances required by Section 2, he added, a court must also find that members of the protected racial class had "less opportunity than other members of the electorate to participate in the political process and to elect representatives of their choice."

The majority assumed that efforts to comply with Section 2 would constitute a compelling interest justifying race-based districts. They further assumed that North Carolina's state legislature believed that a second majority-black district was necessary for compliance with Section 2 and had a strong basis in evidence for that conclusion.

Rehnquist disputed the contention, however, that the Twelfth District was narrowly tailored to further that goal. At a minimum, asserted the chief justice, a Section 2 violation required a "geographically compact" minority, and the Twelfth District clearly possessed no such minority population. Rehnquist also dismissed the appellees' argument that once a state had a strong basis for concluding that it was violating Section 2, it could place a majority-minority district wherever it wished, regardless of whether the district satisfied *Gingles*'s compactness requirement, so long as racially polarized voting was present in the area where the district was placed. The remedy must be provided, he asserted, in the area where a Section 2 violation was found. "For example, if a geographically compact, cohesive minority population lives in south-central to southeastern North Carolina, . . . District 12 which spans the Piedmont Crescent would not address that [Section] 2 violation. The black voters of the south-central to southeastern region would still be suffering precisely the same injury that they suffered before District 12 was drawn. District 12 would not address the professed interest of relieving the vote dilution, much less be narrowly tailored to accomplish the goal."

Justices Bryon White and Harry Blackmun, who had dissented in *Shaw v. Reno*, retired from the bench in 1993 and 1994, respectively. But their replacements, Justices Ruth Bader Ginsburg and Stephen Breyer, joined the two other *Shaw I* dissenters, Stevens and Souter, in dissenting from the Court's ruling in *Shaw v. Hunt*. Stevens first faulted the majority for failing to craft a "coherent" standing doctrine "to justify its emerging and misguided race-based districting jurisprudence." In his judgment, the Court was attempting "to impose a particular form of electoral process" rather than provide redress to the victims of racial discrimination. He could understand how the Republican intervenors could claim injury to their personal political interests; after all, North Carolina's districting plan benefited Democrats rather than Republicans. But the courts had dismissed their partisan gerrymandering claim. To Stevens, the claims of the plaintiffs and their intervenors that they were the victims of racial discrimination were harder to accept. "The injury that these plaintiffs have suffered, to the extent that there has been injury at all," asserted the justice, "stems from the integrative rather than the segregative effects of the State's redistricting plan." But that was hardly the sort of injury to which earlier victims of racial discrimination had been subjected. Under the Court's prior decisions, racially motivated laws violated equal protection only when they affected people of different races differently. Yet in *Shaw*, no members of a particular racial group were being treated less favorably than members of other groups or subjected to treatment stamping them "with a badge of inferiority." To the extent the challenged districts conveyed any stigmatic message, it appeared to affect persons of all races equally. Indeed, Stevens was uncertain whether the message conveyed by race-based districting was "a distressing endorsement of racial separation, or an inspiring call to integrate the political process."

In *Hays*, the Louisiana redistricting case, the Court had limited standing to those who lived in a district claimed to be racially gerrymandered or who, while residing elsewhere, were assigned to a district as a direct result of race-based line drawing. Those plaintiffs, the *Hays* majority had concluded, suffered the harms caused by racial districting to a greater degree than did other state residents — "representational" harms, when such districting prompts officeholders to represent only the majority racial group in their districts, and "stigmatic" harms in terms of the racial hostility such districting may provoke. Stevens, however, found such injuries entirely too speculative to support a grant of standing under the Court's precedents.

Stevens then turned to the majority's holding that, under *Miller*, North Carolina's majority-minority districts were predominantly race based and subject to strict scrutiny. Noting that, in reaching the same conclusion, the district court had applied a less rigorous standard than *Miller* required, the justice recommended that the case at least be remanded to the district court for application of the *Miller* formula. But Stevens also agreed with the state and its intervenors that the challenged districts were not vulnerable to strict review under *Miller*. Chief Justice Rehnquist had relied primarily on two factors in concluding that the challenged districts were predominantly race based — the state's admission that its "overriding" purpose was to create two majority-minority districts, and the Twelfth District's highly irregular shape. But Stevens disputed the notion that the state had subordinated other districting principles to race in its congressional district plan. In defending the Court's position, the chief justice had cited the statement of Gerry Cohen, North Carolina's chief mapmaker, that the "principal reason" for the state's plan was creation of "two majority black districts." But in his dissent, Stevens quoted Cohen's full statement, which was that the "principal reason" for the challenged plan was the creation of two districts that not only were majority black but also "had communities of interest within each one."

Questioning the Court's use of the Twelfth District's bizarre shape as evidence of the overriding racial purpose behind its adoption, Stevens offered several perceptive observations. First, he noted that North Carolina's constitution, unlike the law of many states, does not require electoral boundaries to be geographically compact; the state's creation of a noncompact district was thus hardly a departure from one of its traditional districting principles. The state's failure to draw a compact district in its south-central to southeastern region, as the Justice Department had suggested, was further evidence, in the justice's judgment, that factors other than race drove the districting process. Had race been the predominant motivation, surely North Carolina simply would have adopted the attorney general's recommendation. But that would not have served the Democratic General Assembly's nonracial interests in protecting Democratic incumbents and creating distinct urban and rural communities of interest in separate districts.

Even on the assumption that the challenged plan was predominantly racial, Stevens thought that it easily satisfied the strictures of the compelling interest test. For one thing, the state's "sorry history of race relations . . . surely provide[d]," in his judgment, "an adequate basis for a decision to facilitate the election of representatives of the previously disadvantaged minority." For another, there was North Carolina's desire to avoid the litigation necessary to overcome the attorney general's objection to the initial plan with a single majority-minority district. "It is entirely proper for a State whose past practices have subjected it to the pre-clearance obligation . . . to presume that the Attorney General's construction of the Act is correct" and to adopt a second district rather than launch a court battle.

Even if a desire to avoid litigation was not in itself an adequate justification for the creation of majority-minority districts, added Stevens, the state clearly had an interest in complying with a finding of the attorney general that it reasonably believed could not be successfully challenged in court. Nor was *Miller* an obstacle to such a conclusion on North Carolina's part. Whereas Georgia had simply acquiesced in the attorney general's application of Section 5 of the Voting Rights Act in the *Miller* case, the *Shaw* district court had found that the North Carolina legislature made its own independent assessment, reasonably concluding that a plan with only one majority-minority district would violate Section 5.

Stevens readily agreed that the state had cited nondiscriminatory reasons for initially resisting the creation of a second majority-black district. But the General Assembly had later concluded that such arguments would not satisfy a court, and the trial court had found that judgment reasonable. "I am mystified," declared the justice, "as to why this finding does not deserve our acceptance."

Finally, Stevens maintained that the state had a substantial interest in avoiding the expense and unpleasantness of a Section 2 vote dilution challenge to its original single majority-minority district plan. In his judgment, the legislature clearly had a reasonable basis for fearing that it would lose such a suit. During the redistricting debate in the General Assembly, many districting maps had been presented with African Americans constituting over 50 percent of the population in two districts, and the attorney general had originally denied preclearance on the ground that two geographically compact majority-minority districts (albeit only one majority-black district) could be drawn. Even though many of the maps did not propose especially compact districts, the legislature had reasonably concluded, wrote Stevens, that a federal court might have found some of those unadopted plans enough of a basis for a viable vote dilution suit under the *Gingles* decision. The plaintiffs had won *Gingles*, after all, even though the district they proposed as an alternative to the state's plan was, in the district court's view, "not a model of aesthetic tidiness."

The justice scored as well the majority's conclusion that, even if the state had a compelling interest in avoiding a Section 2 suit, the disputed Twelfth District was not narrowly tailored to further that goal, since it was not placed in an area vulnerable to minority vote dilution claims. To Stevens, the fact that the district was not in an area where a Section 2 vote dilution violation had been established meant only that a federal court could not *require* the state to draw the Twelfth

District in the location the state's legislature had chosen. In its own districting decisions, he declared, a state should have greater discretion than a federal court.

"The Court today," Stevens concluded, "rejects North Carolina's plan because it does not provide the precise remedy that might have been ordered by a federal court, even though it satisfies potential [Section 2] plaintiffs, furthers such race-neutral legislative ends as incumbency protection and the preservation of distinct communities of interest, and essentially serves to insulate the State from a successful [Section 2] statutory challenge. There is no small irony in the fact that the Court's decision to intrude into the State's districting process comes in response to a lawsuit brought on behalf of white voters who have suffered no history of exclusion from North Carolina's political process, and whose only claims of harm are at best rooted in speculative and stereotypical assumptions about the kind of representation they are likely to receive from the candidates that their neighbors have chosen."

In a lengthy dissent for *Bush v. Vera*, the Texas majority-minority districting case decided the same day as *Shaw II*, Justice Souter, joined by Ginsburg and Breyer, registered his objections to the Court's stance in both cases. As he had elsewhere, Souter, like Stevens and others, bemoaned the Court's failure to establish a coherent standard of injury required of plaintiffs in such cases. "If, indeed," he observed, "what *Shaw I* calls harm is identifiable at all in a practical sense, it would seem to play no favorites, but to fall on every citizen and every representative alike." To the extent that racial considerations in districting merely reinforced impressions of racial distinctiveness or the perception that elected officials would represent only the interests of the dominant racial group, such "expressive harms" bore, in Souter's judgment, "virtually no resemblance" to gerrymandering claims accepted in earlier cases — "those involving districting decisions that removed an identifiable class of disfavored voters from effective political participation." Far from constituting "political apartheid," majority-minority districting, declared the justice, neither implied the inferiority of any race nor segregated voters by race. Instead, *Shaw I* had simply "vindicated the complaint of a white voter who objected not to segregation but to the particular racial proportions of the district. . . . Whatever this district may have symbolized, it was not 'apartheid.'"

Souter also took issue with what he considered a related "conceptual inadequacy" in *Shaw I*. It defined the injury suffered by residents of majority-minority districts as reinforcement of the view that members of a racial group will prefer the same candidates at the polls. But the very purpose of the constitutional prohibition against minority vote dilution, Souter insisted, was to allow voters "to make just such a preference effective. . . . If there were no correlation between race and candidate preference, it would make no sense to say that minority voters had less opportunity than others to elect whom they would; they would be part of the mainstream and the winners would be their choices. When voting is thus racially polarized, it is just because of this polarization that majority-minority districts provide the only practical means of avoiding dilution or remedying the dilution injury that has occurred already. *Shaw I* has thus placed those who choose to avoid the long-recognized constitutional harm of vote dilution at risk by casting doubt on the legitimacy of its classic remedy; creation of a majority-minority district 'reinforces' the notion that there is a correlation between race and voting, for that correlation is the very condition on which the success of the court-ordered remedy depends. So it is that the Court's definition of injury is so broad as to cover constitutionally necessary efforts to prevent or remedy a violation of the Fourteenth and Fifteenth Amendments and of [Section] 2 of the Voting Rights Act."

The justice reserved his most pointed observations, however, for the *Miller* Court's finding that majority-minority districts with a "predominantly racial" purpose were subject to strict scrutiny, the standard applied in *Shaw II* and *Bush v. Vera*. Districting decisions, he reasoned, were by nature highly complex, embodying a large variety of considerations and trade-offs. The predominant motive underlying a legislative decision in such a mix was, in Souter's judgment, illusory. In addition, many traditional, racially neutral districting principles could be applied only through consideration of race, especially since race clearly bears a close relationship to other socioeconomic and political factors. Consideration of a population's ethnic composition had long been accepted as an integral and appropriate part of the districting process, he added, and Souter saw little difference between that and the creation of majority-minority districts. "If . . . a legislature may draw district lines to preserve the integrity of a given community, leaving it intact so that all of its members are served by one representative, this objective is inseparable from preserving the community's racial identity when the community is characterized, or even self-defined, by the race of the majority of those who live there. This is an old truth, having been recognized every time the political process produced an Irish or Italian or Polish ward." In Souter's judgment, the traditional interest in protecting incumbents in a racially mixed region was equally intertwined with racial considerations. "Thus," he asserted, "it is as impossible in theory as in practice to untangle racial consideration[s] from the application of traditional districting principles in a society plagued by racial bloc-voting with a racial minority population of political significance, or at least the unrealized potential for achieving it."

The result of the Court's failure to establish a coherent concept of standing or to delineate a means for distinguishing a "predominant" racial objective from the application of traditional, nonracial districting principles, concluded Souter, was arbitrariness. "It is impossible to distinguish what is valid from what is not, or to decide how far members of racial minorities may engage 'in the same sort of pluralist electoral politics that every other bloc of voters enjoys.'" The Court's approach, the justice feared, also undermined the incentive for states with substantial minority populations to attempt to avoid further vote dilution. A state that drew majority-minority districts now risked a *Shaw* suit and a possible court order that it pay attorneys' fees to prevailing plaintiffs; those that did not faced preclearance objections from the Justice Department and Section 2 vote dilution suits. "The States, in short, have been told to get things just right, no dilution and no predominant consideration of race short of dilution, without being told how to do it." The consequence of such a vague standard, declared Souter, was "stalemate, [with] neither the moral force of the Constitution nor the mercenary threat of liability operat[ing] effectively" to produce efforts against continued dilution of minority voter influence.

Justice O'Connor not only spoke for a plurality of justices in *Bush v. Vera* but, in a rare move, also filed a separate concurrence in which she concluded, among other things, that a state's attempts to avoid a Section 2 vote dilution suit constituted a compelling governmental interest that justified majority-minority districts. Combined with that of the four dissenters, her opinion provided a majority for that proposition. In Souter's judgment, this development helped mitigate *Shaw's* "underlying incoherence" somewhat. By limiting a state's use of racial data in creating districts that claimed to serve traditional, nonracial districting principles, he added, the Court was perhaps providing "useful guidance" to legislatures. Even so, a state could never be certain that its use of race in districting to protect a minority incumbent of a particular party would not be held by a court to be "predominantly" racial, rather than partisan, in purpose.

Given the difficulties inherent in their enforcement, Souter favored abandonment of *Shaw* and *Miller*. Of the Court's members, only Justices Antonin Scalia and Clarence Thomas were on record as considering every intentionally created majority-minority district a forbidden racial gerrymander. "A radical transformation of the political selection process in the name of color-blindness [was thus] out of the question." Even confining *Shaw* to cases involving districts with extremely bizarre shapes would not eliminate its intrinsic conceptual and practical weaknesses. The Court, therefore, "should allow for some faith in the political process." After all, Souter reasoned, legislatures in the past had successfully given weight to ethnicity in the districting process, thereby permitting "ethnically identified voters and their preferred candidates to enter the mainstream of American politics." Rather than create a regime of ethnic apartheid and political conflict, such efforts had exerted a moderating influence on ethnic politics and increased the levels of political participation among such groups. "[The] possibility that racial politics, too, may grow wiser so long as minority votes are rescued from submergence," the justice concluded, "should be considered in determining how far the Fourteenth and Fifteenth Amendments require us to devise constitutional common law to supplant the democratic process with litigation. It counsels against the profession that *Shaw* has yet evolved into a manageable constitutional standard."

CHAPTER 7

Forum Shopping

With his victory in *Shaw v. Hunt*, Robinson Everett was now two for two in the Supreme Court. But attorneys for the defendants and defendant-intervenors attributed their opponents' success largely to Tom Farr and the Republican intervenors in *Shaw II*. The GOP had provided much of the financing for expert witnesses and other expenses connected with the litigation, and its willingness to accept race-conscious districting under certain circumstances was obviously more palatable to a majority of the justices than was Everett's tenacious advocacy of completely color-blind line drawing. By not taking the extreme position that Everett obviously preferred, Adam Stein later said, "I think that Tom Farr made the winning argument in the Supreme Court. . . . If the Republicans hadn't intervened, we might have won, because [Farr] . . . had the support of a large law firm and their legal staff, and so on, to really put the whole thing together. And, ultimately, . . . I think his oral argument was kind of the capstone to that, that made it just much more likely that they would have won."

Some thought that Everett's lack of litigation experience had been a detriment to his effectiveness as well. "I don't think Robinson has the kind of litigation experience that Tom Farr has," Tiare Smiley said. "Robinson has done a lot of things, but he's not really a litigator." Several of Everett's courtroom adversaries readily acknowledged, though, his contributions to the plaintiffs' success. "A lot of people," Stein said, "have underestimated Robinson Everett, his canniness and skill, because his style is sort of old-fashioned. I think that's true of people in the attorney general's office, the . . . civil rights side of the voting rights bar, and other people. I think I'm one of the few who think people on our side of the issue have underestimated his [talents] and his ability to figure out how to move the case his way." Everett's style before the Supreme Court, Stein added, "appeared somewhat scattered, sort of barely pulling things together. . . . He did have an edge going into the Supreme Court, and he had a district that the world had made fun of. . . . And he made sure that picture [of the challenged districts] was sitting up there. And that's what he had a hold of, . . . a Court, a majority of which had a strong aversion to any sort of affirmative action. . . . Although he didn't marshal [his arguments] as civil rights lawyers that I've dealt with on this case might think you might, he did it plenty good for his purposes."

Eddie Speas substantially agreed. "Robinson is not the most graceful courtroom trial litigator around. But he is a distinguished, thoughtful fellow. One of the lawyers said at one point, 'You know, Robinson is not the best trial lawyer, and Robinson is not the best appellate lawyer. But the force is with him.' . . . That's very accurate. Robinson in his complaint had captured an idea whose time had come." But Speas was less taken with his opponent's "good old boy [courtroom] image"; he found it "a little bit hard for a Duke law professor to carry that off."

Whatever their impressions of his skill as a litigator, no one doubted Everett's tenacity. The North Carolina house of representatives now had a narrow GOP majority, and the Democrats retained control of the state senate. A few days after the Supreme Court's *Shaw II* ruling, Everett and the other plaintiffs petitioned party leaders in each chamber to promptly enact a constitutionally valid redistricting plan. "Since neither party controls both houses of the General Assembly," Everett reasoned, "neither party will be able to obtain enactment of a redistricting plan that is unfair to the other party. The balance of power helps assure that a plan can be generated, and such a balance may not exist after the 1996 election." The state party primaries had already been conducted, but since the legislature had adopted the 1992 districting scheme in five weeks, Everett argued that a plan could be adopted and new primaries held in time for the fall election.

Leaders in neither party seemed interested in drafting a new plan immediately, however. Although he met with a number of legislators, Everett failed to gain an audience with house speaker Harold Brubaker, a Randolph County Republican, or Democratic senate president pro tem Marc Basnight of Dare County. The General Assembly adjourned June 21 without taking any action on redistricting.

Since the legislature had also left Raleigh without adopting a final budget, Governor Jim Hunt quickly announced that he was calling a special budgetary session. In a July 2 letter, Everett urged the governor to have the legislature also consider redistricting during the special session. The *Charlotte Observer* had recently carried an article about what Everett termed a "color-blind" and "party-blind" districting plan that had been drawn in only two hours with a General Assembly computer — a plan that left Mel Watt and Sue Myrick, a Charlotte area GOP incumbent, the only members of the state's congressional delegation residing in the same district. "In our petition to the General Assembly," Everett observed, "we stated that a good-faith effort to apply traditional race-neutral districting principles could quickly produce a fair and lawful redistricting plan. The *Charlotte Observer* now has proved this point."

The response from the governor was no more helpful than that from legislative leaders. "It's a very contentious issue," Hunt told reporters, "and I just don't think there's time. We'll do, obviously, what the courts tell us to do. If they want to order new districts and put off the election, then we'll do that." State election board director Gary Bartlett contended that a new series of congressional elections would require at least seventy-one days — fifty days if the legislature dispensed with North Carolina's requirement of a runoff in any primary in which the front-runner failed to win at least 40 percent of the vote. And while speaker Brubaker indicated on the eve of the legislature's special session that a house committee would begin considering new redistricting plans, his goal was adoption of a plan for the 1998 elections rather than 1996.

By that point, however, Everett had already asked the district court to require the state to adopt a new redistricting plan and reschedule the primary contests, barring from office any member of Congress elected in 1996 under the discredited 1992 plan. "Our argument," he told reporters, "is that if [the 1992 plan] is unconstitutional, two elections (in 1992 and 1994) [under it] is two too many. You certainly wouldn't want to go for three."

The three-judge district court panel scheduled a hearing on Everett's motion for late July. In an apparent effort to generate public (and thus legislative) sympathy for prompt redistricting, another lawyer for the

Shaw plaintiffs wrote an op-ed piece for the July 14 issue of the *Greensboro News Record*. Concord attorney Martin McGee, who had assisted Everett in drafting the Supreme Court briefs for *Shaw v. Hunt*, countered arguments against quick action by the General Assembly. Since the legislature was already back in session and many redistricting proposals were already on the table, McGee saw no reason why legislators could not act promptly. He conceded the hardships that a new round of primaries would create for candidates but insisted that "redistricting now outweighs the folly of proceeding with an unconstitutional plan." If the General Assembly did not act, the district court might well impose its own redistricting plan, he asserted, quoting the following passage from Justice White's opinion in *Wise v. Lipscomb* (1978): "Legislative bodies should not leave their reapportionment tasks to the federal courts; but when those with legislative responsibilities do not respond, or the imminence of a state election makes it impractical for them to do so, it becomes the 'unwelcome obligation' . . . of the federal court to devise and impose a reapportionment plan pending later legislative action." Even if the district court did not take action, McGee warned, the Supreme Court could reverse the trial court and order new elections.

As the court hearing approached, the General Assembly seemed unlikely to follow McGee's advice. Republican Richard Morgan of Pinehurst, a house committee chairman, unveiled a plan similar to the one the Justice Department had suggested in 1991. At a public hearing on that proposal, however, the acting president of the state NAACP termed it "an insult to the African-American leadership in the House and Senate," who had played no role in the plan's development. Critics also noted that although the two proposed majority-minority districts included a majority of minority residents, each contained more whites than blacks of voting age. Leaders in the state's Democrat-controlled senate made it clear, moreover, that they favored a delay in redistricting until the 1998 elections. Even Everett, though praising Morgan's efforts to accomplish redistricting immediately, indicated that he did not favor the Republican plan and would be submitting several proposals of his own (including the plan drawn by the *Charlotte Observer* and a 1992 proposal of the state League of Women Voters) to the three-judge panel. And on the eve of the hearing, the *Greensboro News Record*, which had carried McGee's call for prompt redistricting, editorialized that any "attempt to redistrict now would create chaos" in the election process. Reasoning that "it's doubtful . . . , given its partisan nature, any legislature can do a good job of drawing congressional or legislative districts," the paper joined others in recommending the creation of an independent redistricting commission.

On July 29, Judges Phillips, Britt, and Voorhees convened once again to hear the *Shaw* litigants' counsel. Assuring the panel of the relative ease with which a new, constitutional plan could be adopted and special elections held, Everett urged the court "to make sure that something is done for the 1996 elections," adding that "otherwise the systematic injury will be perpetuated all the way as a practical matter to 1999."

For the Republican intervenors, Tom Farr declared that "politicians, regardless of the party or color, regardless of the creed, will trample on whoever and whatever when it suits their political interest to do so, and I think everyone in the room will agree to that proposition. . . . Please do not give politicians another victory over the United States Constitution and the voters of this state."

"I must disassociate myself [from that] statement," Judge Britt shot back. "I think you probably allowed yourself to get a little too strong. Certainly politicians are well known for protecting their turf and their interest in how to get things through the General Assembly, particularly in legislative reapportionment, and the Supreme Court has recognized that as a valid reason for actions, but I cast my dissent on the tone [of Farr's remarks]."

Speaking for North Carolina, Eddie Speas stressed the legislature's interest in attempting to adopt a new plan rather than "default" to the court, but he also argued that no redistricting scheme should be adopted in haste. "The state has learned painfully, first from *Gingles* and now from *Shaw* of the consequences of developing a flawed plan, so we believe that care should be exercised here so that the citizens of our state may have a plan that is constitutional that they may use for many years to come." Speas conceded that *Shaw* involved the integrity of North Carolina's elections. He asserted, however, that "we can't begin the election process until there is a plan in place, until there has been an adequate time to adopt a plan, to have it precleared [by the Justice Department] and have it approved by this Court."

"Well," Judge Voorhees interrupted at one point, "the mandate of this Court is to develop a remedy and proceed in conformity with the Supreme Court's opinion. Isn't any delay of the election at odds with that mandate?" Speas responded by citing the Supreme Court's opinion in *Reynolds v. Sims* (1964), a leading reapportionment case, upholding the proposition that electoral relief can be deferred when necessary to prevent "substantial interruption of the elections process."

Judge Phillips then asked the state's attorney what considerations should drive any deadline the court might impose on the legislature for adopting a plan for the next election. Speas gave a general reply, but when Adam Stein rose to speak for the defendant-intervenors, he referred the court to an affidavit filed by Roy Cooper of Rocky Mount, a state senator recently chosen to head that chamber's redistricting committee. In his affidavit, Cooper suggested April 1, 1997, as a deadline within which the General Assembly could act while providing ample time for court challenges before the 1998 election cycle.

Stein devoted his remaining time to citing a variety of problems that court-ordered redistricting for the 1996 election would entail. As one who had cast his first ballot while serving with the military in Germany, he cautioned against curtailment of the time allotted for absentee balloting, particularly for citizens stationed abroad. A truncated process, he argued, would also severely restrict the time needed for the electorate to become familiar with candidates, and candidates with their constituents. He warned, too, of findings related to "voter fatigue," the falloff in voter turnout that abrupt changes in an election schedule might cause. Delay in the November general election date, he added, might adversely affect North Carolina's congressional delegation in terms of committee assignments, participation in the selection of congressional leaders, and the like. Anita Hodgkiss continued Stein's theme, focusing especially on the disproportionately low turnout among African American and poor voters in special elections.

———

The day after the hearing, the panel, by a two-to-one vote split along the same partisan lines as previously, refused to order a special election and instead gave the General Assembly until April 1, 1997, to draw a new map for the 1998 elections. "In order to avoid disruption of ongoing state electoral processes," the majority concluded in a three-page order, "the 1996 primary elections already held for congressional offices are hereby validated. The 1996 election for those offices may proceed as scheduled under state law to elect members of Congress under the existing redistricting plan."

Incumbents Eva Clayton and Mel Watt were elated at the outcome. "The citizens of North Carolina," Watt said, "deserve to have the districts redrawn in a thoughtful and deliberative manner, and not in a crisis-like atmosphere." Senator Roy Cooper indicated that his committee would continue working on a plan after the General Assembly adopted a state budget and adjourned, but he predicted that no plan would be adopted until the legislature's 1997 session, beginning in January. Republican house speaker Harold Brubaker, who previously seemed uninterested in adopting a plan for the 1996 elections, now emphasized that his party had not been in the majority in either chamber when the unconstitutional 1992 plan was adopted. "All along, we have stood ready and willing to correct this problem. We are disappointed that the lower court has decided to relegate the citizens of North Carolina to another two years of unconstitutional representation." But house majority leader Leo Daughtry may have captured the prevailing sentiment on both sides of the legislative aisle. "Everybody here is interested in going home," he said. "Most of us have work to do. For most of us, staying up here is no fun."

When questioned by reporters after the ruling, Everett initially appeared somewhat uncertain whether to appeal to the Supreme Court on the call for special elections, which the Court typically refused to grant. "We don't want to push our luck too hard. If there is a way to appeal and to get some ruling in the near future, I believe we will do so. We don't want to do anything counterproductive for the citizens of the state." On August 9, however, he filed an appeal. Terming the existing districts "dysfunctional," he charged that they tended "to induce — rather than reduce — 'balkanization' and racial animosity." Any disruption that election-year redistricting might cause, he added, would be less harmful to the state than holding another election under the districting plan the High Court had struck down. A three-judge district court in the *Bush* case from Texas, he reminded the justices, had recently redrawn thirteen of that state's thirty congressional districts and voided the results of primaries held in the unconstitutional districts. "At issue," he concluded, "is not only the voters' confidence in the integrity of the electoral process but also their confidence in the integrity of the judicial process."

Without comment, the Supreme Court on August 21 let stand the district court's ruling. Pleased with that decision, North Carolina attorney general Mike Easley expressed relief that the ruling "gives the people's elected representatives enough time to get the districts drawn correctly." He added, "We did not want the federal courts drawing our state districts unless absolutely necessary." Everett's secretary Dorothy Bullock, another of the *Shaw* plaintiffs, attempted to minimize the decision's importance to the overall progress of the litigation. "We won the war," she remarked, "but lost this little skirmish. We worked really hard on this for four years and had hoped we could have new districts for the next election, but we can live with it."

The General Assembly complied with the district court's mandate that redistricting be completed by April 1, 1997. But given the divided party control of its chambers, with a Democratic majority in the senate and a house controlled by the GOP, the task was a delicate process. Senator Roy Cooper chaired the senate redistricting committee; W. Edwin McMahan, a Charlotte Republican, headed the redistricting committee in the house of representatives.

A native of Nash County in eastern North Carolina and a partner in a Rocky Mount law firm, Cooper had won election to the house in 1986 and had been a member of the state senate since 1991. A political moderate who was generally popular among legislators of both parties, he became senate majority leader in 1997 and would win election as North Carolina's attorney general in 2000. Originally from Asheville, Ed McMahan had worked in insurance and banking until 1974, when he became a partner in a Charlotte architectural, development, and engineering firm. When David Balmer, the Charlotte Republican whose plan was used to design the Twelfth District in 1992, left the house to run for Congress (unsuccessfully), McMahan won election to Balmer's seat. In late 1996, speaker Harold Brubaker asked him to chair the house's redistricting committee. "To be very honest about it," he later said, "I didn't really know very much about what I was getting into. [But the speaker] felt . . . that even though I was new to the legislature and only in my second term, that having been in business for thirty years, [with] hopefully a skill in negotiating, that I probably would get along well with members" of both parties in both legislative chambers.

Neither legislator was particularly partisan. Early in his career, Cooper had joined with certain other eastern North Carolina Democrats and legislative Republicans to replace a powerful veteran Democratic speaker with another Democrat more to their liking. And though Cooper later regretted that decision, he enjoyed close ties with members of both parties. McMahan's parents belonged to different parties; his grandfather on his mother's side, he remembered, "would always give me a dime to say I was a Democrat," while his father's family were staunch Republicans. Although a registered Republican, McMahan considered intense partisanship an unfortunate element of politics. On occasion, he had supported Democratic candidates in local races.

Although each chamber had its own redistricting committee, Cooper and McMahan worked closely from the outset. "I don't think Roy ever thought we could get a plan approved on the house side," McMahan later recalled. "He was very, very leery of us ever being able to get a plan approved, to the extent of wanting us to bring it to the house first and vote on it in the house side before he would do it in the senate. . . . [And] we certainly did get down to having some [contentious] moments toward the end of the [process]." But Cooper "was willing to be flexible, and I was willing to be flexible. And I think the best thing we did was to sit down in three or four early meetings and try to make a list of what we thought were the most important things each side needed. And each time we would negotiate, we would go back to what our [original] goals were."

Senator Cooper was adamant from the beginning that creation of a second majority-minority district in the south-central and southeastern portion of the state, which legislative Republicans initially favored, was entirely unacceptable to senate Democrats. The two readily agreed, however, that their primary objective was to maintain the partisan status quo in the congressional delegation. The 1996 elections had resulted in a six-six partisan split in the delegation, and McMahan later said, "without any hesitation," that maintaining that balance was their primary goal. Given the Justice Department preclearance process, of course, "race was one of the factors" in the 1997 redistricting, "but not the predominant factor, as far as I'm concerned."

In late February, Cooper unveiled a senate redistricting plan under which, he told reporters, "all twelve incumbents could have an excellent chance of winning." McMahan announced that the house hoped to produce similar plans soon, possibly including one with a minority district in south-central and southeastern North Carolina. Noting that such an arrangement would hurt the reelection chances of both Mel Watt and another Democratic incumbent, Cooper countered, "we'd have grave concern about that option." A political consultant to Third District GOP congressman Walter Jones complained that the proposed shape of Jones's district under the senate proposal would hurt Jones and enhance the congressional aspirations of senate president pro tem Marc Basnight. But Basnight promptly denied any interest in a congressional bid. "I wouldn't have it if you gave it to me on a plate. I'll never run for Congress. I don't want it. I don't want to go there, except maybe to the zoo, or to the Jefferson Memorial."

Under the 1992 districting plan, forty-six counties were split between two districts, and six among three districts. The senate proposal split only twenty-four counties, and none among three districts. Only about a dozen precincts were to be divided, compared with several dozen under the 1992 scheme. But Everett was not impressed. "The Twelfth District still looks very strange to me," he observed. "The highest compliment I can pay [the new plan] is that it is less bizarre" than the current one.

The plan produced by the GOP-controlled house was very similar to the senate proposal, and in late March, following various modifications, both chambers approved a plan. The scheme adopted contained five solidly Democratic districts and one leaning toward the Democrats, as well as five strong Republican districts and one GOP-leaning district. Eva Clayton's First District retained a slim majority of black residents, but only 45 percent of registered voters were African American. The minority population in the new Twelfth District was 46.6 percent, contrasted with 56.6 percent under the 1992 plan. Previously 160 miles long, it now stretched 105 miles from Greensboro to Charlotte, wider and shorter than its predecessor.

In June, the Justice Department notified state officials that the new redistricting plan had survived the preclearance process, and on September 15, a unanimous district court upheld the plan as well. Since none of the *Shaw* plaintiffs lived in the redrawn Twelfth District, Everett told reporters that it would be "fruitless" to continue with that suit. But he was "pretty confident," he added, that "somebody will pursue it further. I've heard indications that people are upset by it. . . . I'm certainly going to help anybody who had standing to attack it."

Everett's remarks were hardly idle speculation. After the Supreme Court in *Shaw v. Hunt* dismissed the challenge to the First District on the ground that none of the *Shaw* plaintiffs resided there, Martin Cromartie, a resident of the district, intervened as a plaintiff for further proceedings in *Shaw*. A native of Robeson County, Cromartie had moved to Tarboro as a young child. Following college and law school at Duke and Chapel Hill, he practiced law in Tarboro for many years. A chronic illness forced his retirement in the early 1990s, and in recent years, he had been in and out of a variety of hospitals. He now spent most of his time in a Washington, D.C., assisted-care facility for military veterans. Cromartie had first met Everett and his cousin Ned at Duke, and the three had been friends since that time. Although a racial liberal who regularly voted for Eva Clayton, he shared Everett's distaste for majority-minority districting. When his friend first filed the *Shaw* suit, Cromartie had made a small financial contribution to the effort. He now eagerly agreed to Everett's request that he intervene in *Shaw*.

But Cromartie not only intervened in the *Shaw* case after the Supreme Court's 1996 ruling. With Everett as counsel, he and other First District residents also filed a separate lawsuit, *Cromartie v. Hunt*, in the neighboring Pitt County court of U.S. District Court Judge Malcolm Howard, a Reagan appointee and one-time member of President Richard Nixon's Watergate defense team. But the suit was eventually expanded to include plaintiffs from the Twelfth District as well, becoming, like *Shaw*, a statewide challenge to majority-minority districting before a three-judge district court.

In a July 9, 1996, letter to Clayton, the new plaintiff emphasized that his suit was aimed at her district, "but not at you. I hope you believe me when I say that we support you now, and intend to support you in the days and years ahead." He had filed his case, he wrote, because he believed that districting should be "color-blind." He supported *Shaw v. Reno* for the same reason. While the congresswoman might not agree with him "about the way we get there," he added, "I think we can agree that the final battle in the long fight for racial equality will not be won in court or legislature — but will be finally won only . . . in the 'hearts and minds of men [and women].'"

The *Shaw* three-judge panel of two Democrats and one Republican had twice ruled against Everett and his co-counsel. Lawyers in the North Carolina attorney general's office immediately suspected, therefore, that the new *Cromartie* suit, filed by an Everett friend of long standing, was simply a forum-shopping ploy — an attempt to transfer the majority-minority districting dispute to a new district court panel with a possibly more favorable disposition toward the plaintiffs' claims.

Under the doctrine of claim preclusion, litigants can sometimes be prevented from bringing a new suit to relitigate claims previously tried before a different court. Such arguments are rarely successful, nor would they be in the *Cromartie* case. But the state would repeatedly raise the issue during the course of the litigation. While taking a deposition from Martin Cromartie, for example, Norma Harrell, a member of the attorney general's staff, probed him at length about the origins of his suit. "Was there any reason," asked Harrell, "why you preferred to pursue your claims against the 1st District in this second action in which you were the lead plaintiff, . . . rather than continuing through the *Shaw* action, which had been in existence? . . . Did you ever consider that you might not want to have the issues decided by the court that . . . decided in the *Shaw* case?"

"In a way," Cromartie answered, "but I knew that wasn't anything I could do anything about and that was all up to Robinson [Everett]."

"And did you consider that judges that you believed to be of a particular political background or affiliated with the Republican Party versus the Democratic Party would be more likely to be a more favorable forum for you?"

"Sure; but again, I . . . knew I had no influence over that."

"And did you have any view that you would prefer to have the case ultimately decided by a court or a group of judges different from the *Shaw* judges?"

"I don't think that I thought about it in that cohesive a fashion."

"And so you don't recall whether you had that in mind . . . or whether it was talked about or something you thought about when you and the other *Shaw* plaintiffs through your attorneys asked the court, the *Shaw* court, not to rule on the 1997 plan?"

"No I didn't; . . . no."

"You just relied on Robinson Everett, the plaintiff[s'] counsel?"

"Correct."

Everett would later dispute the contention that he had encouraged Cromartie to file a separate suit in a bid to secure a more favorable three-judge panel for continuing his challenge to majority-minority districting, or that he had attempted to persuade the *Shaw* panel not to rule on the 1997 plan. But counsel for the state seemed convinced that that was the sole purpose for the *Cromartie* suit. "It was their counsel's plan," Tiare Smiley later declared. "He had lost to [the *Shaw* panel] two-one twice. He did not want to be in front of that panel [again]. I don't know what Robbie says personally. I'm sure he denies it. The Fourth Circuit [chief judge] appoints the panel, so you're not assured necessarily of anything . . . but certainly there was an opportunity for a different panel. . . . This kind of maneuvering does not make the federal courts look good to the public."

––––––

Whatever the truth regarding the forum-shopping charge, the *Cromartie* suit did go forward, and the three-judge panel selected to hear the case was composed of two Republicans and one Democrat. Judge Voorhees, consistently the lone dissenter on the *Shaw* panel, was joined on the *Cromartie* court by Fourth Circuit Court of Appeals Judge Sam J. Ervin III, a Democrat and son of the late North Carolina senator, and U.S. District Court Judge Terrence Boyle. A New Jersey native and former member of Senator Jesse Helms's staff, Boyle was a 1984 Reagan appointee well known for his opposition to race-conscious districting. Earlier, Durham whites had filed a suit challenging county school board districts as racially gerrymandered. While Earl Britt, the judge assigned the case, was out of the country, Judge Boyle took over, threatening to halt elections under the board districting plan and failing to inform county or state attorneys that he had taken charge of the case. When Judge Britt returned to Raleigh, he resumed control of the case.

On March 31, 1998, the new panel convened in Morganton, Judge Ervin's home, for a two-hour hearing on Everett's motion that the judges rule summarily in his clients' favor or grant a preliminary injunction postponing that year's congressional elections until a full hearing could be held on his challenge to the 1997 districting plan. The Morganton proceedings took place eight weeks after the filing period had opened for candidates, two weeks after primary absentee balloting had begun, and five weeks before the May primary, in which parties would pick their nominees for the fall general election. Everett wanted the elections delayed until a valid districting plan had been adopted.

Litigants can win on a motion for summary judgment only if a trial court is convinced that there is no genuine issue of fact in the case and that those moving for summary judgment are entitled to a ruling in their favor simply as a matter of law. Since the Supreme Court had held in *Miller* and *Shaw II* that majority-minority districting plans were unconstitutional only if they had a predominantly racial purpose and were not narrowly tailored to further a compelling state interest, one might have assumed that a trial would be necessary to determine whether North Carolina's 1997 plan met this test. On Friday, April 3, however, a two-one majority, with Judge Ervin dissenting, granted Everett's motion for summary judgment. The panel further instructed the state to present a schedule for the prompt adoption of a new plan by the following Wednesday and to devise a new schedule for holding party primaries.

Announcing that the state would file an immediate appeal to the Supreme Court, North Carolina attorney general Mike Easley heatedly complained that the situation was "getting ridiculous." His frustration was hardly surprising. Judge Voorhees, after all, had voted to uphold the 1997 plan the previous August in the *Shaw* case but was now voting to strike it down in *Cromartie*. "One judge sat on both courts and voted two different ways. Our state legislature is getting very confusing signals." McMahan echoed the attorney general's sentiments, if not his vehemence. "I didn't expect this. I'm sure this will do nothing but create chaos."

State officials had hoped to get a stay of the district court's order from the Supreme Court, thereby allowing elections to proceed on schedule while an appeal was pending. On April 13, however, the High Court, over the dissents of Justices Stevens, Ginsburg, and Breyer, denied a stay.

The three-judge panel did give the state a victory of sorts, though, in a related suit. In July 1996, Jack Daly, a twenty-four-year-old law student and Republican candidate in a losing bid to become state auditor, began a court challenge to North Carolina's state legislative districts as well as its congressional map. Since he had allowed three elections to pass before bringing his suit, state lawyers argued that his case should be dismissed based on his "unexplained and inexcusable delay." In March, the same three-judge panel hearing the *Cromartie* case rejected the state's contention. On April 17, 1998, however, the court denied Daly's petition to delay the May state legislative primaries until those districts had been redrawn — and little wonder, since he had waited seven months after filing his suit to serve the defendants with legal papers and thirteen months before asking the court to halt the primaries. Under the circumstances, Judge Boyle concluded, Daly and his co-plaintiffs had failed to establish any entitlement to such emergency relief. "The plaintiffs are in no position to now rely on time being of the essence in this court of equity when the plaintiffs' own failure to prosecute their demand for injunctive relief created the current exigency."

The ruling in Daly's case relieved the state from rescheduling state legislative primaries, and no districting was required for statewide races. The *Cromartie* panel gave the General Assembly until May 22, however, to redraw congressional districts. It denied, moreover, attorney general Easley's suggestion that primaries be allowed to proceed as originally scheduled in the eastern part of the state while being rescheduled in the Twelfth District and neighboring districts likely to be affected by the Twelfth's revised shape. Congressional primaries in all districts were to be held under an acceptable redistricting plan and at a time approved by the court.

———

After considerable wrangling, the General Assembly met the district court's May 22 deadline for enacting a 1998 plan. The Justice Department granted preclearance in early June. Later that month, the three-judge panel concluded that race was not the predominant purpose underlying the state's latest redistricting effort, thereby permitting the rescheduled primaries and the November elections to proceed. Ultimately, a five-four Supreme Court majority would reach the same conclusion with respect to the 1997 plan, but through a more protracted process.

In September, the Court agreed to review North Carolina's redistricting dispute a third time. On January 20, 1999, the justices heard oral argument. Facing Everett on this occasion was his Duke law school colleague Walter Dellinger, a constitutional specialist who had served as acting solicitor general in the Clinton administration. An assistant to the solicitor general also appeared as a friend of the court supporting the state appellants. Dellinger emphasized primarily that the record of the case did not support the three-judge panel's grant of summary judgment to the plaintiffs. Everett contended that the 1997 plan was so similar to the 1992 plan struck down in *Shaw v. Hunt* that its predominantly racial purpose was self-evident. Given the two schemes' close resemblance, he thought it "ridiculous" for the state to claim that its goal in drawing the 1997 district lines was predominantly political rather than racial. "These judges . . . looked at this evidence, considered it in the context, and realized there was nothing in the post hoc [statements] of the legislators. . . . They were giving ex post facto rationalizations . . . designed cleverly to — to cover . . . the true motive, the predominant motive."

Justice Antonin Scalia had clearly lost his patience with what he viewed as the intransigence of North Carolina officials. "Do [courts]," he exclaimed at one point in the proceedings, "have to pretend that this is not a legislature that has been pulled kicking and dragging into . . . drawing a fair district?" But as many as five members of the Court, including the chief justice, indicated their concern that the district court majority had issued a summary judgment for the plaintiffs without giving the defendants the benefit of a trial. Several noted, for example, that such judgments were normally reserved for cases in which the facts were not in dispute, a category into which they clearly did not place *Cromartie*.

Everett got the message. Following oral argument, he conceded that the Court "might order it back [to the district court] for a full-scale trial instead of summary judgment," adding, "I guess the thing that is a little depressing is that whatever happens, we're going to be litigating this for quite a while in one form or another."

Everett's fear proved correct. On May 17, 1999, a unanimous Court — speaking through Justice Clarence Thomas, no less — reversed the district court and held that a trial must be held on the factual questions raised in the case. The limited record in the case to that point, Thomas observed, allowed inferences to be drawn favoring a finding that either a racial or a political purpose had been the predominant consideration underlying enactment of the 1997 redistricting plan. A trial was thus necessary to resolve the issue. "Even if the question whether appellants had created a material dispute of fact was a close one," added Thomas, "'the sensitive nature of redistricting and the presumption of good faith that must be accorded legislative enactments' . . . would tip the balance in favor of the District Court making findings of fact."

On November 29, the district court convened for the *Cromartie* trial. Judge Ervin had died in September. Ordinarily, three-judge courts consist of one court of appeals judge and two district court judges. But probably because no North Carolinian was then sitting on the Fourth Circuit bench, that court's chief judge designated U.S. District Court Judge Lacy Thornburg to join Judges Boyle and Voorhees on the panel. A Democrat and 1995 Clinton appointee who had served as North Carolina's attorney general from 1984 to 1992, the new member of the court had made a losing gubernatorial bid in 1992.

Since the 1997 redistricting plan had been a bipartisan effort, adopted by a Democratic state senate and GOP-controlled house, the Republican Party had elected not to intervene in the *Cromartie* plaintiffs' behalf. But the *Shaw* defendant-intervenors, represented chiefly by Adam Stein, also participated in the *Cromartie* suit.

During the three-day trial, Everett presented a number of legislators and ex-legislators who testified that, in their judgment, race, not politics, had driven the redistricting process. Laypersons, including Everett's cousin Reuben of Salisbury, a retired banker and businessman, attested to the difficulties the Twelfth District's design created for constituents in terms of contact with their representative and the representative's visibility in the district. Much of the plaintiffs' case, however, was devoted to the testimony of Ronald E. Weber, a University of Wisconsin–Milwaukee political scientist who had appeared as a plaintiffs' expert in many districting cases. Drawing primarily on party registration records and elaborate statistical analyses, Weber concluded that the General Assembly had been driven predominantly by race in adopting the 1997 plan. He also testified that no majority-minority district based on a regard for compactness and other traditional redistricting principles could be created in North Carolina, given its relatively dispersed minority population.

To bolster their contention that the 1997 plan had been driven primarily by politics rather than race, the state called Senator Roy Cooper, Representative Ed McMahan, and Gerry Cohen, the General Assembly's chief mapmaker. All testified that although race had obviously been a consideration in the redistricting, especially given the Voting Rights Act and preclearance requirements, the predominant factors in the legislature's line drawing had been political concerns such as incumbency protection and the state's interest in creating districts reflecting distinct rural and urban communities of interest.

The state also had its own expert at the trial. He was David Peterson, president of a Durham statistical consulting and computer software development firm and recently retired from the Duke faculty, where he had taught variously in the business school, law school, and Department of Statistics for over twenty years. Relying on voting patterns as well as racial demographics and party registration patterns, Peterson had examined the Twelfth District's entire boundary, comparing areas outside the district with those inside. He found a strong correlation between an area's racial composition and party preference, with a high Democratic vote in heavily black districts but much more variation in party preference in precincts with low black representation. Focusing on what he termed "divergent boundary segments" — those areas where blacks were more numerous inside the Twelfth District but Democrats were more numerous outside, and those areas where blacks were more numerous outside the district but Democrats were more numerous inside — he concluded that the legislature had included more heavily Democratic precincts in the Twelfth District than heavily black precincts. In his judgment, therefore, the data supported a political explanation for the 1997 plan's configuration.

An affidavit Peterson filed in the case had apparently impressed the justices on *Cromartie*'s first trip to the Supreme Court, particularly since, unlike Weber, he had examined data relating to all the boundaries surrounding the Twelfth District in reaching his conclusion. Peterson's analysis and finding of a high correlation between the race of voters and their party preference, Justice Thomas had observed, "support an inference that the General Assembly did no more than create a district of strong partisan Democrats."

The Court obviously did not intend to suggest that it accepted Peterson's conclusions, but only that factual issues remained in the case that required a trial to resolve. The plaintiffs continued to vigorously contest the statistician's credentials as a redistricting expert, as well as the data and analysis on which his conclusions were based. In *Daubert v. Merrell Dow Pharmaceuticals* (1993), the Supreme Court had construed a federal rule of evidence in laying down standards for the admissibility of expert opinion, and Everett had filed a *Daubert* challenge to Peterson's status as an expert witness. Since Peterson relied in part on data not available to the General Assembly when its redistricting plans were first drawn, the plaintiffs' counsel also argued that the defense witness's conclusions were irrelevant to the issue of legislative motive. Instead, Everett charged, they were simply another element in the "post-hoc rationalizations" being offered by the state in its effort to convince the courts that the districting that the Supreme Court had earlier condemned as a predominantly racial scheme had become, via modifications in the Twelfth District's shape, a primarily partisan political enterprise.

The state's lawyers obviously disagreed with the plaintiffs' assessment of Peterson's credentials and analysis. "David," Eddie Speas later said, "is one of the best expert witnesses I have ever seen and one of the most accomplished statisticians I know. We have used him as an expert witness in cases extending over many years . . . big class action suits. David has been our expert, and a very . . . able expert." In fact, added Speas, Peterson regularly conducted seminars for federal judges in the use of statistics in litigation. Nor was the state's attorney impressed with Everett's "post-hoc rationalization" thesis. "Any time intent is an issue, as it is in these cases, this kind of evidence is not properly viewed as a 'post-hoc rationalization,' but as some scientific or independent confirmation of the story [legislators] told in the first place. The purpose of the evidence was to provide some independent confirmation of the testimony of the legislative officials . . . that race did not predominate" in the districting process.

Another issue prominent in the 1999 trial was what Everett termed the "smoking e-mail." Douglas Markham, a North Carolina native and Houston attorney involved in the Texas redistricting litigation, was providing significant support at this stage of the North Carolina suit. Seth Neyhart, a 1999 Duke law graduate, also assisted Everett, his former professor, in the *Cromartie* case. A resolutely conservative Republican, the former Lutheran seminarian and pastor was as vigorously committed to a color-blind Constitution as his mentor was. "The way to achieve a color-blind society where everyone is treated as an individual and not as a member of a racial or an ethnic group," Neyhart remarked, "is not to try to figure out which group has been wronged at some time in the past and try to redress that wrong with a specific remedy just for that particular group. That just perpetuates the racial divisions and the balkanization of our society. Instead, the law should forbid racial discrimination for whatever purpose."

Immediately after joining Everett's firm in August, Neyhart began devoting much of his time to the *Cromartie* suit. He and Douglas Markham did "a lot of the grunt work preparing for the trial. Judge Everett is still refusing to enter the computer age. So I did a lot of work with him in preparing for depositions and getting documents ready and researching witness statements. . . . Gerry Cohen [alone] is a full-time job."

In the rush of preparing for the trial, the plaintiffs' counsel had postponed requesting documents from Gerry Cohen for possible use at trial until shortly before they were scheduled to question the legislative mapmaker in a pretrial deposition session. "There wasn't time for [Gerry] to go through the [material requested] and see what was there," Neyhart recalled. "So I know [he] pretty much just printed out everything on his computer and stuck it in a big pile. And he showed up [for the deposition] with it."

During the seventh or eighth hour of Cohen's nine-hour deposition at the attorney general's office on September 17, Everett began thumbing through a batch of e-mails the witness had provided the plaintiffs. Suddenly, Neyhart remembers, "he stopped, and I get this elbow, and he pointed at [one of the e-mails], and I looked at it and did a double take." The e-mail to which their attention had been drawn was dated February 10, 1997. It was a message from Cohen to Senator Cooper, who was heading the senate committee drafting the 1997 redistricting plan, and to Leslie Winner. It read: "By shifting areas in Beaufort, Pitt, Craven and Jones counties, I was able to boost the minority percentage in the First District from 48.1 percent to

49.25 percent. . . . I have moved the Greensboro black community into the 12th District, and now need to take about 60,000 voters out of the 12th District."

To Everett, the e-mail was conclusive evidence that race rather than politics had actually driven the redistricting process. During the trial, he questioned Cooper and Cohen closely about the message's meaning. Cooper testified that he did not remember the e-mail but that the principal purpose of shifting black and white voters from one district to another was partisan — to ensure the six-six party balance in the state's congressional delegation. Race was a consideration, he conceded, but primarily because African American voters were also the state's most reliably Democratic voters. Cohen adopted the same stance. But in his closing argument, Everett declared, "I think this is a smoking gun. They do not refer to the Greensboro Democratic community — community of Democrats. They refer to the Greensboro black community and that's what they were doing. They were thinking in terms of race. The Supreme Court said you can not use race as a proxy for politics."

Just as the *Shaw* district court of two Democrats and one Republican had consistently sided with the state, the *Cromartie* panel of two Republicans and one Democrat was not disposed to change its mind after the November trial. On March 7, 2000, Judges Boyle and Voorhees ruled, over Judge Thornburg's dissent, that although North Carolina's First District had been constitutionally redrawn, the Twelfth District remained an unconstitutional racial gerrymander. The Twelfth District's "primary characteristic," Judge Boyle declared for the majority, was "its 'racial archipelago,' stretching, bending and weaving to pick up predominantly African-American regions while avoiding many closer and more obvious regions of high Democratic registration, but low African-American population."

Boyle and Voorhees accepted plaintiff expert Weber's characterization of defense expert Peterson as "unreliable" and "irrelevant," while fully embracing Weber's contentions. Weber, wrote Boyle, "showed time and again how race trumped party affiliation in the construction of the 12th District and how political explanations utterly failed to explain the composition of the district." As Weber had argued, the judge concluded, the state could have drawn "a much more compact, solidly Democratic 12th District . . . had race not predominated over traditional political considerations in the redistricting process."

The majority's finding of a predominantly racial purpose "was further bolstered," in Boyle's view, by Senator Cooper's "allusion to a need for 'racial and partisan balance'" in the 1997 plan. Cooper had asserted that whereas "partisan balance" referred to the interest in maintaining a six-six partisan split in the state's congressional delegation, "racial balance" was not intended to suggest a ten-two district split between whites and African Americans. That assertion, Boyle declared, was simply "not credible."

Boyle and Voorhees also concurred with Everett's depiction of the "smoking gun" e-mail. "The Cooper-Cohen e-mail," asserted Boyle, "clearly demonstrates that the chief architects of the 1997 plan had evolved a methodology for segregating voters by race, and that they had applied this method to the 12th District." The e-mail's specific references to "black" Greensboro neighborhoods and plans to "improve" the First District by "boost[ing] the minority percentage" were evidence the mapmakers were applying computer technology to create districts that were just under 50 percent minority and thus, as Cooper had told legislators at one point, could escape the strict scrutiny to which racial gerrymanders were subject under *Miller* and *Shaw II*. "Using a computer to achieve a district that is just under 50% minority," concluded Boyle, "is no less a predominant use of race than using it to achieve a district that is just over 50% minority."

While concurring with the majority's decision upholding the First District, Judge Thornburg vigorously dissented from its ruling striking down, yet again, the Twelfth District. Stressing the "substantial deference" federal courts have traditionally accorded state legislatures in congressional apportionment, Thornburg scored his colleagues' "unwarranted intrusion" into the legislative process. He also rejected the majority's conclusion that the Twelfth District constituted a racial gerrymander subject to strict judicial scrutiny. "Numerous motives and influences," he argued, were inherently at work in legislative decision making. Given that environment, judicial efforts to discern whether a given factor predominated over others in the districting process was risky business. Courts generally accepted incumbency protection as a legitimate redistricting objective, and pursuing that goal by ensuring the six-six partisan split in the state's congressional delegation made it necessary for the General Assembly to preserve the Twelfth District as a Democratic stronghold. "In creating such a district," wrote Thornburg, "common sense as well as political experience dictated ascertaining the strongest voter-performing Democratic precincts in the urban Piedmont Crescent. That many of those strong Democratic performing precincts were majority African-American, and that the General Assembly leaders were aware of that fact, is not a constitutional violation. Those precincts were included in the Twelfth District based primarily upon their Democratic performance, not their racial makeup."

Thornburg was as unimpressed as his colleagues were taken with Weber, the plaintiffs' expert witness. Noting that Weber had indicated during the trial that legislatures, in his judgment, could not be trusted to draw district lines, the dissenting judge charged that bias permeated his testimony, undermining both his criticism of Peterson, the state's expert, and his own assertions that race rather than politics had driven adoption of the 1997 redistricting plan. "His 'hired gun' mentality and obvious prejudice against legislatures fulfilling 'the most vital of local functions,'" Thornburg declared, "attest to the unreliability of his conclusions." In his judgment, moreover, Weber's arguments did "little to advance Plaintiffs' position." All the Twelfth District's majority-black precincts were "among the highest, if not the highest, Democratic performing districts in that geographic region." Thus, although Weber could point to other high-performing Democratic precincts left out of the disputed district, Thornburg could not understand why, given the General Assembly's goal of incumbency protection, "any of the *highest* performing [and largely African American] Democratic precincts should be excluded from the Twelfth District," thereby weakening Mel Watt's chances for reelection. Further noting Weber's "incorrect belief" that mapmakers had access only to racial demographic data, when they also could see political breakdowns of voter registration and voter performance on their computer screens, Thornburg argued that "this error, [Weber's] failure to account for other potential factors, the flaws in his arguments, and his ingrained personal bias [against redistricting by legislatures] combine[d] to undermine his subsequent conclusions and criticisms." The judge applauded, in contrast, the expert testimony of Peterson, "the unbiased statistician whose opinions were referenced by the Supreme

Court in" its first *Cromartie* opinion. Perhaps, Thornburg concluded, the General Assembly would simply readopt the 1998 plan, which the panel had approved. "Otherwise," he lamented, "for the fifth time in 10 years, North Carolina's legislature must undergo the arduous task of reaching a consensus on the diverse and inherently political issue of congressional redistricting."

Fearful that the district court's latest ruling would again disrupt the election process, state officials asked the panel to stay its decision pending their appeal to the Supreme Court. Judges Boyle and Voorhees denied a stay, but on March 17 the Supreme Court reversed, allowing the May primaries to be held as scheduled. Several days later, the Court also denied Everett's motion that the state's appeal be heard on an expedited basis, enabling the justices to issue a decision in the case before its summer recess.

On November 27, 2000, two days short of a year after the district court trial, the Supreme Court heard oral argument for a second time in the *Cromartie* case. Walter Dellinger again appeared for the state, Adam Stein for the defendant-intervenors, and Robinson Everett for the plaintiffs. Earlier, counsel for the state appellants had conducted a moot court session at Dellinger's Washington law office to prepare for their appearance before the justices. Dellinger was fearful, Adam Stein later recalled, that the justices would bombard him with questions about his clients' preclusion, or forum-shopping, claim. "He was saying, 'Look, the Supreme Court is a bunch of academic nerds, . . . and they're apt to jump into [that], and I won't get to what's important.' He devoted a lot of time preparing for questions on that issue."

As it turned out, the justices did not ask Dellinger a single question about claim preclusion. Instead, soon after he began his argument, several members of the Court interrupted with questions about the standard to be applied by the Court in deciding whether to reverse the district court. Under well-established precedent, an appeals tribunal can overturn a trial court's findings of fact only if they are "clearly erroneous." When Dellinger's argument appeared to suggest a departure from that rigorous standard, Justice O'Connor interrupted. "It is possible that as a fact finder I would not have found the facts as the court below did, and yet the court below appears to have believed one expert over another and made findings that may have been within its power to make, and how are we to upset that?" Dellinger responded that there was "simply nothing probative" underlying the district court's conclusions. Elaborating, he noted that at one point the trial panel had concluded that all splits of counties between the Twelfth District and other districts invariably occurred along racial rather than political lines. That, Dellinger declared, was "simply not true."

"But, you know," the chief justice then observed, "you've got factual findings here, and if they're supported by some evidence, even though, as Justice O'Connor said, perhaps we would not have made those findings, they're not clearly erroneous."

Later, Dellinger was explaining that the most heavily African American precincts were also the most reliably Democratic; thus their inclusion in the Twelfth District could have had a predominantly partisan rather than racial purpose. Justice Kennedy countered that Dellinger was "basically saying that race can be used as a proxy for partisan affiliation," which, the justice noted, was contrary to *Shaw II* and *Miller.* The state's counsel disagreed. "With all due respect, Justice Kennedy, that is exactly not the case. This is a districting process in which the state used voting statistics of how people actually voted, not the color of their skin . . . , in constructing this district. . . . Instead of using racial[ly] encoded census blocks, they used precinct voting day election returns. . . . It is the appellees and the court below which point out to you that those districts are African-American."

Justice Scalia soon brought up the "smoking gun e-mail." The state was claiming, the justice observed, that the e-mail's reference to the Greensboro "black" community was "just shorthand for those portions of Greensboro that were reliably Democratic." Although conceding that this might have been true, Scalia thought "certainly the other interpretation is a reasonable one as well, in which case it becomes evidence that predominantly they were trying to put together a district that had predominantly black voters in it." To reach that conclusion, Dellinger replied, one would "have to read [the e-mail] as being an explanation of the motive for the move, and you would have to assume that you attributed that to the whole legislature, not to the staff or to the two recipients, and you have to assume that that would be evidence of the predominance of race. I simply don't think it will bear that kind of weight. A stray remark like this."

Particularly in statements to the press, Everett had begun comparing state redistricting plans adopted after the Court struck down the 1992 scheme to the "fruits of the poisonous tree" excluded from criminal trials on illegal search and seizure grounds. Just as unconstitutionally seized evidence, and evidence derived from unlawful searches, was excluded from trials, Everett reasoned, the newer districting plans could be considered essentially derived from the earlier, tainted plan and equally unconstitutional. The plaintiffs' counsel did not refer directly to that analogy during oral argument in *Cromartie*. But when Justice O'Connor asked him about the presumption of good faith and proper motives traditionally accorded legislators, he expressed doubt that courts should indulge such a presumption when legislators "start from an unconstitutional base." The state's assertion that its plan was political rather than racial was, in his judgment, simply "a nice dodge."

Justice Ginsburg asked Everett about the state's communities-of-interest defense, appearing sympathetic to that argument in support of the Twelfth District's shape. When the lawyer responded that the splitting of a city, such as Charlotte, in a districting plan was "irreconcilable" with the concept of a distinct urban community of interest, Ginsburg was unpersuaded. "I can think of some areas of this city that might have more in common with areas of, say, Boston than with each other."

Justice Breyer expressed concern about the emphasis Everett, his expert Weber, and the district court had placed on party registration rather than actual voting patterns in concluding that race, not politics, had driven North Carolina's latest redistricting decisions. "What this Court said" when it first heard *Cromartie*, asserted Breyer, was that the parties should focus on voting, not registration, "because a lot of registered Democrats vote Republican." Yet the district court had continued to stress "registration, registration, registration," grounding its findings "on the very thing we said not to use." Everett responded, however, that considering all the evidence in context, "it seems to us unmistakably clear that this Court which was familiar with the motives of the workings of the General Assembly came to a permissible conclusion."

On April 18, 2001, the Court handed down its second decision in the *Cromartie* case, now technically known as *Easley v. Cromartie*, since

Mike Easley had replaced Jim Hunt as governor the previous January. The "clearly erroneous" standard the state was obliged to meet to secure a reversal of the district court's decision was onerous — but not insurmountable. Justice O'Connor had joined the five-four majority in striking down North Carolina's redistricting plan in *Shaw v. Hunt*, but a rumor had been circulated that she originally voted to uphold the 1992 plan, only later changing her mind and becoming the fifth vote for a ruling against the state. Whatever the truth of that story, the justice now joined the *Shaw II* dissenters to uphold the 1997 redistricting plan.

Speaking for the *Cromartie* Court, Justice Breyer conceded that an appellate tribunal can review a district court's factual findings only to discover clear error, "asking whether 'on the entire evidence' the Court is 'left with the definite and firm conviction that a mistake has been committed.'" He also concluded, however, that a trial court's findings must be subject to "extensive review" when, as in *Cromartie*, "there was no intermediate court review" of a district court's decision, "the trial was not lengthy, the key evidence consisted primarily of documents and expert testimony, and credibility evaluations [of witnesses and other evidence] played a minor role" in the court's decision. That review had convinced the majority, wrote Breyer, that only a "modicum of evidence" supported the district court's conclusion that race had dominated politics in the 1997 line drawing.

The district court had relied heavily on the analysis and conclusions of Weber, the plaintiff's expert, rather than on those of Peterson, to support its finding that the 1997 plan had a predominantly racial rather than partisan purpose. The Supreme Court majority, however, was less impressed with Weber, who had based his conclusions mainly on party registration figures, than with Peterson, who had used voting data, thus taking into account the substantial degree to which white registered Democrats in North Carolina regularly voted Republican. Given the much greater rate at which African American Democrats, compared with their white counterparts, actually voted for Democratic candidates, Breyer concluded that the state's clustering of blacks into the Twelfth District did not necessarily establish a predominantly racial purpose; it was just as likely to have been motivated by the legislature's desire to create a safe Democratic seat in the district. The justice attached little weight, moreover, to Senator Cooper's statement to a legislative committee that the challenged plan would satisfy the need for "racial and partisan" balance, or to the Cooper-Cohen e-mail. Cooper's statement indicated, at most, only that race had been one consideration underlying the 1997 plan, not the "predominant" factor. Although the e-mail offered "some support" for the district court's conclusion, Breyer observed, it was not sufficient to overcome the majority's finding of clear error.

Justice Thomas, joined by Chief Justice Rehnquist and Justices Scalia and Kennedy, dissented. Thomas thought that the majority had a queer notion of the clear-error rule. The Court, the justice conceded, had cited pertinent cases and "couch[ed] its conclusion in 'clearly erroneous' terms." But those "incantations," he declared, were mere "empty gestures" in view of the majority's decision to subject the district court findings to "extensive review."

Nor could Thomas accept Breyer's rationale for purporting to apply the clear-error rule yet subjecting the trial court's decision to rigorous scrutiny. If the absence of intermediate appeals court review justified the Court's approach, as Breyer claimed, the dissenting justice wondered why the Court had made no mention of that fact in earlier cases, including *Shaw* and *Miller*, which had had no intermediate appellate review before going to the Supreme Court. There was simply no support in the law, Thomas asserted, for the majority's suggestion that the first appellate court to review a trial court's fact-finding should subject those findings to more stringent scrutiny than ordinarily allowed under the clear-error standard.

The justice was equally unimpressed with the majority's notion that rigorous review of the district court's decision was necessary because the trial had not been "lengthy." Even if a trial's duration should affect the standard of appellate review, which Thomas seriously doubted, such a consideration was hardly appropriate for *Cromartie*, in which the proceedings had lasted three days and included the testimony of twelve witnesses, as well as the submission of hundreds of pages of deposition testimony, expert statistical analyses, and other documentary evidence. To the Court's assumption that the district court's findings were entitled to less deference because the key evidence was expert testimony requiring no traditional determinations about the credibility of witnesses and other evidence, Thomas also had a ready retort. The trial court, he asserted, had indeed made an unflattering assessment of Senator Roy Cooper's credibility. Its interpretation of the Cooper-Cohen e-mail as evidence supporting the plaintiffs' racial gerrymandering claim, added the justice, was probably "influenced by its evaluation of Cohen as a witness" as well.

But the best evidence, in Thomas's judgment, that the majority was merely giving the clear-error standard lip service, while actually subjecting the district court's findings to stringent scrutiny, was the Court's close examination of the trial record. "I do not doubt this Court's ability to sift through volumes of facts or to argue its interpretation of those facts persuasively," the justice declared. "But I do doubt the wisdom, efficiency, increased accuracy, and legitimacy of an extensive review that is any more searching than clear error review."

Applying what he considered to be the correct standard, Thomas found the district court's reading of the evidence clearly permissible, whatever his own evaluation of the facts of the case might have been. "If I were the District Court, I might have reached the same conclusion that [this] Court does. . . . But I am not the trier of fact, and it is not my role to weigh evidence in the first instance. The only question that this Court should decide is whether the District Court's finding of racial predominance was clearly erroneous. In light of the direct evidence of racial motive and inferences that may be drawn from the circumstantial evidence, I am satisfied that the District Court's finding was permissible, even if not compelled by the record."

———

Given the usual strictures of the clear-error rule, Everett had been reasonably confident of another Supreme Court victory in *Cromartie*, and the shift in Justice O'Connor's vote came as a great surprise. Everett had not been aware of the rumor that O'Connor had originally sided with the state in *Shaw v. Hunt*. He did know, of course, that in *Bush v. Vera*, the Texas redistricting case, O'Connor had not only filed a plurality opinion striking down that state's majority-minority districting but also written a separate concurrence making clear her view that a state's attempt to comply with the Voting Rights Act constituted a compelling interest that justified certain forms of race-conscious line drawing. But Everett had interpreted the justice's questions during oral argument as generally favorable to his position and considered her defection a major blow. "I thought that as a practical matter," he later said, her shift "had the effect of in many ways undercutting the real effect of the earlier *Shaw* ruling."

Eddie Speas had been cautiously optimistic, too. Although theoretically obliged to review election cases on appeal, the High Court had ways of avoiding full review of such suits — either dismissing them for failing to raise a "substantial" federal issue or summarily affirming the lower court. When the Court had scheduled *Shaw v. Reno* for full review on the redistricting litigation's first trip to Washington, Speas and his colleagues had approached that hearing with some trepidation, fearful that the Court would not have granted a full hearing simply to uphold the trial panel's ruling in the state's favor. Speas had seen the Court's willingness to grant full review to the *Cromartie* district court's most recent decision favoring the plaintiffs as a more optimistic sign, and he had not been disappointed.

As this book was being completed, North Carolina's General Assembly debated congressional and state legislative redistricting required by the 2000 census — a process complicated by the state's gain of a thirteenth House seat and an unsuccessful Utah court challenge to the increase in the North Carolina congressional delegation. Following extensive negotiations, the legislature adopted redistricting plans for the U.S. House and General Assembly. However, Republicans charged that the state legislative plans violated a state constitutional provision forbidding districting schemes that split counties, and they persuaded a state judge to strike down the newly drawn legislative districts and postpone the 2002 state primaries until the General Assembly adopted revised plans. At this writing, that case was pending in the courts.

Given Justice O'Connor's stance in the most recent *Cromartie* decision, further racial gerrymandering challenges to North Carolina's congressional districts appeared more problematic. Even so, no one was likely to underestimate Robinson Everett's tenacity. In February 2001, he appeared before a legislative committee, urging consideration of bills proposed by GOP legislators to create an independent redistricting commission and take politics — racial, partisan, or otherwise — out of the process. Partisan redistricting deadlocks had led to the adoption of such bodies in other states, and Everett hoped that North Carolina might take the same approach. Nor had the *Cromartie* decision weakened his resolve. "Absolutely not!" he declared when asked whether he had ruled out further litigation several months after the Court's ruling, and the General Assembly seemed bent on adopting what he thought "pretty clearly will be a Democratic gerrymander." He suggested, however, that in any future suit he might resort to the state courts and provisions of the North Carolina constitution, rather than the federal courts, to challenge both partisan and racial gerrymandering in the latest round of redistricting, especially since Republicans now occupied a majority of seats on the state's supreme court.

In part, Everett conceded, he was "inclined to threaten litigation as forcefully as possible with a view to getting [the state] to do the right thing." He also acknowledged that the GOP's decision not to intervene in the *Cromartie* suit had posed a financial hardship, especially since the Supreme Court's reversal of the trial court meant that the state would not be ordered to reimburse the plaintiffs for expenses connected with the suit. Given Everett's track record, however, his threats of further litigation could not be dismissed as idle gestures.

Whatever the future direction of court action, debates over majority-minority redistricting are hardly likely to cease. Redistricting litigation of the *Shaw-Cromartie* variety has generated a tremendous volume of scholarly and related commentary focusing not only on the constitutional issues raised in such cases but also on the redistricting process, competing conceptions of fair representation, proposed alternatives to the current system of legislative elections, and the ultimate impact of majority-minority districts on the electoral fortunes of Democrats and Republicans, as well as minority political influence. Lani Guinier, President Clinton's controversial nominee to head the Justice Department's civil rights division, has proposed, for example, cumulative voting — giving voters multiple votes and allowing them to distribute their votes in any combination they choose — as a way of increasing minority voter influence without resort to gerrymandering.

Everett and other critics of majority-minority redistricting often cite political scientist Carol Swain's *Black Faces, Black Interests: The Representation of African Americans in Congress* in support of their contention that majority-black districts may undermine rather than enhance minority political influence. Swain draws on Hanna Pitkin's distinction between "descriptive representation," in which legislators and their constituents share demographic characteristics, and "substantive representation" of constituents' goals without regard to racial or ethnic heritage in challenging the proposition that only African Americans can represent black interests effectively. Instead, she argues, blacks should form coalitions with whites in seeking to increase their political clout rather than isolate themselves — and their electoral strength — in a few majority-minority districts.

Everett obviously finds Swain's thesis persuasive, but especially so in view of her race and background. An unwed African American mother from Roanoke, Virginia, Swain overcame her humble roots and earned a doctorate in political science at Chapel Hill, where she studied with Everett's old friend Professor William Keech. On completing graduate study, Swain first took a position at Duke but refused to accept a tenure-track (and potentially permanent) post there based on the school's affirmative action policy; she moved instead to Princeton, where she ultimately obtained tenure. To Everett, Swain exemplifies the ability of disadvantaged minorities to succeed without the assistance of race-conscious policies. She declined to be a witness in *Shaw*, but Everett drew heavily on her defense of substantive rather than descriptive representation in his challenge to majority-minority districts. "She said," he later recalled, "I don't have any reason to hate white men. They've helped me a lot. She's a very principled person." Everett regrets that critics see a sort of racism in Swain's stance. He wrote several letters in an effort to get her — and an explanation of her views — a slot on Charlie Rose's PBS interview program. He never got a reply. "She seemed sort of sad that people viewed things as they did," he recently said.

Others have emphasized the risks inherent in efforts to maximize minority officeholding. Political scientist Abigail Thernstrom stressed in an influential 1987 book "the danger that categorizing individuals for political purposes along lines of race and sanctioning group membership as a qualification for office may inhibit political integration." She also contended that the Voting Rights Act had been extended far and, in her judgment, inappropriately beyond its original purpose of preventing racial discrimination at the polls, becoming instead a weapon for ensuring minority electoral success. In a 1997 work, she and her husband Stephen Thernstrom pursue a broader theme, arguing that African American gains in education and employment were greater before the adoption of affirmative action programs than afterward.

Literature supportive of majority-minority redistricting and critical of court challenges to such measures matches in volume and intensity that on the other side of the issue. In *Colorblind Injustice: Minority Voting Rights and the Undoing of the Second Reconstruction*, UNC historian J. Morgan Kousser objects to what he considers Thernstrom's "radical reinterpretations" of the Voting Rights Act, as well as the "revolutionary" reading given the equal protection guarantee in *Shaw v. Reno* and its progeny. Kousser ridicules Everett's claim in a *Shaw* brief that since no court had ever determined that North Carolina had engaged in racially discriminatory congressional districting, "there was no constitutional violation to be remedied by establishing two majority-minority districts." Charging that Everett offered "no evidence whatever" to support his contentions, the historian details repeated racial gerrymandering directed against minority voters in the state from the end of Reconstruction through the 1980 redistricting cycle. "Was the redistricting of 1991–92 . . . an unnecessary special privilege for blacks — unnecessary because they could compete and be represented equally without it, and special because no white politicians had ever received districts tailored for them and had never considered the race of the voters when deciding how to separate them into districts?" To Kousser, the answer was obvious — and ample justification for majority-minority redistricting.

Stanford law professor Pamela Karlan, who clerked for Justice Blackmun, one of the *Shaw v. Reno* dissenters, may be the most persistent critic of the *Shaw-Cromartie* plaintiffs and their counterparts in other suits. In amicus briefs and scholarly commentaries that are regularly cited by counsel for states, Karlan has challenged the fairness of analogies drawn between majority-minority districts — which, after all, were the most racially integrated in the nation — and South African apartheid. Like state counsel, she does not understand how courts can hear such cases, given the usual rules of standing. How, she wonders, were the constitutional rights of *all* voters (whatever their race) personally and directly injured simply by the shape and racial composition of the districts in which they resided? "Essentially," she has observed, "*Shaw [v. Reno]* provides individual citizens and lower federal courts hostile to black political power with a roving warrant to challenge the results of the political reapportionment process."

As the intense differences among litigants, counsel, judges, politicians, and scholars make clear, majority-minority district schemes, like affirmative action programs generally, raise agonizingly difficult constitutional and policy questions. Even Justice John Marshall Harlan, who propounded the notion of a "color-blind" Constitution in his *Plessy* dissent, was hardly an opponent of all color-conscious laws. In *Plessy*, Harlan was attacking segregation directed at a "degraded" race only recently elevated from slavery and widely assumed to be inherently inferior to its white counterpart. He opposed policies based on presumptions of racial superiority and the *Plessy* majority's cynical assumption that such laws were intended to treat both races equally, when actually they were designed to perpetuate slavery in fact if not in form, albeit under the "thin disguise" of "separate but equal." And he supported the Freedman's Bureau and related color-conscious efforts to correct the pernicious effects of the "peculiar institution."

It is doubtful that Justice Harlan would have regarded majority-minority redistricting in the same critical light — particularly against the backdrop of nearly a century in which no African American won a single congressional seat in North Carolina. Given the persistence of racially polarized voting, the defeats minority candidates almost invariably suffer in substantially white districts, and the heavy toll such patterns exact in terms of minority morale, a modern Harlan might well have embraced majority-minority districts in much the same way he endorsed the benevolent race-conscious efforts of his day, whatever his *Plessy* references to constitutional color blindness.

Arguably, once the Supreme Court accepted race-conscious redistricting — merely forbidding "predominantly racial" gerrymandering, rather than all consideration of race in the apportionment process — the prospects of future judicial intervention in such matters diminished considerably. Redistricting is an exceedingly complex process, entailing consideration of a virtually limitless variety of demographic, geographic, and political factors. It is also a field in which courts traditionally have accorded states the widest latitude and presumption of good faith, so long as they adhere to population equality principles and avoid diluting the electoral strength of disadvantaged racial groups. Given that deference — and the legislative ingenuity in crafting nonracial as well as racial reasons for adopting majority-minority districts — courts are unlikely to find many post-*Cromartie* redistricting plans "predominantly" racial and constitutionally invalid.

Whatever the future of majority-minority districting litigation, however, race-conscious policies of any sort remain a nagging source of national concern. One need not accept the notion of an entirely color-blind Constitution to question whether race-based policies designed to eliminate the impact of past discrimination do not instead merely prolong racial hostilities, postponing the day when, as Martin Luther King, Jr., said, people "will not be judged by the color of their skin but by the content of their character."

January 1991	North Carolina General Assembly convenes; Dan Blue is elected the first African American speaker of the state house of representatives.
July 1991	General Assembly adopts 1991 congressional redistricting plan, with one majority-minority district (District One).
September 1991	Congressional districting plan is submitted to U.S. Justice Department for preclearance under Section 5 of the 1965 Voting Rights Act, as amended.
December 1991	Justice Department objects to the congressional plan, as well as to state legislative districting plans.
January 1992	General Assembly adopts a congressional districting plan with two majority-minority districts (Districts One and Twelve).
January 1992	1992 plan is submitted to Justice Department for preclearance.
February 1992	Justice Department grants preclearance to the 1992 congressional and state legislative districting plans.
February 1992	North Carolina Republican Party and other plaintiffs file U.S. district court suit, *Pope v. Blue*, challenging the congressional plan as an invalid partisan gerrymander.
March 1992	Three-judge district court dismisses *Pope v. Blue*; U.S. Supreme Court denies application for injunction and stay of the district court's order.
March 1992	Robinson O. Everett, Ruth O. Shaw, and three other plaintiffs file *Shaw v. Barr* in U.S. district court, challenging the 1992 congressional plan, which Everett, as chief counsel, contends is an unconstitutional racial gerrymander based on a misinterpretation of the Voting Rights Act.
April 1992	Three-judge district court dismisses *Shaw v. Barr*; plaintiffs appeal to U.S. Supreme Court.
September 1992	U.S. Supreme Court dismisses *Pope v. Blue*, the GOP partisan gerrymandering challenge to the 1992 congressional plan.
November 1992	Eva Clayton (District One) and Melvin Watt (District Twelve) are elected the first African American members of Congress from North Carolina since 1902.
April 1993	U.S. Supreme Court hears oral argument in *Shaw*.

June 1993	Supreme Court, in *Shaw v. Reno*, reverses, five to four, the district court's dismissal of *Shaw v. Barr*; remanding the case for trial and holding that a redistricting plan so irrational on its face that it could be understood only as an effort to segregate voters into separate districts by race can be upheld as constitutional only if narrowly tailored to serve a compelling state interest.
September 1993	District court authorizes twenty-two black and white voters of the First and Twelfth Districts to intervene as defendants in *Shaw*.
November 1993	District court authorizes eleven Republican voters to intervene as plaintiffs in *Shaw*.
March 1994	District court denies plaintiffs a preliminary injunction in *Shaw*, thus allowing congressional elections to proceed on schedule.
March–April 1994	Trial is conducted before Judges Phillips, Britt, and Voorhees.
August 1994	District court dismisses suit, now called *Shaw v. Hunt*, two to one, with Voorhees, the only Republican on the panel, the lone dissenter; majority holds the plan to be a racial gerrymander, but narrowly tailored to serve the state's compelling interest in complying with the Voting Rights Act. Plaintiffs announce their intention to appeal.
December 1995	U.S. Supreme Court hears oral argument.
June 1996	Supreme Court, in *Shaw v. Hunt* (*Shaw II*), dismisses the challenge to the First District on the ground that none of the plaintiffs has standing (none resides there), but declares the Twelfth District unconstitutional as a "predominantly racial" gerrymander that was not narrowly tailored to serve a compelling state interest.
July 1996	Everett acquires litigants and files *Cromartie v. Hunt*, a racial gerrymander challenge to the First District; action in that suit is delayed pending the outcome of *Shaw* in the district court.
July 1996	*Shaw* district court prohibits the state from conducting congressional elections after 1996 under the 1992 plan struck down in *Shaw II*; General Assembly is given until April 1, 1997, to adopt an acceptable new plan.
March 1997	General Assembly adopts a new congressional redistricting plan.
June 1997	Justice Department grants preclearance.
September 1997	*Shaw* district court dismisses the suit.

{ *Race and Redistricting* }

October 1997	Everett files an amended complaint in *Cromartie*, including Twelfth District residents and challenging the 1997 plan as "fruit of the poisonous tree" — the 1992 plan.
March 1998	New three-judge district court holds a hearing in *Cromartie*.
April 1998	*Cromartie* district court, two to one, grants summary judgment for the plaintiffs; finding a clear constitutional violation and no facts in dispute, the majority forbids congressional elections to be conducted until the state adopts yet another plan.
April 1998	U.S. Supreme Court refuses to stay the district court's order.
May 1998	General Assembly adopts a 1998 congressional plan.
June 1998	Justice Department grants preclearance.
June 1998	District court approves the 1998 plan.
January 1999	U.S. Supreme Court hears oral argument in *Hunt v. Cromartie*.
May 1999	Supreme Court, nine to zero, reverses the district court and remands the case for trial, holding that sufficient factual issues were in dispute to make the panel's ruling for the plaintiffs on summary judgment inappropriate.
Nov.–Dec. 1999	Trial is conducted before Judges Boyle, Voorhees, and Thornburg in district court on the constitutionality of the 1997 redistricting plan.
March 2000	District court, two to one, with Judge Thornburg, the only Democrat on the panel, dissenting, again holds the 1997 plan unconstitutional.
November 2000	U.S. Supreme Court hears oral argument.
April 2001	Supreme Court, five to four, reverses the district court, holding that the 1997 plan was a predominantly partisan rather than racial gerrymander and thus was not subject to strict judicial review.

RELEVANT CASES

Abrams v. Johnson, 521 U.S. 74 (1997)
Allen v. State Board of Elections, 393 U.S. 544 (1969)
Batson v. Kentucky, 476 U.S. 79 (1986)
Beer v. United States, 425 U.S. 130 (1976)
Brown v. Board of Education, 347 U.S. 483 (1954) *(Brown I)*
Brown v. Board of Education, 349 U.S. 294 (1955) *(Brown II)*
Bush v. Vera, 517 U.S. 952 (1996)
Chisom v. Roemer, 501 U.S. 380 (1991)
Clark v. Roemer, 500 U.S. 646 (1991)
Daubert v. Merrell Dow Pharmaceuticals, 509 U.S. 579 (1993)
Davis v. Bandemer, 478 U.S. 109 (1986)
Drum v. Seawell, 250 F. Supp. 922 (M.D.N.C. 1966)
Freeman v. Pitts, 503 U.S. 467 (1992)
Gaffney v. Cummings, 412 U.S. 735 (1973)
Gomillion v. Lightfoot, 364 U.S. 339 (1960)
Growe v. Emison, 507 U.S. 25 (1993)
Hunt v. Cromartie, 34 F. Supp. 2d 1029 (E.D.N.C. 1998)
Hunt v. Cromartie, 526 U.S. 541 (1999)
Hunt v. Cromartie, 133 F. Supp. 2d 407 (E.D.N.C. 2000)
Hunt [Easley] v. Cromartie, 121 S. Ct. 1452 (2001)
Johnson v. DeGrandy, 512 U.S. 997 (1994)
Metro Broadcasting v. FCC, 497 U.S. 547 (1990)
Miller v. Johnson, 515 U.S. 900 (1995)
Mobile v. Bolden, 446 U.S. 55 (1980)
Morris v. Gressette, 432 U.S. 491 (1977)
Perkins v. Matthews, 400 U.S. 379 (1971)
Plessy v. Ferguson, 163 U.S. 537 (1896)
Pope v. Blue, 809 F. Supp. 392 (W.D.N.C. 1992)
Powers v. Ohio, 499 U.S. 400 (1991)
Reynolds v. Sims, 377 U.S. 533 (1964)
Richmond v. J. A. Croson Co., 488 U.S. 469 (1989)
Rogers v. Lodge, 458 U.S. 613 (1982)
Rome v. United States, 446 U.S. 156 (1980)
Shaw v. Barr, 808 F. Supp. 461 (E.D.N.C. 1992)
Shaw v. Hunt, 861 F. Supp. 408 (E.D.N.C. 1994)
Shaw v. Hunt, 517 U.S. 899 (1996)
Shaw v. Reno, 509 U.S. 630 (1993)
Smith v. Allwright, 321 U.S. 649 (1994)
South Carolina v. Katzenbach, 383 U.S. 301 (1966)

Thornburg v. Gingles, 478 U.S. 30 (1986)
United Jewish Organizations v. Carey, 430 U.S. 144 (1977)
United States v. Hays, 515 U.S. 737 (1995)
Wesberry v. Sanders, 376 U.S. 1 (1964)
Whitcomb v. Chavis, 403 U.S. 124 (1971)
White v. Regester, 412 U.S. 755 (1973)
Wise v. Lipscomb, 437 U.S. 535 (1978)
Wright v. Rockefeller, 376 U.S. 52 (1964)

BIBLIOGRAPHICAL ESSAY

The principal primary sources for this book were the court records and briefs for the *Shaw* and *Cromartie* cases, including judicial opinions, transcripts of hearings and oral arguments, transcripts of the 1994 *Shaw* and 1999 *Cromartie* trials, selected depositions, and other documents. The Kathrine R. Everett Papers in the Southern Historical Collection at the University of North Carolina at Chapel Hill provided insights into the personal and political background of Robinson O. Everett, chief counsel for the *Shaw* and *Cromartie* plaintiffs. Newspaper articles, especially in the *Raleigh News and Observer* and *Greensboro News Record*, were useful sources of information regarding key personalities and events. Recorded interviews, conducted either in person or by telephone, were also extremely helpful, adding substance, background, and color to the public record. Interviewed for the study were Robinson O. Everett (August 7, 2000, and October 11, 2001); Dan T. Blue (October 24, 2000), speaker of the North Carolina house of representatives when the litigation first arose; Thomas Farr (October 25, 2000), counsel for Republican plaintiff-intervenors in the *Shaw* case; W. Edwin McMahan (December 21, 2000), Republican chair of the state house redistricting committee at one stage of the redistricting process; Seth Neyhart (January 23, 2001), Everett's associate in the *Cromartie* suit; Ruth O. Shaw (September 15, 2000), a *Shaw* plaintiff; Melvin Shimm (September 14, 2000), a *Shaw* plaintiff; Tiare Smiley (September 19, 2000), counsel with the North Carolina attorney general's office; Eddie Speas (October 26, 2000), chief deputy attorney general of North Carolina; and Adam Stein (December 29, 2000), attorney for defendant-intervenors in the litigation.

The following books and articles were among the most useful secondary sources: T. Alexander Aleinikoff and Samuel Issacharoff, "Race and Redistricting: Drawing Constitutional Lines after *Shaw v. Reno*," *Michigan Law Review* 92 (December 1993): 588; David A. Bositis, ed., *Redistricting and Minority Representation* (Washington, D.C.: Joint Center for Political and Economic Studies, 1998); Christopher M. Burke, *The Appearance of Equality: Racial Gerrymandering, Redistricting, and the Supreme Court* (Westport, Conn.: Greenwood Press, 1999); Chandler Davidson and Bernard Grofman, eds., *Quiet Revolution in the South: The Impact of the Voting Rights Act, 1965–1990* (Princeton, N.J.: Princeton University Press, 1994); Bernard Grofman and Chandler Davidson, eds., *Controversies in Minority Voting: The Voting Rights Act in Perspective* (Washington, D.C.: Brookings, 1992); Bernard Grofman, Lisa Handley, and Richard G. Niemi, *Minority Representation and the Quest for Voting Equality* (Cambridge: Cambridge University Press, 1992); Lani Guinier, *The Tyranny of the Majority: Fundamental Fairness in Representative Democracy*

(New York: Free Press, 1994); Pamela Karlan, "All over the Map: The Supreme Court's Voting Rights Trilogy," in *Supreme Court Review — 1993* (Chicago: University of Chicago Press, 1993), 245–287; J. Morgan Kousser, *Colorblind Injustice: Minority Voting Rights and the Undoing of the Second Reconstruction* (Chapel Hill: University of North Carolina Press, 1999); David Lublin, *The Paradox of Representation: Racial Gerrymandering and Minority Interests in Congress* (Princeton, N.J.: Princeton University Press, 1997); Paul Luebke, *Tar Heel Politics 2000* (Chapel Hill: University of North Carolina Press, 1998); Frank R. Parker, "The Constitutionality of Racial Redistricting: A Critique of *Shaw v. Reno*," *District of Columbia Law Review* 3 (1995): 1; Richard H. Pildes and Richard G. Niemi, "Expressive Harms, 'Bizarre Districts,' and Voting Rights: Evaluating Election-District Appearances after *Shaw v. Reno*," *Michigan Law Review* 92 (1993): 483; Mark E. Rush, ed., *Voting Rights and Redistricting in the United States* (Westport, Conn.: Greenwood Press, 1998); David A. Strauss, "The Myth of Colorblindness," in *Supreme Court Review — 1986* (Chicago: University of Chicago Press, 1986), 99–134; Carol M. Swain, *Black Faces, Black Interests: The Representation of African Americans in Congress*, enlarged ed. (Cambridge: Harvard University Press, 1995); Abigail M. Thernstrom, *Whose Votes Count? Affirmative Action and Minority Voting Rights* (Cambridge: Harvard University Press, 1987); Stephen Thernstrom and Abigail Thernstrom, *America in Black and White* (New York: Simon and Schuster, 1997).

INDEX

Everett, Robinson, *continued*
  on *United Jewish Organizations v. Carey*, 46
Exclusionary purpose, 37

Farr, Thomas
  career of, 84–87
  on compactness, 92
  on *Pope v. Blue*, 85, 111
  on post-*Shaw* redistricting, 168
  Republican Party and, 86–87
  Shaw v. Hunt and, 90, 101–102, 110, 127–128, 164
  Shaw v. Hunt cross examination, 111–114, 118
  Shaw v. Hunt opening statement, 91–93
  Shaw v. Hunt Supreme Court arguments, 146–147, 148–149
  Souter, David and, 148–149
FCC, Metro Broadcasting v. See Metro Broadcasting v. FCC
Ferguson, James, 89
Ferguson, Plessy v. See Plessy v. Ferguson
Ferguson, Stein (Firm), 11, 88, 89, 90, 123
Fifteenth Amendment, 4, 6, 36, 48, 58
Fifth Amendment, 34
Fifth District, 101
First Amendment, 24
First District
  1992 Democratic primary, 94
  Cohen-Cooper e-mail and, 183–184, 185, 192
  equal protection claim and, 50
  Jones, Walter and, 115
  Lichtman, Allan on, 119–120
  litigants from, 147, 153
  population of, 20
  post-*Shaw* redistricting and, 173

rural areas, 110, 111, 113–114, 120–121
shape of, 13, 17, 21
Third District and, 114–115
whites in, 120
Fitch, Milton F. (Toby), Jr.
  life and career of, 83, 115–116
  redistricting plan and, 11, 18, 19
  Shaw v. Hunt and, 91, 93, 115–118
Fourteenth Amendment
  O'Connor, Sandra Day on, 75
  Pope v. Blue and, 24
  Shaw v. Barr and, 34, 36, 48
  Shaw v. Reno and, 58
Fourth Circuit Court of Appeals, 23–24
Fourth District, 113
Freeman v. Pitts, 45–46
Froelich, Jake, 125
Frost, Robert, 43

Galifianakis, Nick, 54
Gantt, Harvey
  election of, 106, 111
  Helms-Gantt Senate race, 94–95, 106, 124
  Watt, Melvin and, 20, 126
Gardner, James C., 20
Gender differences, 33
General Assembly. *See* North Carolina legislature
Geographically compact areas. *See* Compactness requirement
Georgia, 5, 6, 139–142
Gerrymanders, 21
  partisan, 2–4, 11, 22, 23–24, 85
  political, 99–100, 111
  racial, 33, 37, 75, 76, 93, 135
Gingles, Ralph, 87
Gingles, Thornburg v. See Thornburg v. Gingles
Ginsberg, Ben, 9–10, 53, 54

212　　　{ *Race and Redistricting* }

Ginsburg, Ruth Bader, 156, 160, 189
Gomillion v. Lightfoot, 4, 58, 74, 77, 151
Good faith defense, 68, 189
Graham, Frank Porter, 27–28
Greensboro, North Carolina, 183–184, 185, 188
Gressette, Morris v. See Morris v. Gressette
Grofman, Bernard, 55–56, 101
Gunier, Lani, 90, 195

Harlan, John Marshall, 45, 62, 197–198
Harrell, Norma, 175–176
Hasidic Jews, 37
Hate crimes, 32
Hawke, Jack, 22
Hays, United States v. See United States v. Hays
Hefner, William, 14, 108–109
Helms, Jesse, 54, 57, 58, 85
election of, 106
Helms-Gantt Senate race, 94–95, 106, 124
Hess, Michael, 53, 54–55, 95–97, 121–122, 146
Hodgkiss, Anita, 87, 104–105, 123–127, 169
Hoey, Clyde, 63
Hofeller, Thomas, 95–100
Howard, Malcolm, 174
Hunt, Cromartie v. See Cromartie v. Hunt
Hunt, Jim, 166, 190
Hunt, Sam, 19, 23
Hunt, Shaw v. See Shaw v. Hunt
Hunter, Howard, Jr., 14

Incumbent protection
Cohen, Gerry on, 111, 112
Cromartie v. Hunt and, 185–186

Democratic Party, 14, 22, 87, 109, 112, 127–128
Hess, Michael on, 55
Justice Department on, 17
in post-*Shaw* redistricting, 172
Powell, Jefferson on, 127–128
Republican Party, 14, 112
Souter, David on, 148–149, 162
Indiana, 23
Injury in fact, 130, 145
Intent: vs. effect, 1, 41–42
invidious, 41–42, 43, 46, 69
Interest, compelling, 132, 158

Jews, 37, 105–107. *See also United Jewish Organizations v. Carey*
Johnson, Miller v. See Miller v. Johnson
Jonas, Charles, 85
Jones, Walter B., Jr., 14–15, 20, 115, 173
Jones, Walter B., Sr., 14
Jones, Woodrow, 84–85
Jurors, peremptory challenge of, 32–33, 45
Justice Department
on the 1991–1992 redistricting plan, 15–18, 20
on the 1997 redistricting plan, 173
Democratic Party on, 18–19
on majority-minority districts, 9–10, 15–16
Miller v. Johnson and, 139, 141–142
Rehnquist, William on, 155
Shaw v. Barr and, 36–38
Shaw v. Hunt and, 148
See also Attorney General; Preclearance requirements

Karlan, Pamela, 197
*Katzenbach, South Carolina v. See
    South Carolina v. Katzenbach*
Keech, William, 196
Kennedy, Anthony
    on compactness, 151–152
    on *Easley v. Cromartie*, 188, 191
    on *Miller v. Johnson*, 140–141
    on *Shaw v. Hunt*, 151–152
    on *Shaw v. Reno*, 69, 73, 137,
        140–141
    on *Thornburg v. Gingles*, 151–152
*Kentucky, Batson v. See Batson v.
    Kentucky*
King, Martin Luther, Jr., 198
Kneedler, Edwin, 62, 70–71
Kousser, J. Morgan, 196–197
Ku Klux Klan, 27

Lake, I. Beverly, 28
Lancaster, Martin, 14, 108, 114–115
Law Students Civil Rights Research
    Council, 88
Lawyers' Committee for Civil
    Rights under Law, 59
Lee, Howard, 108
Lichtman, Allan, 118–123
*Lightfoot, Gomillion v. See Smith v.
    Allwright*
*Lipscomb, Wise v. See Wise v.
    Lipscomb*
Literacy tests, 5, 6
Louisiana, 5, 148
Lumbee Indians, 19–20

Majority-minority districts
    1991–1992 redistricting plan and,
        13
    constitutionality of, 83
    Cunningham, Dayna on, 94–95
    Eisele, G. on, 39
    Fitch, Toby on, 116–117

intent of, 46, 161–162
    Justice Department on, 9–10,
        15–16
    Kousser, Morgan on, 196–197
    Miller v. Johnson and, 139–140
    in Mississippi, 146
    multiple, 16, 17, 19–20, 113,
        134–135, 139
    population of, 20, 113
    post-*Shaw* redistricting and, 167
    racial discrimination and, 77,
        161–162
    Republican Party and, 9–10, 16,
        18–19, 138
    Scalia, Antonin on, 163
    shape of, 13–14, 15, 16, 20, 21–23
    single, 15, 36
    Souter, David on, 162
    Swain, Carol on, 195–196
    in Texas, 146, 160–163
    Thomas, Clarence on, 163
    Thornburg v. Gingles standards
        for, 149–150
    urban vs. rural, 116, 120–121
    voting rights and, 50, 59
    White, Byron on, 37
    See also Compactness
        requirement; First District;
        Twelfth District
MALDEF (Mexican American
    Legal Defense and Educational
    Fund), 59
Markham, Douglas, 182–183
Marshall, Thurgood, 6
McDonald, Laughlin, 16, 137
McGee, Martin, 167
McGovern, George, 28, 29
McMahan, W. Edwin, 171, 172,
    181
McMillan, James B., 11
Mecklenburg County, North
    Carolina, 103